Teaching Reading, Writing, and Spelling

All You Need to Succeed

Virginia Talbot

CORWIN PRESS, INC.
A Sage Publications Company
Thousand Oaks, California

For information:

Corwin Press, Inc.
A Sage Publications Company
2455 Teller Road
Thousand Oaks, California 91320
E-mail: order@corwin.sagepub.com

SAGE Publications Ltd.
6 Bonhill Street
London EC2A 4PU
United Kingdom

SAGE Publications India Pvt. Ltd.
M-32 Market
Greater Kailash I
New Delhi 110 048 India

Printed in the United States of America

Library of Congress Cataloging-in-Publication Data

Talbot, Virginia.
    Teaching reading, writing, and spelling: All you need to succeed
/ author, Virginia Talbot.
      p.   cm.
    Includes bibliographical references and index.
    ISBN 0-8039-6591-5 (cloth: acid-free paper). — ISBN
0-8039-6592-3 (pbk.: acid-free paper)
    1. Language arts—Handbooks, manuals, etc. 2. Reading—Phonetic
method—Handbooks, manuals, etc. I. Title.
LB1576.T22 1997
372.6'044—dc21   97-4609

This book is printed on acid-free paper.

97 98 99 00 01 02 03 10 9 8 7 6 5 4 3 2 1

Production Editor: Diana E. Axelsen
Production Assistant: Denise Santoyo
Typesetter/Designer: Christina M. Hill
Indexer: Mary Mortensen
Cover Designer: Marcia R. Finlayson

Contents

Acknowledgments

Special thanks to:
Lloyd Homer, Shirley Bell, Linda Nield, and Kathie Stroud.
Illustrators: Ivan Avila and Miguel Avila, High School Freshmen; Orland, California.

"Clap, Clap, Clap!" by Dee Lillegard, from *September to September: Poems for All Year Round.* Copyright © 1986 by Regensteiner Publishing Enterprises, Inc. Reprinted by permission of Childrens Press.

"Drinking Fountain," by Ethel Jacobson, from *Poetry Place Anthology.* Copyright © 1983 by Edgell Communications, Inc. Reprinted by permission of Scholastic Inc.

"Exactly Right," by Laura Arlon, from *Poetry Place Anthology.* Copyright © 1983 by Edgell Communications, Inc. Reprinted by permission of Scholastic Inc.

"The First-Day Game," by Dee Lillegard, from *September to September: Poems for All Year Round.* Copyright © 1986 by Regensteiner Publishing Enterprises, Inc. Reprinted by permission of Childrens Press.

"Friendship's Rule," by M. Lucille Ford, from *Poetry Place Anthology.* Copyright © 1983 by Edgell Communications, Inc. Reprinted by permission of Scholastic Inc.

"A House for One," by Laura Arlon, from *Poetry Place Anthology.* Copyright © 1983 by Edgell Communications, Inc. Reprinted by permission of Scholastic Inc.

"Learning," by M. Lucille Ford, from *Poetry Place Anthology.* Copyright © 1983 by Edgell Communications, Inc. Reprinted by permission of Scholastic Inc.

"Mabel Murple," by Sheree Fitch, from *Toes in My Nose.* Text copyright © 1987 by Sheree Fitch. Reprinted by permission of Boyds Mills Press.

About the Author

Virginia Talbot recently retired after 37 years of teaching. She has taught in all of the primary grades, including, most recently, 17 years in the first grade. The teaching of reading in the primary grades has become her specialty. In her classroom, she demonstrated her teaching techniques to many visiting groups of student teachers and veteran teachers from surrounding schools.

As word of her successful practice spread, she was frequently invited to demonstrate her techniques to teachers in their classrooms. She has lectured on her methods for teaching beginning reading at the California State Teacher's Reading Conference, Northern California reading conferences, student teacher seminars at California State University, Chico, and on closed-circuit educational television. In addition, she conducted inservice workshops for teachers and classroom aides on the topic "How to teach reading, writing, and spelling."

Talbot is also the author of an article published in the *Grade Teacher* titled "Using Parent Aides in the Classroom." Honors bestowed on her include Glenn County Educator's Hall of Fame, Glenn County Teacher of the Year, Candidate for California Teacher of the Year, Masonic Lodge Teacher of the Year, Northern California Reading Teacher Award, and Orland High School Alumna of the Year.

Talbot holds a B.A. degree from the University of the Pacific, Stockton, California. Although retired, she continues to provide guidance to teachers and other educators on effective methods for teaching language.

CORWIN
PRESS

1

Introduction

A Balanced Approach

First you "learn to read" and then you "read to learn."

With this book, you will be prepared to teach beginning reading, writing, and spelling. No other teaching manuals or spelling books are needed. Good reading skills are taught by using the children's own language, structured phonics, basal readers, books, poems, and songs. Writing, spelling, listening, and speaking are emphasized because they are an integral part of the reading process (whole language).

Resources Included

1. A systematic phonics guide and techniques for making phonics "fun"
2. Reading and writing lesson plans for the first 20 days of school
3. Transparency and duplicating masters for teaching manuscript writing
4. Detailed reading homework assignments
5. Prepared letters to be sent to parents
6. How to use different colors and the chalkboard to teach reading

7. Twenty poems to use for reading and enjoyment
8. How to use tape recorders, flashcards, and pocket charts effectively
9. How to use magnets in the teaching of sentence writing
10. How to teach spelling in the primary and intermediate grades

Who Can Use This Book

This manual is written for anyone teaching reading, writing, and spelling. It provides *first-grade* teachers detailed lesson plans for the first 20 days of school plus lessons, techniques, and activities to use throughout the school year. *Kindergarten* teachers will find ideas that can be used for students who are ready to read and write. *Second- and third-grade* teachers will find ways to review skills and work with slower students.

Reading specialists, teachers of *special education*, *intermediate grade* teachers, teachers of *illiterate adults*, and parents who are *home-schooling* will all be able to use many of the methods and techniques contained in this text.

What the Book Covers

• **Chapter 2** is a complete resource for using phonics in reading and spelling. Sample words are listed for each of the phonetic sounds. A technique for teaching the blending of sounds is also included.

• **Chapter 3** has 26 items that can be prepared before a school year begins.

• **Chapters 4 through 23** contain detailed lesson plans for how to teach reading, writing, and spelling the first 20 days of first grade. The reading and writing objectives are provided for each day with a systematic plan for teaching phonics. Items that need to be prepared before the school day begins are included. Other grades may use many of the ideas presented, such as the proper sequence for teaching phonics, ideas for writing daily messages on the chalkboard, teaching formation of letters, and poems for each of the 20 days.

• **Chapter 24** discusses how to build on the skills already introduced in the first 20 days of school. Included are: (1) formation of upper-case letters; (2) writing last names; (3) mastering the vowel code; (4) mastering 100 instant words; and (5) how to teach reading with books, poems, and songs.

• **Chapter 25** contains plans on how to teach 50 phonograms, such as <u>th</u>, <u>ow</u>, and <u>eigh</u>. There are short stories that feature 18 of these special sounds.

• **Chapter 26** has plans on how to teach spelling without a regular spelling book. There is a detailed format for continuing to teach spelling throughout the grades using phonics and the spelling rules that are provided.

• **Chapter 27** demonstrates seven important steps to use when teaching the reading of any story. Included in these seven steps are pre-reading strategies, vocabulary development, comprehension skills, and follow-up activities.

• **Chapter 28** has many suggestions for teaching methods and techniques to use with children who are still at the readiness level and are not yet ready to begin a formal reading program. Besides first grade, these suggestions can be helpful at the kindergarten level and for children with reading disabilities.

• **Chapter 29** contains vocabulary games to play with the total class, reading groups, or individuals. The objective for each of the games is to have children learn to read words in isolation, to learn the meanings of words, or both.

• **Chapter 30** contains many reading strategies that were not included in the previous chapters, such as teaching reading comprehension, deciphering words, and guided silent reading. You should be familiar with this chapter as it contains many techniques to be used beginning with the first day of school.

• **Chapter 31** contains ideas for involving and training parents in helping their children with reading homework. Included is a method for recording books that are taken home to read.

• **Chapter 32** has a progressive, step-by-step method for teaching creative writing. Proper sentence structure, punctuation, and spelling are emphasized.

How to Use This Book

How you use this book depends on the grade level and the abilities of the students you are teaching. First-grade teachers can use the ideas and lesson plans in the sequence presented. Other teachers may select and adapt lessons and activities to fit their own needs.

It is essential to thumb through the entire book first in order to get an overview of the skills being taught and the sequence in which they are introduced. Each day's instructions reinforce and build on the students' prior learning. To pick and choose isolated lessons may not always be effective if there are skills that are needed before that specific activity is introduced.

The methods and techniques presented in this book are intended to be used with students ready to begin formal reading, writing, and spelling. It is assumed children have had sufficient instruction in the pre-writing and pre-reading (reading readiness) activities that are usually part of a kindergarten curriculum. Such activities would include developing fine motor skills, distinguishing letters from numbers, knowing that the spoken word can be written by using letters, knowing that individual letters have specific sounds (sound-symbol relationship), and introduction to (not mastery of) consonant sounds. If introduction to consonant sounds is not part of the school's kindergarten curriculum, then it may be necessary to incorporate additional activities into the daily lesson plans as each consonant is introduced. These activities may include having children find objects and say words that begin with each consonant sound, find objects in magazines that begin with specific sounds, and draw objects for each of the sounds.

Because the use of phonics is important throughout this book, it is the subject of the second chapter, "What You Need to Know About Phonics."

The teaching of phonics is no more than teaching the individual sounds for the consonant and vowel letters and special combinations of these letters (phonograms, or digraphs). Teachers (and aides!) should study this chapter and become familiar with these sounds. Practice the oral blending "Say It Fast" technique. During the school year, use Chapter 2 as a reference guide for examples of words that are needed when teaching specific sounds. *Suggestion:* Parents may be given a copy of the entire chapter, so that they can better understand the sounds being taught and can assist their child at home.

The methods and techniques for actually teaching phonics are covered in detail as they are introduced in this book. All letters and their sounds (consonants and vowels) are introduced in the lesson plans for Days 2 through 18. The sequential order for introducing the letters (and sounds) is according to letter formation (see *Letter Formations* on pages 39-40). This sequential order is preferred because there is a definite progression in learning to form letters (Johnston, 1995). The vowel code is taught on Days 15 through 19. Phonograms are introduced in Chapter 25, "Teaching the Special Sounds of Phonograms."

The teaching of phonograms and formal spelling dictation begin simultaneously, after the introduction of consonant sounds and the vowel code. Thus, Chapter 25 and Chapter 26, "Teaching Spelling Through Dictation," should be used together.

The intent of Chapter 30, "More Reading Strategies," is to incorporate the teaching strategies that did not seem to fit into any of the preceding chapters. The teacher should become familiar with the ideas presented in this chapter and plan to use them whenever appropriate. One section of particular importance is titled "Reading to Children." The ideas presented are applicable for the first day of school for all primary grades.

In order to avoid too much repetition, cross-referencing is utilized throughout the book. This should be especially useful for teachers who are not necessarily following any sequential order. If a lesson needs further explanation, the cross-reference should further clarify the activity.

Some chapters have reproducible forms included at the ends of the chapters. These reproducibles are discussed somewhere within that chapter and have as a cross-reference: "(see end of chapter)." Other reproducibles do not necessarily belong in only one chapter, so they are included at the end of the book under "Additional Resources." *Note:* For easier use, some reproducibles could be enlarged on the copier.

One final suggestion to help find lessons and ideas quickly: Prepare and secure your own index tabs either on the pages that you will frequently need, such as the Vowel Code, or on the first page of each chapter.

I have found that the methods and activities presented in this book work well for me. But this is not the only way. If your school or district has certain preferences for other ways to teach phonics, reading, writing, or spelling, you can easily modify the time line, strategies, and forms in this book to fit the needs of your own school or district.

To teach reading, writing, and spelling is quite a challenge! I hope this book will help all teachers be successful. Good luck!

2

What You Need to Know About Phonics

Anyone teaching reading and spelling must have a thorough knowledge of phonics. Phonics is the study of speech sounds and the relationship between sounds and the letters that represent those sounds. This chapter provides an overview of the topic and will be referred to in the daily lessons and other chapters of the book.

The English language is said to be 85% phonetic; that is, 85% of the words are spelled and read as they sound when spoken. There should be a systematic plan for teaching phonics from the very beginning, thus assuring greater success for accurate and independent readers and spellers. However, phonics should not be overemphasized. Children need to enjoy reading, and they must comprehend what they read.

Sounds

Learning the letter sounds, rather than the names of the letters, is essential for maximum success in phonics. Although knowing letter names usually helps in learning the consonant sounds, there are a few exceptions. One exception is the letter "**y**." If the sound of "**y**" corresponded to the name of the letter, one would assume its sound to be /**w**/ as in "*wagon*."

Spelling

Spelling should be taught by sounding out, not by saying the names of the letters. In learning a foreign language, one needs to learn to "think" in that language. Translating from one language to another slows down the process. In the same way, changing from letter "names" to "sounds" slows down the spelling process. Children need to think "sounds" from the beginning.

In the upper grades, phonetic principles should be explained when there are lists of spelling words and when spelling errors have been made in writing. Teaching phonics can be rewarding and fun!

Consonants

Consonants are taught before vowels. Consonant letters and sounds are introduced in many preschools and are emphasized in many kindergarten programs, but the sounds may not be mastered by all incoming first graders. Review and mastery of consonant sounds is the goal in first grade. Children should be able to identify each consonant letter and know the sound(s) for the letter. When they see the letter, they should be able to say the sound(s). Following is a list of consonants with a word example of the sound:

/**b**/ *book*

/**c**/ *cat, city* (two sounds)

/**d**/ *dog*

/**f**/ *fish*

/**g**/ *goat, giraffe* (two sounds)

/**h**/ *horse*

/**j**/ *jar*

/**k**/ *kite*

/**l**/ *lamp*

/**m**/ *moon*

/**n**/ *nest*

/**p**/ *pig*

/**qu**/ (needs both letters)

 queen (/**kw**/)

 antique, conquer (/**k**/)

/**r**/ *rake*

/**s**/ *sun, is* (two sounds)

/**t**/ *turtle*

/**v**/ *vase*

/**w**/ *wagon*

/**x**/ *x*-ray (/**ks**/)

 xylophone (/**z**/)

/**y**/ *yellow* (beginning of a word)

 be-*yond* (beginning of a syllable)

/**z**/ *zoo*

Note: The letter "**c**" makes the /**s**/ sound if followed by an "**e**" (c*e*nt), an "**i**" (c*i*ty), or a "**y**" (bicycl*e*). The letter "**g**" usually makes the /**j**/ sound if followed by an "**e**" (g*e*ntle), an "**i**" (g*i*raffe), or a "**y**" (g*y*m). Some exceptions are "geese" and "girl."

Vowels

Vowel sounds are more varied than consonant sounds. Good readers and spellers need to know the many sounds that vowels can make. There are fewer exceptions than some may think. The five vowels are "**a**," "**e**," "**i**," "**o**," and "**u**." The letter "**y**" is *usually* a vowel. The only time that "**y**" is not a vowel is at the beginning of a word or syllable (e.g., "*yellow*" and "*beyond*").

Unlike most consonants, all of the vowels have more than one sound. If first graders are expected to read and spell words using the different sounds of a vowel, such as "*can*," "*name*," and "*all*," then they should be taught all of the sounds for each of the vowels from the beginning (see *Day 2: Sounds of Aa* on pages 32-33; *Day 6: Sounds of Oo* on page 54, etc.). This is in contrast to first teaching short vowels (ă ĕ ĭ ŏ ŭ), then long vowels (ā ē ī ō ū), and finally, the two-dot vowels (ä ö ü). Children who are taught all of the vowel sounds from the beginning will have the tools for becoming early independent readers and are more likely to spell entire words from the beginning, rather than leaving out unknown vowel sounds (Johnston, 1995).

Vowel Code

Using a vowel code is very helpful in learning the vowel sounds. A vowel code (ă, ē, ö) is simply using markings to denote sounds. Knowing the vowel code is a great tool for helping to unlock new and unfamiliar words. The markings for the vowel code are:

ă (*at*)	**ĕ** (*get*)	**ĭ** (*it*)	**ŏ** (*on*)	**ŭ** (*up*)
ā (*ate*)	**ē** (*me*)	**ī** (*ice*)	**ō** (*go*)	**ū** (*use*)
ä (*want*)		**ö** (*do*)	**ü** (*put*)	

Note: The vowel "**i**" has the /ē/ sound in many words. Examples are s*ki*, p*o*l*i*ce, p*i*ano, and mach*i*ne. If the reader first tries both vowel sounds (/ĭ/ and /ī/), the context of the sentence should help to figure out the correct word.

The vowel code markings are taught for the first time on Day 15 (see *Vowel Code* on page 96). The markings for the letter "**a**" are introduced on Day 15, the letter "**e**" on Day 16, the letter "**i**" on Day 17, the letter "**o**" on Day 18, and the letter "**u**" on Day 19. Reading words with vowel code markings also begins on these days.

Vowel Code Examples

/ă/   bag, and, cap, math, after, alligator, January
/ā/   ate, apron, wave, table, baby, famous, cradle
/ä/   want, water, father, ball, fall, walk, talk, haha
/ĕ/   ten, best, went, yes, left, elephant, yellow, gentle
/ē/   he, me, she, here, Pete, delicious, redo, return
/ĭ/   is, in, him, six, winter, middle, dinner, penguin
/ī/   ice, side, mine, five, find, giant, minor, trial
/ŏ/   on, not, hop, frog, shop, pond, monument, October
/ō/   no, go, home, rose, most, over, open, cold, notice
/ö/   do, to, two, who, move, prove, lose, shoe
/ŭ/   up, us, cut, funny, sun, jump, punish, crumble
/ū/   use, cute, huge, tube, rule, June, fuchsia, music
/ü/   put, pull, full, push, bush, would, could, should

The vowels "**a**," "**e**," and "**o**" can say the /ŭ/ sound. Whenever these three vowels say the /ŭ/ sound, they are not marked. Examples:

"**a**"   a, again, alone, above, was, what, umbrella, syllable
"**e**"   the, elephant, linen, fluent, elevator, eleven
"**o**"   from, come, love, brother, above, does, of, color

Vowel "y"

- The letter "**y**" appears in three phonograms:

    /**ay**/ (m<u>ay</u>); /**oy**/ (t<u>oy</u>); /**ey**/ (k<u>ey</u>, th<u>ey</u>)

- When "**y**" is at the end of a one-syllable word, it says /ī/:
    my, by, sky, try, why, shy, fly, dry, cry

- When "**y**" is at the end of a two- (or more) syllable word, it says /ē/:
    bun-ny, ba-by, cran-ber-ry, in-fin-i-ty
    Exceptions: sup-ply, re-ply, Ju-ly

- When "**y**" is in the middle of a word, it usually says /ĭ/ or /ī/:
    /ĭ/: bicycle, mystery, physical, anonymous, Plymouth
    /ī/: style, type, analyze, psychologist, gyrate

Phonograms

A blend is when two or more letters blend together but each retains its *original sound*. For example, "**spr**" is a blend. The separate sounds—/s/ /p/ /r/—have not been changed. In contrast, a phonogram (also known as a digraph) is when two or more letters go together to make a *special* sound. For example, the phonogram /**th**/ makes a completely different sound than the separate sounds of /**t**/ and /**h**/. To show that the letters belong together for a *special sound*, a phonogram may be underlined in a word when instructing (<u>th</u>is). Phonograms are not introduced until all consonant sounds and the vowel code have been taught. Prior to this, words with phonograms are "sight words." The phonograms listed do not necessarily have to be taught in the order given. Many phonograms have more than one sound (k<u>ey</u>, th<u>ey</u>); thus, phonograms can have vowel code markings to indicate which sound to use (k<u>e̯y</u>, th<u>a̅y</u>). *Note:* An x over a letter means "silent." A star (*) under a letter means "an exception to its usual sounds."

List of All Phonograms

1. /**sh**/   <u>sh</u>e, <u>sh</u>ip, <u>sh</u>allow, fi<u>sh</u>, fla<u>sh</u>card
2. /**th**/   <u>th</u>is, <u>th</u>en, <u>th</u>at (voiced)   <u>th</u>ing, <u>th</u>row, wi<u>th</u> (voiceless)
3. /**ch**/   <u>ch</u>in, <u>ch</u>eek   s<u>ch</u>ool, <u>Ch</u>ristmas   ma<u>ch</u>ine
   (k over "ch" in school, Christmas; sh over "ch" in machine)
4. /**wh**/   <u>wh</u>at, <u>wh</u>en, <u>wh</u>ite   <u>wh</u>o, <u>wh</u>ole
   *(x over o in who; x over o in whole; * under each)*
5. /**ay**/   m<u>ay</u>, pl<u>ay</u>, cr<u>ay</u>on, m<u>ay</u>or
6. /**ai**/   <u>ai</u>m, <u>ai</u>lment, m<u>ai</u>l, s<u>ai</u>lor
7. /**oo**/   z<u>oo</u>, s<u>oo</u>n, l<u>oo</u>se   g<u>oo</u>d, b<u>oo</u>k, h<u>oo</u>d   fl<u>oo</u>d
   (ö over oo: zoo, soon, loose; ü over oo: good, book, hood; u over oo: flood)*
8. /**ow**/   n<u>ow</u>, br<u>ow</u>n fl<u>ow</u>er   sn<u>ow</u>, yell<u>ow</u>, <u>ow</u>ner
   (ō over ow: snow, yellow, owner)
9. /**ou**/   <u>ou</u>t, f<u>ou</u>nd   th<u>ou</u>gh, d<u>ou</u>gh   s<u>ou</u>p, thr<u>ou</u>gh
   (ō over ou: though, dough; ö over ou: soup, through)
   fam<u>ou</u>s, c<u>ou</u>ntry   c<u>ou</u>ld, w<u>ou</u>ld, sh<u>ou</u>ld
   (ŭ over ou: famous, country; ü over ou: could, would, should)
   y<u>ou</u>r, f<u>ou</u>r, c<u>ou</u>rse, c<u>ou</u>rt, m<u>ou</u>rn
   (or over ou: your, four, course, court, mourn)
10. /**ee**/   gr<u>ee</u>n, sh<u>ee</u>t, f<u>ee</u>l
11. /**ea**/   <u>ea</u>t, d<u>ea</u>l, cr<u>ea</u>m   br<u>ea</u>d, inst<u>ea</u>d   gr<u>ea</u>t, st<u>ea</u>k
    (ē over ea: eat, deal, cream; ĕ over ea: bread, instead; ā over ea: great, steak)
12. /**ar**/   c<u>ar</u>, st<u>ar</u>, f<u>ar</u>m, M<u>ar</u>ch   c<u>ar</u>rot, M<u>ar</u>y, sh<u>ar</u>e, Febru<u>ar</u>y
    (ā over ar: carrot, Mary, share, February)

                        or   or   or   er   er

w<u>ar</u>m, w<u>ar</u>, w<u>ar</u>den   calend<u>ar</u>, mol<u>ar</u> (unaccented)

                                               er   er

13. /**or**/   f<u>or</u>, <u>or</u>ange, m<u>or</u>ning   doct<u>or</u>, flav<u>or</u> (unaccented)

14. /**oy**/   b<u>oy</u>, Cordur<u>oy</u>, <u>oy</u>ster, j<u>oy</u>ful

15. /**oi**/   <u>oi</u>l, <u>oi</u>ntment, sp<u>oi</u>l, j<u>oi</u>n

                                                      ār   ār   ār

16. /**er**/   h<u>er</u>, moth<u>er</u>, pap<u>er</u>, m<u>er</u>chant   v<u>er</u>y, wh<u>er</u>e, Am<u>er</u>ica

17. /**ir**/   f<u>ir</u>st, d<u>ir</u>t, squ<u>ir</u>m

18. /**ur**/   p<u>ur</u>ple, t<u>ur</u>tle, p<u>ur</u>se

19. /**ear**/   <u>ear</u>ly, <u>ear</u>n, l<u>ear</u>n, h<u>ear</u>d, <u>ear</u>th

                                      ē

Exceptions: <u>ear</u>, f<u>ear</u>, h<u>ear</u> (/<u>ea</u>/ + /**r**/)   b<u>ear</u>, w<u>ear</u> (silent "e" + /**ār**/)

20. /**wor**/   <u>wor</u>k, <u>wor</u>m, <u>wor</u>ld, <u>wor</u>se

21. /**oa**/   g<u>oa</u>t, b<u>oa</u>t, f<u>oa</u>m, l<u>oa</u>n

22. /**ing**/   r<u>ing</u>, sw<u>ing</u>, k<u>ing</u>, someth<u>ing</u>

23. /**ph**/   ele<u>ph</u>ant, tele<u>ph</u>one, Rudol<u>ph</u>

                                        d   d   t   t

24. /**ed**/   paint<u>ĕd</u>, glid<u>ĕd</u>   mail<u>ed</u>, color<u>ed</u>   look<u>ed</u>, rak<u>ed</u>

25. /**ck**/   bla<u>ck</u>, de<u>ck</u>, pi<u>ck</u>, ro<u>ck</u>, stu<u>ck</u>

                       xx   xx   g   g   f   f

26. /**gh**/   thou<u>gh</u>t, bou<u>gh</u>   <u>gh</u>ost, <u>gh</u>etto   enou<u>gh</u>, cou<u>gh</u>

27. /**igh**/   l<u>igh</u>t, s<u>igh</u>t, ton<u>igh</u>t

28. /**eigh**/ <u>eigh</u>t, sl<u>eigh</u>, w<u>eigh</u>

              ö   ö   ö   ū   ū   ō

29. /**ew**/   n<u>ew</u>, bl<u>ew</u>, st<u>ew</u>   f<u>ew</u>, m<u>ew</u>   s<u>ew</u>

                                                         *

              ö   ö   ö   ū   ū

30. /**ue**/   bl<u>ue</u>, cl<u>ue</u>, tr<u>ue</u>   h<u>ue</u>, c<u>ue</u>

31. /**ui**/   fr<u>ui</u>t, s<u>ui</u>tcase, j<u>ui</u>ce

32. /**aw**/   s<u>aw</u>, str<u>aw</u>, <u>aw</u>ful

33. /**au**/   <u>au</u>to, <u>Au</u>gust, h<u>au</u>l

              ē   ē   ē   ā   ā

34. /**ey**/   mon<u>ey</u>, monk<u>ey</u>, hon<u>ey</u>   th<u>ey</u>, wh<u>ey</u>

35. /**wr**/   <u>wr</u>ite, <u>wr</u>ong, <u>wr</u>inkle

36. /**kn**/   <u>kn</u>ow, <u>kn</u>ee, <u>kn</u>it

37. /**gn**/   <u>gn</u>at, <u>gn</u>aw, si<u>gn</u>

38. /**ps**/   <u>ps</u>alm, <u>ps</u>ychology

39. /**dge**/   ba<u>dge</u>, he<u>dge</u>, bu<u>dge</u>

              ē   ē   ā   ā   ā

40. /**ei**/   rec<u>ei</u>ve, dec<u>ei</u>t   v<u>ei</u>n, r<u>ei</u>ndeer, th<u>ei</u>r

		$\bar{e}$	$\bar{e}$	$\bar{i}$	$\bar{i}$
41.	/**ie**/	f<u>ie</u>ld, p<u>ie</u>ce		p<u>ie</u>, l<u>ie</u>	
42.	/**ought**/	b<u>ought</u>, th<u>ought</u>			
43.	/**aught**/	c<u>aught</u>, t<u>aught</u>			
44.	/**tion**/	na<u>tion</u>, vaca<u>tion</u>, correc<u>tion</u>			
45.	/**sion**/	mi<u>ssion</u>, pa<u>ssion</u>	televi<u>sion</u>, divi<u>sion</u>		
46.	/**tient**/	pa<u>tient</u>, quo<u>tient</u>	*Note:* effi<u>cient</u>		
47.	/**cial**/	spe<u>cial</u>, fa<u>cial</u>, ra<u>cial</u>			
48.	/**tial**/	par<u>tial</u>, mar<u>tial</u>, pala<u>tial</u>			
49.	/**tious**/	cau<u>tious</u>, ficti<u>tious</u>, ostenta<u>tious</u>			
50.	/**cious**/	deli<u>cious</u>, spa<u>cious</u>, pre<u>cious</u>			

Note: The last seven phonograms start with "**ci**," "**si**," or "**ti**" at the beginning of the second or third syllable. These phonogram sounds all begin with /**sh**/. *Note:* I use the word *phonogram* rather than "digraph"—it seems to go with *phonics* (*phon*ogram). In my classrooms, this similarity was pointed out to the children, and they quickly learned the word and the concept.

Oral Blending

In oral blending, two or more letters are blended together, but each retains its original sound. The goal in oral blending is to hear each sound isolated in a word and then to say the entire word with its sounds blended. Readers must learn to take isolated sounds and "say it fast." This is the ultimate skill that is needed for using phonics in reading and spelling.

Compound words are used first to begin teaching oral blending. Practice with approximately ten compound words a day until the skill is mastered (see *Oral Blending Word Lists* on page 14). For easy reference, have the list of ten words written on a 4" × 6" file card. Additional lists may be planned around themes, such as animals, objects in the classroom, or students' names.

Compound Words. The teacher says each word in a compound word separately and the students "say it fast." The choral reading technique is used. In choral reading, everyone recites (on a given signal) at precisely the same time.

Teacher:	"**foot**" (pause) "**ball**"
Teacher:	"**Say it fast.**"
Students:	"**football**"

If a rhythm is established, the students have no difficulty responding in unison. No one should say the word before or after the entire class.

Syllables. When the majority of the students are ready to move on, change compound words to syllables in words: first, two-syllable words; then, three-syllable words; finally, multi-syllable words. Examples:

Teacher:	"ti" (pause) "**ger**"	"**grass**" (pause) "**hop**" (pause) "**per**"
Teacher:	"**Say it fast.**"	"**Say it fast.**"
Students:	"**tiger**"	"**grasshopper**"

Individual Sounds. When teaching the blending of individual sounds, it is best to use words with only three sounds first: c-a-t, b-u-g, th-a-t. The next list would have four isolated sounds: h-e-l-p, j-u-m-p, f-a-s-t. Gradually the list becomes more difficult: th-ir-s-t-y, g-ar-d-e-n, m-a-g-i-c.

"Reading" Sounds. Once the vowel code has been taught, the students can begin learning to "read" the sounds and then "say it fast." The teacher needs to do a lot of demonstrating of this technique ("my turn" vs. "your turn"). Eventually the students can read and blend without demonstrations. Many children enjoy the challenge of blending difficult words.

To teach oral blending in reading, the words are written with vowel code markings on the chalkboard. Example:

Teacher:	"**My turn.**" "**f**"-"**ī**"-"**n**"-"**d̆**"
Teacher:	"**Say it fast.**"
Students:	"**find**"

The next step would be for the children to blend without a demonstration:

Teacher:	"**Your turn. Get ready.**"
Students:	"**f**"-"**ī**"-"**n**"-"**d̆**"
Teacher:	"**Say it fast.**"
Students:	"**find**"

Note: Teacher moves a pointer finger under each letter that is being sounded. When a word is said "fast," the pointer finger moves "fast" under the word.

Oral Blending Word Lists

Compound Words. (1) foot-ball   (2) to-day   (3) sun-shine   (4) out-side
(5) for-got   (6) play-house   (7) some-thing   (8) good-night   (9) ear-ache
(10) pop-corn

Two-Syllable Words. (1) moth-er   (2) sis-ter   (3) thun-der   (4) flow-er
(5) piz-za   (6) chil-dren   (7) cray-on   (8) fun-ny   (9) pen-cil   (10) un-der

Three-Syllable Words. (1) ham-bur-ger   (2) Hal-low-een   (3) cal-en-dar
(4) di-no-saur   (5) oc-to-pus   (6) Sat-ur-day   (7) Sep-tem-ber
(8) Thanks-giv-ing   (9) gin-ger-bread   (10) won-der-ful

Multi-Syllable Words. (1) Jan-u-ar-y   (2) tel-e-vi-sion   (3) caf-e-ter-i-a
(4) re-fri-ger-a-tor   (5) hip-po-pot-a-mus   (6) ther-mom-e-ter   (7) rhi-no-cer-os
(8) el-e-va-tor   (9) a-pol-o-gize   (10) pep-per-o-ni

Three-Sound Words. (1) c-a-t   (2) b-u-g   (3) d-o-g   (4) s-i-t   (5) h-a-ve
(6) sh-i-p   (7) r-e-d   (8) f-u-n   (9) b-o-x   (10) g-oa-t

Four-Sound Words. (1) m-i-l-k   (2) j-u-m-p   (3) c-o-l-d   (4) h-a-n-d   (5) t-r-a-p
(6) k-e-p-t   (7) f-a-s-t   (8) d-e-s-k   (9) g-r-ee-n   (10) t-ea-ch-er

Multi-Sound Words. (1) s-i-l-v-er   (2) z-e-b-r-a   (3) g-ar-d-e-n   (4) f-a-m-i-l-y
(5) b-r-o-th-er   (6) v-a-l-e-n-t-i-ne   (7) p-r-e-s-e-n-t   (8) s-e-v-e-n
(9) a-n-i-m-a-l   (10) f-i-n-i-sh

Sight Words

Sight words are not taught phonetically. They cannot be sounded out. Sight words need to be memorized. Common sight words are:

- **eye:**   This word looks like two eyes with a nose in between
- **one:**   "**on**" with an "**e**"
- **once:**   "**one**" with a "**c**"
- **of:**   Chant: " '**o**' '**f**' spells '**of**' "
- **does:**   Explain: the root word "**do**" + "**e**" "**s**"
- **ocean:**   Begins and ends right, with three silly waves (**cea**) between
- **sure:**   The "**h**" got lost in /**sh**/! (Same for the word "sugar.")

Note: Children love to use their imaginations, so add humor whenever possible.

Common Silent Letters

t	of*t*en, whis*t*le, cas*t*le, lis*t*en, ca*t*ch
n	colum*n*, autum*n*, hym*n* (follows the letter "**m**")
b	clim*b*, lam*b*, lim*b* (follows the letter "**m**")
	de*b*t, dou*b*t (precedes the letter "**t**")
h	*h*our, *h*onest, *h*onor (beginning of a word)
w	t*w*o, to*w*ard, *w*ho (not the /**wh**/ phonogram)
l	ta*l*k, wa*l*k, cou*l*d, wou*l*d
u	g*u*ess, b*u*ilding, b*u*y
c	s*c*ene, s*c*ientist, s*c*ent

Phonetic Pronunciation to Decipher Words

Sometimes words that do not follow any rules can first be pronounced phonetically. Then, in context, the phonetic pronunciations will help to decipher the actual words. Examples:

wăs   <u>wh</u>ăt   wŏmăn   b<u>ee</u>n   s<u>ai</u>d   măny   quarrĕl

3

Before School Begins

Activities From A to Z

This chapter has 26 suggestions for activities that may be prepared before the first day of school. The more that can be planned and prepared before the year begins, the better. Read through this chapter and select ideas to try.

A. Time Line. Develop a time line for teaching reading, writing, and spelling for the entire school year. The time line will indicate dates for introducing specific areas of instruction, such as the vowel code, phonograms, and formal spelling. If used in sequential order, this book provides a time line for the first grade. Details can be added as the year progresses.

B. Letters to Students. A week before school, send a letter to your students, welcoming them to your class. Sample letter:

Dear _____,

> *School begins next Tuesday, September 3rd. I am looking forward to having you in my first-grade class.*

The school day begins at 8:30 a.m. On Tuesday, you may come into our room anytime after 8:00 a.m. I will be waiting for you in Room 14, which is by the office.

Bring a happy smile. First grade will be fun!

Your teacher,

_____

Note: Allowing students into the classroom early on the first day of school decreases the confusion that happens if everyone arrives when the bell rings. It helps to make the first day go smoother.

C. Alphabet—Display and Flashcards. Every primary grade needs to display the alphabet. Purchase a horizontal alphabet wall chart that has accompanying pictures that begin with the sounds of each of the 26 letters. The pictures for the vowels should all begin with a short vowel sound (see *Alphabet Display* on page 32). The formation of letters should correspond to those being taught in the classroom. If needed, a letter can be changed by covering it with another.

Put up the entire alphabet chart and then cover each letter with construction paper. The impact is much greater if each letter is uncovered as it is introduced. In first grade, it takes approximately four weeks to teach the alphabet. The letters are not presented in alphabetical order. They are introduced according to similar writing formations: first, round letters that begin at 2 o'clock; then, letters that begin with a tall line; then, letters that begin with short and slanted lines; and, finally, letters that begin by going across (see page 115). (Second-grade teachers can also cover each letter on an alphabet display; however, the introduction of the letters will be accelerated, perhaps one week instead of four.) Prepare two sets of flashcards; one set for the lower-case letters and another set for the upper-case letters. Write the letters large enough to be seen by the entire class.

D. Color Words—Display and Flashcards. Color words also need to be displayed in the lower primary grades. Each color word should also have an accompanying picture using that particular color. Again, the impact is much greater if each color is added to the display as it is introduced. The only word shown on the first day of school is the color-word "red." It takes eight days to teach the eight colors in a primary color-crayon box. Write the color words on eight separate flashcards, beginning each word with a lower-case letter.

E. Number Words—Display and Flashcards. Number words should also be displayed. Number words are not taught until the eight color words have been completed. Because each number word will be introduced one at a time, do not put them on a single chart. *Suggestion:* Write each number word on a sentence strip. The sentence strip should have a picture illustrating that particular number. Write the words on eleven separate flashcards ("one," "two," . . . "ten," "zero"). "Zero" is taught last because the concept of "zero" should be developed after mastering the other numbers.

F. Homework Flashcards. Duplicate a set of the eight color-word flashcards (see *Color Words* on page 243) on tagboard for each child. Cut the words apart. Put one "red" card into a small envelope for each child. Write the child's name on the envelope, along with the heading: *Color Words.*

Group the remaining cards by color and store them in clear, resealable storage bags. Repeat this same procedure with the number words (see *Number Words* on page 244).

Place the "one" and "two" cards into a small envelope for each child. Write the child's name on the envelope, along with the heading: *Number Words.* Group the remaining cards by number and store in resealable storage bags.

G. Homework Letter and Envelope. Duplicate the letter to parents about flashcard homework (see *Homework Letter 1* on page 237). Send it home the first day of school, along with the first homework assignment, flashcard "red." Prepare large envelopes the students can use to transport homework to and from school. Reinforce all of the sides and the flap with wide tape. Each envelope needs the child's name, the school's name, and the room number. *Note:* If available, use interdepartmental envelopes. Also, the envelope is not necessary until Day 15—the first time homework needs to be returned to school.

H. Name Tags. Prepare three name tags for each child:

1. Name tags for the children to wear the first day of school.
2. Desk tags to place at each child's desk.
3. Names to be put into a pocket chart.

I. Pocket Charts. Purchase at least two pocket charts. A pocket chart holds individual words or sentence strips behind clear plastic pockets. Put up one of the charts. Write two headings: **Boys** . . . **Girls.** Insert the headings in the top pocket. On the first day of school, tell the children to find their own names and place them under the correct heading.

J. Vowel Code Posters. Prepare pictures to be used when teaching the vowel code (see *Vowel Code Posters* on page 245). First, cut apart the five pictures (apple, elephant, igloo, octopus, umbrella) leaving the "codes" under the pictures. On tagboard, enlarge and reproduce each poster separately. Color the pictures and laminate the five posters. *Note:* If needed, change pictures to match vowel pictures on *your* alphabet display.

K. Clock Poster. Make a large round clock face on a 12″ × 18″ poster board. The number 2 on the clock needs to be emphasized in some way: different color, surrounded by sunrays, or underlined.

L. Handwriting Papers. Papers may be duplicated daily or all in advance. Each copy needs a transparency. The *handwriting* (H.W.) papers in this book (see Resources H.W. 1-24 on pages 252 through 275) are prepared for "traditional" manuscript. There are many different manuscript programs and variations within each. In traditional manuscript, such as Palmer, letters do not slant sharply to the right, and there are no curves going up at the end. This manuscript resembles printed text, and most letters may be formed either without lifting or with minimum lifting of the pencil. If your school teaches "modern" manuscript, such as D'Nealian (letters slant sharply to the right, and there are curves going up at the end), you may use the papers provided by your school or prepare your own set by following the format and the order for introducing the letters to the students outlined in this book. For an explanation of why certain letters are formed in a specific way, see *Letter Formations* on pages 39-40.

Note: Examples of teacher writing in the chapters are written in traditional manuscript, although some illustrations of process have a slight slant to the right and reflect my own personal writing style. Handwriting papers and other forms for students are traditional manuscript (without a slant).

M. Name-Writing Papers. These papers are needed the second day of school. Duplicate handwriting papers (see lined paper on pages 246-251), one for every two students. Fold each paper in half, and write two children's names on the top line. Put a dot where each letter begins. Repeat until all names have been written, two per page. Duplicate at least five copies of each paper. Save all of the masters in case some children will need more practice.

Cut the copies apart and paper-clip each name together. Arrange them alphabetically, ready to begin using on Day 2.

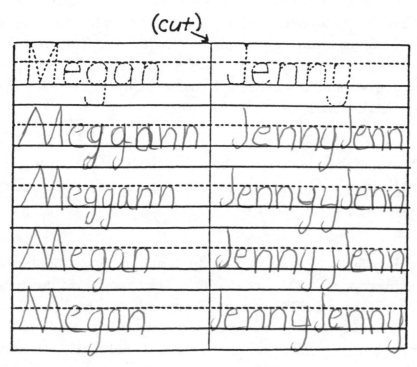

Figure 3.1. Name Writing

N. Individual "Mailboxes." Plan an area that may be used for "mailboxes," one per child. Homework and other papers that need to be sent home are placed into these individual cubicles. The students may put homework and papers that are returned into these same cubicles; however, it may be more convenient for the teacher if all returning papers are placed into one special container. *Suggestion:* Build the "mailboxes" out of wood, much like a bookcase. Each cubicle should be wide enough to hold a large homework envelope. This bookcase may be placed by one side of the door, cubicles facing the door for easy access. It could be used as a room divider.

O. Bookshelves. Library books in the primary grades are best displayed with the covers showing. A bookcase built like a magazine rack is suitable for this type of display. In many classrooms, these bookshelves can be placed under the chalkboard ledge. This is often lost space anyway. One shelf can be built midway down, and the second shelf can be at floor level. The shelves do not have to be very wide, but each shelf will need a little lip across the front to keep the books in place.

P. Teacher's Reading Table. Plan a place for the teacher to work with reading groups. Needed are a large table, chairs, large pocket chart, and a chalkboard.

Whenever possible, the students should face the pocket chart and chalkboard. In other words, avoid having them sit with their backs to these two items.

Q. Library Books. To start the school year, choose at least two books for each student in the classroom. Because most of the children are not yet proficient readers, the books should have a lot of pictures. Some books may be placed in baskets in order to be easily accessible to children at their desks. The remaining books should be placed on the library bookshelves.

R. VIP Corner. Each child should have a turn to be the "Very Important Person" (VIP) for an entire week. The teacher can be VIP for the first week of school. The classroom aide, student teachers, custodian, principal, librarian, nurse, and school secretary may also be honored. A place needs to be prepared with a small table and a bulletin board. On the table, the VIP may display collections, hobbies, a baby book, souvenirs, favorite books, and so forth. The bulletin board can feature pictures of the family, pets, trips, and special events. When class enrollment is stabilized, prepare a VIP calendar for the entire year. Whenever possible, the VIP week should correspond with the child's birthday. Summer birthdays may be scheduled whenever there is an available week. The VIP calendar should be sent home with the child's week highlighted. A letter of reminder is sent home the Friday before the child's week is to begin (see *VIP Letter* on page 242). Reading and writing are part of the VIP program (see "mascot" journal on page 74 and *VIP Chart Story* following).

S. VIP Chart Story. Every VIP should have a chart story written about him or her (see *Kendra Gates's VIP story* on page 73). At the beginning of the year, the story is read to the class. Later, the students are able to read the story with little or no help. Because the teacher is the VIP the first week of school, this chart story may be written before school begins. VIP stories may be rewritten on smaller paper and placed into a cumulative binder.

T. Class Rules. Everyone has their own ideas about class rules. In the early primary grades, it is best for the teacher to establish the rules. Rules should be written, and the students should learn to read them. It is best to have no more than six rules (see *Class Rules* on page 28). Each rule may be written on a sentence strip and put up as it is introduced, or all of the rules may be written on a single piece of chart paper as they are being introduced. The rules should be taught one at a time during the first week of school. Two rules may be introduced on the same day, but at separate times of the day, thus emphasizing the rules and having ample time to read (and reread) them.

U. Tape-Recorded Books. Many books with accompanying tapes can be purchased, especially through children's book clubs. However, there is no need to be limited to purchased tapes. Tapes can be made to go with any book. The teacher (or other qualified reader) simply reads the book into a tape recorder. Plan an introduction and use a signal when it is time to turn the page. Tape-recorded books may be used at a listening center, as a free-time activity, to help develop fluency in reading, and for homework.

V. "I Want to Learn" Chart. Using a large chart paper and a black marking pen, write the heading: "In first [or second or third] grade, I want to learn." In black pen, write numbers down the left side of the paper. Place this paper up at the front of the room. During the first or second day of school, solicit ideas from the students as to what they would like to learn. If possible, write the sentences in a pattern, using different colored pens. Color coding is a great technique to use with beginning readers. For example:

Solicited Ideas	Color Key
1. <u>How to</u> *read books*	<u>How to</u> = brown
2. <u>How to</u> *write stories*	*Italics* = red
3. <u>How to</u> *ride a horse*	
4. <u>About</u> *dinosaurs*	<u>About</u> = blue
5. <u>About</u> *outer space*	*Italics* = red

W. Costumes. Children in the primary grades should have the opportunity to put on a lot of plays. The plays do not have to be elaborate . . . the simpler, the better. Plays should be part of the reading and writing process. Prepare a large box and start your collection of costumes. Items to include are hats, jewelry, masks, shirts, bandannas, and aprons. *Suggestion:* Teachers may sometimes get free items at garage sales at the end of the day.

X. Home-Reading Books. Collect books for homework. Arrange the books into an order, beginning with the easiest and ending with the most difficult to read. Use a numbering system to designate reading levels and to track when a book has been checked out. Place labels on the outside top right-hand corner of each book. Using a permanent marking pen, number the books to indicate 10 reading levels: Level 1 is for the easiest books, and Level 10 is for the most difficult books. By using decimal points, each book has a different number for checking out. For instance, **1.1** is the first book in Level 1 and **6.3** is the third book in Level 6 (see *Numbering the Books* on page 209). New books can easily be added to the collection.

Y. Poems. Start a collection of poems. Look for poems that can be read to the class, poems good for children to read and memorize, and poems that can be used for choral readings. Classify the poems: teacher reads, children read, and choral readings or themes such as animals, family, and holidays.

Z. Free-Time Activities. When children finish all assignments early, they need to know what to do. At the beginning of the school year, this can be chaotic. Some children will hurry and not do their best, in order to get to the "fun stuff." Children wandering around the room and visiting with others will distract those trying to finish. Start planning and collecting materials that can be used during free time. *Suggestions:*

1. **Library Books:** Reading (looking at) books may be required as the first activity after finishing assignments or learning centers. Baskets of books may be placed at each desk area (tables or rows). The children may select only books that are in their designated basket. The baskets are rotated until each area has had access to them.

2. **Tape Recorders:** Have available at least four children's tape recorders. The children may either listen to books being read on tapes or read their own stories into the tape recorder. Children find listening to themselves read is quite a treat!

3. **Writing:** Have writing paper available and encourage children to write, especially after sentence and story writing have been introduced into the curriculum. Free-time writing is neither corrected nor critiqued. Nevertheless, free-time writing is praised!

4. **Coloring:** Many children love to draw and color their own pictures. However, children can go through lots and lots of paper. Establish from the beginning what paper to use and what to do with it when finished. *Suggestion:* Have backs of old papers available for free-time pictures. Students may place these pictures in their "mailboxes" and take them home at the end of the day for their families to enjoy.

5. **Clay:** Order modeling clay, one stick per child. Put the clay into small resealable storage bags. Make mats for clay by cutting vinyl tablecloth material into 12" × 12" squares. Establish rules for using clay. *Suggestions:* Clay stays on the mat; no pounding and no putting objects into the clay. Encourage the children to form letters and numbers out of the clay. Occasionally, suggest specific objects to be formed, such as a turkey, a snowman, or a dinosaur.

6. **Pattern Blocks:** Fill large resealable storage bags with pattern blocks (wooden tanagrams). See that the bags have an equal amount of each of the different patterns. Prepare one bag per child or for two children to share.

Laminate black construction paper for each child. The patterns look great on the paper, and it serves as a working area on a desk or on the floor.

7. **Unifix Cubes:** These can be bagged and distributed in the same way as the pattern blocks. Make sure that the bags have an equal amount of each of the different colors.

8. **Jigsaw Puzzles:** Purchase boxes of puzzles (remember garage sales). First graders should have mostly puzzles with 60 pieces or less. Those with 24 pieces are good because children can usually complete them in less time. Jigsaw puzzles may be assigned as "learning center" activities. Puzzles may be assembled on framed bulletin boards or large cookie sheets. These "boards" may be placed on the floor and moved whenever needed. Unfinished puzzles may be saved on them.

9. **Games:** Purchase games and toys such as Checkers, Dominoes, Go Fish, Old Maid, and Lincoln Logs. It is best if these games are played only during a total-class "free time." Because some slow-working children may seldom have free time, once a week plan for a total-class "free time" (no assignments). During this time, many children like to play "school." Encourage them to "read the walls" (use a pointer stick and read chart stories, bulletin boards, and anything written on the chalkboards). *Note:* A deck of playing cards for each student is excellent for a variety of math activities.

4

First Day of School

Reading and Writing Objectives

1. Read names.
2. Read the color-word "red."
3. Read messages that are written on the chalkboard.
4. Read two class rules.
5. Listen to daily poem and stories.
6. Begin choral reading.
7. Participate in composing and reading chart: "In first [second] grade, I want to learn."

Before the School Day Begins, Prepare the Following:

1. Write names for name tags, desk tags, and the pocket chart (see *H. Name Tags* on page 18).
2. Prepare pocket chart with heading: Boys . . . Girls
(see *I. Pocket Charts* on page 18).
3. Put "red" on the bulletin board and have flashcards available (see *D. Color Words* and *F. Homework Flashcards* on pages 17 and 18, respectively).
4. Select books and the daily poem to read.
5. Select two class rules to introduce (see *Class Rules* on page 28).
6. Prepare chart for: *"In first [second] grade, I want to learn"* (see *V. "I Want to Learn" Chart* on page 22).
7. Plan assessment papers and free-time activity.

On the first day of school, it is helpful to have the assistance of another adult for at least the first hour of the day. It is also advisable to allow the children to come into the classroom before the bell rings. If arrivals are staggered, the first hour will usually go more smoothly. The helping adult can take pictures of each student (most children are dressed in their best on the first day) and help them to find their name tags, desk tags, and names to put into the pocket chart. Reading names is the first reading activity in first grade. *Suggestion:* Have multiple pictures developed of each child. These pictures may be used in a variety of writing activities throughout the school year, including VIP chart stories.

THE FIRST SCHOOL DAY BEGINS

Soon after the bell rings and the children are settled in their seats, the teacher may write the first message on the chalkboard. The teacher reads the words aloud as they are being written. A sample teacher message is:

Dear Class,

Welcome to Room 14!

First grade will be fun.

Your teacher,

_____

After writing the letter, the teacher should read it one more time, with expression, pointing to the words as they are read (tracking). *Suggestion:* Write a "Dear Class" letter every day of the school year. Write it on the chalkboard prior to the beginning of the school day. Read the letter to begin the day, and then read the poem (see *A Poem a Day,* below). The letters may be recopied onto paper and put into a binder titled "Dear Class." As the children become proficient readers, they will enjoy rereading the letters.

A Poem a Day. Beginning each day with a poem is a good habit to establish. Listening to poems being read will eventually lead to learning to read poems. A good poem for the first day of school is *The First-Day Game:*

The first day of school
There are lots of new faces.
The first day of school
There are new things and places.
Corners to peek in
And pictures to see,

Things I can touch
And new things that touch me.
But the first day of school
My favorite game
Is "What shining face
Goes with each different name?"

—*Dee Lillegard*

Reading Names. The next reading activity is to read all of the names in the pocket chart. The children raise their hands as their own names are read. Go back and read the names one more time, asking the children to read them with you. The teacher may hesitate just a little with each name, to see if anyone can read the names without assistance (informal assessment).

Choral Reading. Next, teach the children to read the color-word "red." This is the only color up on a front bulletin board (see *D. Color Words* on page 17). The children will also be learning how to choral read. In choral reading, everyone reads together, just as everyone sings a song together. No one goes ahead or lags behind.

The choral reading procedure is: The teacher says "Get ready" and taps under each word as it is read. In this instance, the teacher says "Get ready" and then taps under the word "red" on the bulletin board. Repeat this procedure until everyone reads the word in perfect unison. Next, show the flashcard with the word "red." Say "Get ready" and tap the flashcard.

Intersperse this activity a few more times throughout the day. At the end of the day, each child takes home a "red" flashcard in an envelope and the homework letter (see *F. Homework Flashcards* and *G. Homework Letter and Envelope* on page 18). The responsibility of homework begins on the first day of school! If "mailboxes" are to be used (see *N. Individual "Mailboxes"* on page 20), be sure to allow time at the end of the day to discuss their use.

Teacher Message. The teacher may write messages throughout the day. Writing messages on the chalkboard is an effective technique for teaching reading and for modifying behavior. Because most first-grade students are not yet proficient readers, the beginning messages must be very simple. As the year progresses, the messages should be appropriate to the reading capabilities of the majority of the students. Challenge their capabilities!

A first-grade teacher message for the first day of school could be: The teacher draws a happy face on the chalkboard, large enough to write everyone's name inside. Throughout the day, as you notice a child who is exemplifying good behavior, write that child's name inside the happy face. Say the child's name after writing it. If possible, include all children by the end of the day. Begin the next day by again reading all of the names. Then erase just the names and repeat the same procedure.

Storytime. At least three books should be read the first day of school, at three different times of the day. At storytime, it is good to have the younger children sit on the floor close to the reader. The children must be taught to sit and listen. Their hands must be kept to themselves. Their eyes should be on the reader or on the book that is being read. Teaching good listening skills is important.

Good students are good listeners! Suggested books to read on the first day of school have the "red" theme:

1. *Red Is Best* by Kathy Stinson
2. *The Lion and the Little Red Bird* by Elkisa Kleven
3. *Clifford, the Big Red Dog* by Norman Bridwell

Class Rules. At two separate times during the day, introduce two of the class rules. Display one rule and see if anyone can read it (informal assessment). Discuss the rule and practice chorally reading it. Later in the day, reread the first rule and introduce the second rule in the same way. Whenever a rule is not being followed, read the rule again. *Suggested rules:* (1) Use materials the right way. (2) No visiting during worktime. (3) Raise your hand for help. (4) Don't hurt anyone (body or feelings). (5) Clean up after yourself. (6) Mind all teachers.

Assessment. If time allows, assign three papers to assess student capabilities. These may be worked on at three separate times of the day or may be finished on the second day of school. Place these papers in the individual student portfolio folders. In order to show changes and progress during the year, selected papers are placed in the portfolios. Classroom testing papers should also be included. The first three assessment papers of the school year may be:

1. Write their names five times on lined writing paper.
2. Write their numbers on graph paper as far as they can go.
3. Draw a picture of themselves.

Because the children will eventually have independent worktime while the teacher works with reading groups, it is important to teach them how to work independently. The process should begin the first day of school with the first papers. Discuss: (1) how to use pencils and crayons, (2) why there is no unnecessary visiting during worktime, (3) where to put finished papers, and (4) how to use free time.

Free Time. The children will finish the assigned papers at different times. They must know what to do when they have finished. It is best to have only one new choice per day, until all of the free-time activities have been introduced. On this first day of school, prior to assigning the first assessment paper, introduce library books as the only choice during free time. Because many of the children are not yet proficient readers, talk about how to look at pictures in a book. Demonstrate how to study the pictures and to think about the story that the pictures are telling. If books are placed in baskets (see *Q. Library Books* on page 21), then the getting and returning of books needs to be discussed.

VIP Corner. Sometime during the day, the teacher should share a few items from the VIP table. At the end of the week, there will be a VIP chart story to read (see *R. VIP Corner* and *S. VIP Chart Story* on page 21).

"I Want to Learn" Chart. Solicit ideas from the children as to what they want to learn in school this year. Use two different colored pens to write these ideas on a large chart paper (see *V. "I Want to Learn" Chart* on page 22). The teacher reads aloud as each idea is being written. If possible, compose the ideas into patterns. For instance:

In first grade, I want to learn:	**Color Key**
1. <u>How to</u> *read books.*	<u>How to</u> = brown
2. <u>How to</u> *write names.*	<u>About</u> = blue
3. <u>About</u> *snakes.*	*Italics* = red
4. <u>About</u> *volcanoes.*	

"How to" and "About" begin the two patterns and will usually work with any of the children's ideas. This completed chart is used for choral reading.

Today the children read only the two patterns (brown and blue), and the teacher reads the endings (red).

Teacher:	**"Get ready"**	*Teacher:*	**"Get ready"**
Children:	**"How to"**	*Children:*	**"About"**
Teacher:	**"read books."**	*Teacher:*	**"snakes."**

Note: The teacher "tracks" during the entire reading of the chart.

Before the end of the school year, try to accomplish all of the ideas. ("How to ride a motorcycle" is an impossible objective for first graders!)

5

Day 2

1. Read names.
2. Read the color-word "yellow."
3. Read yesterday's chart story: *"I want to learn."*
4. Read two more class rules.
5. Learn sounds for **Aa**: /ă/ /ā/ /ä/.
6. Listen to daily poem and stories.
7. Begin learning to write "clocks."
8. Practice writing own names.

It may be impossible to complete everything that was planned for the first day. (It is always better to have too much planned rather than not enough!) Incorporate anything not completed the previous day into the next day's schedule. Always review and build on previous lessons.

BEFORE THE SCHOOL DAY BEGINS, PREPARE THE FOLLOWING:

1. Add "yellow" to the bulletin board and have flashcards available (see *D. Color Words—Display and Flashcards* on page 17).
2. Put **Aa** on the alphabet display and have flashcards available (see *C. Alphabet—Display and Flashcards* on page 17).
3. Rearrange names into ABC order, still separating Boys . . . Girls.

4. Select daily poem and stories to read.
5. Display poster-board "clock" (see *K. Clock Poster* on page 19).
6. Select two more class rules to introduce.
7. Duplicate name-writing papers (see *M. Name-Writing Papers* on page 19).
8. Duplicate Handwriting Paper 1 and transparency (see *L. Handwriting Papers* on page 19 and *Resources* on page 252).
9. Plan practice-work papers and free-time activity.
10. Add more VIP pictures and items.

THE SECOND SCHOOL DAY BEGINS

A Poem a Day. Read a poem to begin the day. *Suggestion:*

Clap, clap, clap! (Clap 3 times.)	Clap, clap, clap!
My hands make noise.	And now we're through.
Clap, clap, clap!	Quiet hands! (Fold hands.)
Let's hear the boys.	Quiet face! (Point to face.)
Clap, clap, clap!	Let's have quiet every place!
Now girls clap, too.	Shhhhh! (Say till all are quiet.)

—*Dee Lillegard*

Note: Chanting this poem together is a good way to begin each day. It helps to get the children quiet and settled. Then read the new poem for that day.

Reading Names. For a few more days, attendance may be taken by reading the names in the pocket chart. Arranging the names in ABC order helps find the names quickly and establishes a pattern for remembering them. At first, it may be easier to keep the names under the "Boys . . . Girls" headings.

Later, the headings should be removed and the names arranged in a single ABC listing. When taking attendance, the teacher reads the names the first time through. The names of absent children may be turned over. During a second reading, the teacher and the children read the names together.

Color Words. The teacher introduces the new color word, "yellow." Stand near the "color" bulletin board and say "Get ready" while tapping under the word "yellow." The children choral read: "Yellow." Repeat the process, alternating between "red" and "yellow." Show and tap the flashcard "yellow" as the children read the new word. Repeat the process, alternating between the two flashcards, "red" and "yellow." Review the flashcards several times during the day. At the end of the day, send home the "yellow" flashcard (see *F. Homework Flashcards* on page 18).

Teacher Message. Continue the same type of message on the chalkboard. Choral read, then erase the names in yesterday's happy face. Throughout the day, keep looking for good behavior and write names inside the happy face.

Little stars (*) may be added to some names to encourage the continuance of good behavior. Use the choral reading technique when reading the names.

As soon as a name is written, say "Get ready" and tap under the name. Read the name two times, so that everyone has the opportunity to read it correctly.

"I Want to Learn" Chart. The teacher reads the entire "I want to learn" chart. Review the beginning patterns: "How to" and "About." Read the chart again, but this time the children read the beginning patterns and the teacher reads the endings. Choral read it one more time. This time see if some of the children can read the endings without the teacher reading. The teacher should hesitate and give the students time to try on their own before offering assistance.

Alphabet Display. In teaching the alphabet, it is important to emphasize "sounds" rather than the letters' names. It is advisable to display each letter as it is introduced, rather than showing the entire alphabet at the onset (see *C. Alphabet—Display . . .* on page 17). Purchase an alphabet display that has a picture with each letter. For example, the letter **Aa** might have a picture of an apple, and the letter **Bb** might have a picture of a ball. The vowel pictures should all begin with short-vowel sounds, such as ăpple, ĕlephant, ĭgloo, ŏctopus, and ŭmbrella. *Note:* Having a picture of *ice* cream instead of an *i*gloo does not follow the recommended short-vowel pattern. *Note:* Letters are introduced according to letter formation. Today only the letter **Aa** is showing. It is introduced first because the lower-case "a" is the first of the similarly formed 2-o'clock letters (**a, c, d, f, g, o, q,** and **s**) to be taught. Because consonant sounds are usually worked on in kindergarten (see *How to Use This Book* on page 3) and because all words must have at least one vowel, interspersing vowels with consonants leads to a quicker learning and usage of phonics in reading and spelling (Johnston, 1995).

Sounds of Aa. To teach the sounds of **Aa,** first point to the picture on the alphabet display and say: "apple." Then point to **Aa** and say the three sounds: "/ă/ /ā/ /ä/" (see *Vowel Code* on pages 8-9). Repeat this procedure several times. Then say, "Your turn" and have the children say, "Apple /ă/ /ā/ /ä/" Teach all three sounds of the vowel (ă, ā, ä). Do not teach only the short vowel sound /ă/. Words such as "căn," "nāme," and "wänt" appear early on in reading, so the three vowel sounds need to be introduced from the beginning (Johnston, 1995). On Day 15, the teacher presents reading words using all three /a/ vowel sounds (see page 97).

Next, show the "**a**" flashcard. Both the manuscript writing and typewriter printing of the letter should be on the flashcard. Demonstrate by saying the picture and then the sounds, even though the picture is not on the flashcard. Picture association helps those children who may have difficulty in remembering the sounds.

Storytime. During the day, read books to the children. Continue to establish good listening habits. It is also important to work on reading comprehension skills (see *More Reading Strategies* on page 191). Suggested books that have the "yellow" theme:

1. *Yellow Button* by Anne Mazer
2. *Yellow, Yellow* by Frank Asch
3. *Curious George* (man with a yellow hat) by H. A. Rey

Mascot. A stuffed animal, such as "Clifford" or "Curious George," could be a class mascot. The mascot may go home with students during each of their special VIP weeks. A writing assignment may be part of the mascot's home visit (see *"mascot" journal* on page 74). Books about the mascot may be read for many succeeding days.

Writing Clocks. A clock is an excellent prop to use in teaching beginning writing. Children need to get into the habit of starting certain letters at 2 o'clock. These letters are **a, c, d, f, g, o, q,** and **s.** Starting at 2 o'clock makes the transition to cursive writing much easier. On the poster-board clock (see *K. Clock Poster* on page 19), the teacher puts a pointer finger on the circle by 2 o'clock and slowly goes around the circle, counter-clockwise, *chanting:* "Put your finger at 2:00. Up to 12:00. Down to 6:00. Back to 2:00. Lift up your finger." The voice may go up and down at the appropriate times. Repeat this process several times, having the children chant along with the teacher. Then choose a few children to come up and be the teacher (put pointer finger at 2 o'clock and go around the clock) as everyone else chants. Draw two horizontal writing lines on the chalkboard, low enough for the children to reach. Write about six circles (clocks) between the two lines. Each circle should touch both lines. The teacher points to where 2:00 would be on the first circle. Let children come up and find 2:00 on the other circles.

Handwriting Paper 1. The children are now ready to write their own "clocks" (see *H.W. 1* on page 34). Both halves of this reproducible are identical, so duplicate half of the number needed and cut the papers in half.

The teacher uses an overhead projector and writes on a transparency as the children write on their papers. Everyone should say the chant, as it helps to remember which direction to go. When writing, chant the word "pencil" instead of "finger." Children need to be taught to hold their pencils correctly. They should sit tall when they write, with their chairs close to the desk. Both hands are used in writing. One hand holds the pencil, and the other hand holds the paper. When letters are written incorrectly, the bad habits are often hard to break. *Suggestion:* Until everyone has been individually instructed in writing his or her own name, the teacher writes each child's name (including the starting dots) on the first line of each handwriting paper (see *H.W. 1* example below). The children simply trace over the teacher's printing of the name.

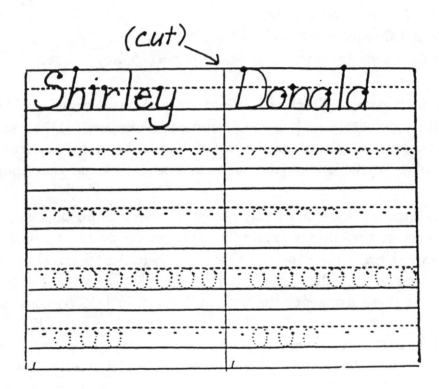

Figure 5.1. Handwriting Paper 1

Note: The pencil starts where the dot is placed. Line 2 is for tracing. Line 3 includes tracing and writing their own half circles. Line 4 is for tracing. Line 5 includes tracing and writing their own "clocks."

Suggestions:

1. Do not allow erasing with any of the handwriting papers. Reasons for this are:
   a. When children are erasing, they are not watching.
   b. Children need to learn to "think" before they write.
   c. They are just learning, so perfection is not expected. (To reinforce the no-erasing rule, teacher may purposely make errors on the transparency. The errors are not erased. Instead, the teacher moves on and tries again.)
2. When correcting writing papers, look for a best writing, and put a happy face or star above it. If no "best" is apparent, then the teacher may write correctly over one, to show what it should have looked like.
3. The teacher should never move away from the overhead projector to help individual students. Moving away is disruptive for the other students and takes too much time. Helping individuals should be done at some other time. It is great if there is an aide in the classroom to give individual help!

Class Rules. Read yesterday's rules and then introduce two more class rules at two different times during the day. The teacher reads and discusses the rules. The students practice reading with the teacher. *Note:* At this point, the children read everything as sight words. They memorize, because most of the children do not yet have enough phonetic skills to use while reading.

Free Time. Before giving out the first practice-work paper, introduce a new free-time activity, such as clay or Unifix cubes. Discuss all the rules pertaining to this new activity. Tell the children that today they have two choices for free time: read a library book or do the new activity. When introducing a new free-time activity, allow enough time after the last practice-work paper for everyone to have a chance to work with the activity. *Caution:* Children must always do their "best" with all assignments. From the beginning, do not let them hurry and be sloppy in their work just so that they have time for the "fun" activities. This discourages lots of "flitting around."

Practice-Work Papers. During the morning, find time to do at least two practice-work papers. A suggestion is to have papers that reinforce yesterday's color-word, "red." Because the children are not yet ready to write independently, coloring and cut-and-paste papers are something that they may be taught to work on by themselves. Some schools and/or teachers may not approve of duplicated papers; however, independent assignments must be selected with care. Work should be challenging and meaningful, yet not beyond the capabilities of the majority of the students. Don't expect the children to write independently until they have been taught some necessary writing skills. Also, children need to have activities that can be completed independently without disturbing others. If a teacher expects to have minimum interruptions while working with reading groups, the early teaching of independent work habits is essential.

Writing Names. In first grade, having an aide is a must at the beginning of the year. If your school does not have paid aides, solicit parents or friends to help out. The aide begins working with children individually to watch them write their names on the name-writing papers (see *M. Name-Writing Papers* on page 19). With a colored pen, the aide goes over the printed name on the top writing line, starting each letter at the dot. The formation of each letter is discussed. Then the aide watches and helps the children write their names on the remaining lines. Encourage touching the lines, as most first graders, with practice, are ready to write on lines. Continue this process for as many days as it takes for all of the children to be proficient at writing their own names.

VIP Corner. Finally, sometime during the day, the teacher should share more of the VIP items.

6

Day 3

READING AND WRITING OBJECTIVES

1. Review previous lessons.
2. Read the color-word "blue."
3. Introduce sounds for **Cc** and **Dd.**
4. Continue to write "clocks."
5. Read final two class rules.
6. Begin oral blending.
7. Listen to daily poem and stories.

BEFORE THE SCHOOL DAY BEGINS, PREPARE THE FOLLOWING:

1. Add "blue" to the bulletin board and have flashcards available.
2. Put **Cc** and **Dd** on the alphabet display and have flashcards available.
3. Select daily poem and stories to read.
4. Duplicate Handwriting Paper 2 and transparency.
5. Plan practice-work papers and free-time activity.
6. Select final two class rules.
7. Select ten compound words for oral blending (see *Oral Blending* on page 12 and *Oral Blending Word Lists* on page 14).
8. Prepare letter to parents about participating in the classroom (see *Volunteer-Aide Letter* on page 241).

THE THIRD SCHOOL DAY BEGINS

A Poem a Day. Begin the day by reading a poem. *Suggestion:* "Quiet"

> I can be as quiet as a spider or an ant.
> Quiet as a butterfly;
>   don't tell me that I can't.
> I can be as quiet as a little fleecy cloud.
> Quiet as a snowflake;
>   now that isn't very loud.
> I can be as quiet as a baby chick asleep,
> Quieter than that!
>   How quiet can *you* keep?

—*Walter L. Mauchan*

Reading Names. Take attendance by reading the names in the pocket chart.

Teacher Message. The format for messages written on the chalkboard may start to change. For instance, do not draw a big happy face today. Instead, write: "Good listening, John!" and draw a small happy face after the message. Read it out loud after writing it. If there is enough room on the chalkboard, leave the message up all day. Repeat the pattern throughout the day with other students . . . "Good listening, Sue!" and so forth.

Class Rules. Read the four class rules that were introduced the first two days of school. Add the final two rules at two different times during the day. Remember to reread whenever a rule needs reinforcing.

"I Want to Learn" Chart. Read the chart *"In first grade, I want to learn . . . "* First, practice yesterday's choral reading pattern in which the children read the beginning patterns ("How to" and "About") and the teacher reads the endings. Next, the teacher reads the beginning patterns and the children read the endings. Finally, the children choral read alone.

Storytime. Read library books to the children. If there is a class mascot, read another book from that series (*Clifford* or *Curious George*). Suggested books to read for the third day of school have the "blue" theme:

1. *I Want a Blue Banana!* by Joyce Dunbar and James Dunbar
2. *Blue Sea* by Robert Kalan
3. *Blue Tortoise* by Alan Rogers

Color Words. The teacher stands by the "color" bulletin board and teaches the new color word, "blue." Practice reading "blue" on the flashcard. Read all three color-word flashcards (red, yellow, and blue), changing the order each time. Send the "blue" flashcard home for homework.

Sounds of Cc and Dd. Review the three sounds of **Aa,** first naming the picture. Point to the **Cc** on the alphabet display. Name the picture and say the sound: "/k/." *Caution:* This is a single sound: /k/ and *not* /kŭ/. Remember to point to the picture as you say it, and point to the letters when you say the sound. Now say "Your turn," and the children respond, saying the picture and the sound. Repeat this process several times. (The letter "c" has another sound, /s/; however, only one sound is introduced at this time.) Next, move to the **Dd** and repeat the same teaching procedure: Say the picture and then the sound "/d/." Review the sounds of the three letters that are now showing on the alphabet display. Someone might notice that there is a space where the **Bb** should be. Keep it a "mystery" as to why that happened (learning all of the 2-o'clock letters first). Wait until all of the 2-o'clock letters are taught to solve the "mystery." *Note:* The various letter formations are detailed in the next section of this chapter.

Do not forget to introduce the "c" and "d" flashcards. Always use the same procedure: Say the "picture" and then the sound. Practice by continuously mixing up the three flashcards. *Note:* Make a game out of the practice sessions. See if you can "trick" them (get them to make an error). *Suggestion:* Do not spend a lot of time soliciting words that begin with the sounds being taught. That skill should have been thoroughly worked on in kindergarten and would take too much time now. The children should have opportunities to review beginning sound skills in practice-work activities and in reading groups, especially the low reading group.

Letter Formations. With the exception of "f," "k," "t," and "x," all of the lower-case letters are written without lifting the pencil, thus easing the transition to cursive writing. The advantages of forming certain letters as done in this book are:

"e": Most traditional manuscript programs form the "e" by first making a "c" and then lifting the pencil to add the horizontal line in the middle. This is not advisable because the "c" has to begin lower than 2:00 (at 3:00) for the line to be properly placed, and the letter is easier to form in one continuous line without lifting the pencil.

"k": Writing the two slanted lines without lifting the pencil (rather than using two separate strokes) is preferable and allows for an easy transition to cursive writing.

"q": The "tail" at the end may either curve up or be a short slanted line pointing to the letter "**u**" (which always follows a "**q**"). The slanted line pointing to the "**u**" (q) is not as likely to be reversed as a curve (ɋ), which can possibly be reversed to follow the same direction as the curve at the end of a "**g**" (ɡ). It is important to use a "tail"; otherwise, the "**q**" looks like a backwards "**p**," which may lead to another reversal problem.

"t": It is preferable to begin with a tall line letter because no other letters begin between the middle and top lines. It should cross on the middle line, just like the "**f**." Consistency is important!

"y": Most traditional manuscript programs form a "**y**" using a *short* slanted line and then a *long* slanted line (ʏ). Many children will often reverse this letter (ⱱ). The modern (but not slanted) manuscript formation of a "**y**" using a "**u**" with the "tail" of a manuscript "**g**" (ɥ) is preferable as it is formed without lifting the pencil, it is not likely to be reversed, and it is helpful in the transition to cursive writing.

2:00 letters:	a, c, d, f, g, o, q, s
Tall line letters:	b, h, k, l, t
Short line letters:	i, j, m, n, p, r, u, y (ɥ)
Slanted letters:	v, w, x
Letters that begin by going across:	e, z

Free Time. Prior to discussing the first practice-work paper, introduce another free-time activity, such as jigsaw puzzles (see *8. Jigsaw Puzzles* on page 24). There must be enough puzzles for the entire class to work on them at the same time, about three children per puzzle. Tell the children that they now have three choices for free time.

Practice-Work Papers. Plan time for assigning two or three practice-work papers. Try to include one new type of paper each day, preparing the children for working independently in the future. The teacher should monitor the work, thus establishing good work habits. The aide continues working with the individual name-writing papers. Children who learned how to write their names correctly the previous day may be given a second paper to complete independently. The teacher should watch them write at least one name to be sure they are still forming all letters correctly.

Writing Clocks. Review 2 o'clock on the poster-board clock. Draw some circles (clocks) between horizontal lines on the chalkboard. Put your pointer finger where 2 o'clock should be on the first circle and erase the circle with your finger, *chanting:* "Put your finger at 2:00. Up to 12:00. Down to 6:00. Back to 2:00. Lift up your finger." Select children to come up to the chalkboard to erase the remaining circles (using their pointer fingers) with everyone chanting in the same manner (children enjoy the process and are eager to participate). This gives the students a "feel" for the way the circle is formed and helps avoid their incorrect reversal of the direction of letters later on.

Handwriting Paper 2. This paper is very much like Handwriting Paper 1. It also needs to be cut in half. Learning to write circles is important and takes practice. The teacher writes on a transparency with an overhead projector as the students write on their papers. On line 2 find 2 o'clock and trace the circle. Complete the circles on lines 3 and 4. Students make their own circles on line 5. Spacing can be difficult. Tell the children to go far enough to have room to make a circle—not too far, yet not too close. Demonstrate on the transparency what is meant by "too far" and "too close."

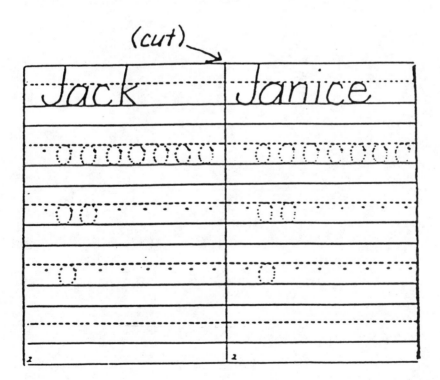

Figure 6.1. Handwriting Paper 2

Oral Blending. It is time to begin oral blending. See *Oral Blending* on pages 12 to 13 for detailed instructions. Select ten compound words to use for this first oral blending lesson (see *Oral Blending Word Lists* on page 14).

VIP Corner. Continue showing more pictures and/or items from the VIP table. At the end of the week, be prepared to read your VIP chart story. If the first week of school is a three-day week, then the chart story should be put up and read today.

Volunteer-Aide Letter. Send home the volunteer-aide letter (see *Resources* on page 241) soliciting the participation of parents in the classroom. This volunteer program begins on Day 20. Prior to that day, the teacher needs to meet with the volunteers to tell them what they will be doing in the classroom, the class rules, and other pertinent information. *Suggestion:* Once the program begins, write specific directions for that day's activities. These directions may be put on a clipboard and left by the door for the parents to read as soon as they arrive in the room.

7

Day 4

Reading and Writing Objectives

1. Review previous lessons.
2. Read the color-word "green."
3. Learn to write the lower case "**a.**"
4. Listen to daily poem and stories.
5. Continue oral blending with compound words.

Before the School Day Begins, Prepare the Following:

1. Add "green" to the bulletin board and have flashcards available.
2. Select stories to read, planning vocabulary development and comprehension questions (see *More Reading Strategies* on page 191).
3. Select daily poem.
4. Rearrange names in the pocket chart into alphabetical order with the boys and girls intermingled (no headings).
5. Plan practice-work papers and free-time activity.
6. Duplicate Handwriting Paper 3 and transparency.
7. Select ten more compound words for oral blending.
8. Add last items to the VIP table (five-day week).
9. Prepare for color mixing: yellow + blue = green (see pages 44-45).

THE FOURTH SCHOOL DAY BEGINS

A Poem a Day. Most poems require some discussion before and after about the messages that they convey. "Friendship's Rule" has a message that can be repeated many times throughout the school year.

> Our teacher says there is a rule
> We should remember while at school,
> At home, at play, whate'er we do,
> And that's the rule of friendship true.
> If you would have friends, you must do
> To them the kindly things that you
> Would like to have them do and say
> To you while at your work and play.
> And that's the rule of friendship true;
> It works in all we say and do.
> It pays to be a friend polite,
> For friendship's rule is always right.

> —*M. Lucille Ford*

Reading Names. Take attendance by reading the names in the pocket chart. Ask whether anyone notices the change. Explain that the names are no longer separated into two separate lists. This alphabetical order should remain constant, unless there are changes in the enrollment.

Color Words. Teach the fourth color word, "green." First introduce the word at the bulletin board. Practice all of the color words. Then practice all four color-word flashcards, frequently changing the order. Send home the "green" flashcard for homework. *Suggestion:* The first three color words that were introduced are the primary colors: red, yellow, and blue. Next, the secondary color words are to be taught. Although the following are neither reading nor writing activities, these science lessons do incorporate the thematic approach to teaching.

Mixing Colors. Colors can be mixed in many different ways. *Suggestions:*

1. Using a clear plastic glass, put yellow food coloring into some water. Add blue food coloring. Yellow + blue = green
2. Put yellow liquid tempera paint into clear, resealable storage bags, one per student. Add blue liquid tempera paint. Carefully seal the bag. Let the

children "squish" the bags to mix the colors. These bags may go home if they are inserted inside another resealable storage bag.

3. Put yellow frosting (purchased in a tube) on graham crackers. Add blue frosting. The children blend the frostings with their fingers to make the new color, "green." They get to eat this science experiment, so have plenty of napkins available!

4. Add drops of red, yellow, and blue food coloring to ice cube trays. Fill the trays with water and freeze. Melt yellow and blue ice cubes together to make green. Save the remaining ice cubes to make orange and purple later.

5. Have the children color a picture using only blue and yellow crayons. By using one color over the other, green will appear in the picture.

Storytime. Suggested books for today have the "green" theme:

1. *Green Eggs and Ham* by Dr. Seuss
2. *Those Green Things* by Kathy Stinson and Deidre Betteridge
3. *Little Blue and Little Yellow* by Leo Lionni (mixing colors!)
4. *Where Are You, Little Green Dragon?* by Klaus Baumgart

Sounds. No new sounds are introduced today. Review the sounds of the letters learned so far. First practice by using the alphabet display. Then use the flashcards, changing the order of the flashcards several times.

Writing the Letter "a". Because the letter "a" is a clock letter, review on the chalkboard four circles, *chanting* as you write: "Put your pencil at 2:00. Up to 12:00 . . . " Draw three horizontal lines on the chalkboard. The middle line should be dotted, just like primary writing paper. The letter "a" is written between the dotted line and the baseline. It is a short 2-o'clock letter, which means that it begins at 2 o'clock under the dotted line. The *chant* is the same, except at the end: "Put your pencil at 2:00. Up to 12:00. Down to 6:00. Back to 2:00. Down to the baseline." D'Nealian writers might say: "Curve down and out at the baseline." Write at least six lower-case "a" letters on the chalkboard. Then repeat the technique of erasing with a pointer finger. Demonstrate with the first "a," chanting as you erase. Select children who are watching to erase remaining letters correctly.

Handwriting Paper 3. This paper is for writing clocks, short lines, and the letter "a." From now on, it will be assumed that the teacher will use the appropriate transparency on the overhead projector with each handwriting paper. The children must watch whenever the teacher demonstrates on the transparency. The teacher and the students always chant as each letter is being written.

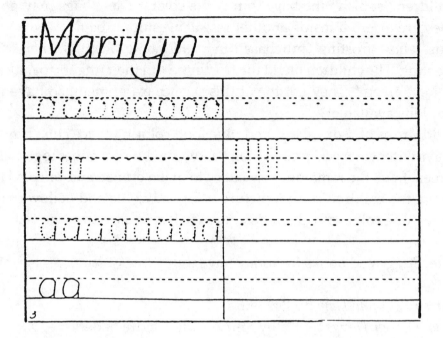

Figure 7.1. Handwriting Paper 3

Note: The letter "**a**" is a "clock" and a short line. In writing, straight lines always go down, not up. Line 4 is for tracing and writing the letter "**a.**" Line 5 is for writing an "**a**" without 2:00 dots for guidance. (Review spacing.)

"Break-Out" Activities. Handwriting papers can take quite a while to complete. Take a break somewhere in the middle. Have the children stand and do some moving activities, such as (1) Simon Says; (2) warm-up exercises; (3) motion songs such as "This Old Man," "I'm a Little Teapot," and "She'll Be Coming Round the Mountain."

Teacher Message. The messages should gradually become more complex; however, until a majority of the students are proficient readers, the same message pattern should be written each time during any given day. Perhaps today, the message pattern could read: "Shawn is a good listener!" and "Jimmy is a good listener!" After writing the message the first time, the teacher reads it out loud. The second time the same message pattern is written, the teacher says "Get ready" and only the children read it.

"I Want to Learn" Chart. Read the chart story. Many of the children may now be able to read the entire chart with little or no assistance. Select some of these children to read one sentence alone. Do not expect this chart to be mastered by all students.

It may be set aside and not worked with every day; however, it should not be taken down until the space is needed. During total-class free time, encourage the children to use pointers (a stick for "tracking" while reading charts) and to read anything on the walls (and chalkboard). Children enjoy "reading the walls."

Free Time. Plan another new free-time activity. This is the last time that this reminder will be included in the daily lesson plans. *Reminder:* Add one activity per day until all the activities have been introduced. Always allow enough time on the day of introduction for everyone to work with the new activity. If free-time activities are thoroughly explained and monitored at the beginning of the year, the remainder of the year will be a "piece of cake." *Suggestion:* After all the free-time activities have been introduced, establish a format as to what the children are to do when they have all of their work finished. Reading a library book could always be the first free-time activity, and then they can choose one other activity. If the second activity is finished, then they must return to reading a book before starting a third activity. This format establishes reading as the top priority. *Reminder:* Keep reminding the children what it takes to read (look at) a book.

Other Daily Activities. Sometime during the day, find time to:

1. Work on practice-work papers and writing names.
2. Read all class rules.
3. Continue oral blending with ten additional compound words.
4. Continue with the VIP activities. *Suggestion:* Monday through Thursday are for showing items. Friday is for reading the chart story.

8

Day 5

READING AND WRITING OBJECTIVES

1. Review previous lessons.
2. Read color-word "orange."
3. Write the letters "**a**," "**c**," and "**d**."
4. Learn sounds for **Ff** and **Gg.**
5. Decorate names for art.
6. Listen to daily poem and stories.
7. Practice oral blending with two-syllable words.
8. Practice reading teacher's VIP chart story.

BEFORE THE SCHOOL DAY BEGINS, PREPARE THE FOLLOWING:

1. Add "orange" to the bulletin board and have flashcards available.
2. Put up **Ff** and **Gg** and have flashcards available.
3. Select daily poem and stories to read.
4. Plan practice-work papers and free-time activity.
5. Duplicate Handwriting Paper 4 and transparency.
6. Select ten two-syllable words for oral blending.
7. Write names for art (see example on page 51).
8. Write VIP chart story (see *S. VIP Chart Story* on page 21).
9. Assemble items for color mixing: yellow + red = orange.

THE FIFTH SCHOOL DAY BEGINS

Reading Names. Take attendance by reading the names in the pocket chart.

A Poem a Day. The Mother Goose rhyme "There Was a Little Green House" might follow the introduction of the color-word "green."

There was a little green house,
And in the little green house
There was a little brown house,
And in the little brown house,
There was a little yellow house,

And in the little yellow house,
There was a little white house,
And in the little white house,
There was a little heart.

Suggestion: Make the four houses out of construction paper, with the green house being the largest and the white house being the smallest. Also make a tiny red heart. Put small magnetic strips on the top two corners of each house and on the back of the heart. Place them in order, one over the other, on a large metal cookie sheet. Remove each house at the appropriate time. Let the children get involved in reciting the poem and in removing the houses.

Color Words. Teach the fifth color word, "orange." Practice the five flashcards. Send the "orange" flashcard home for homework.

Oral Blending. Two-syllable words may now be used for oral blending.

Sounds of Ff and Gg. Review all sounds learned so far. Introduce the sounds /f/ and /g/. Remember to say the picture before the sound. Because they look different, write both the manuscript and typewriter "**g**" on the flashcard.

Writing the Letters "c" and "d." Draw three horizontal writing lines on the chalkboard. On the lower line, write "**a**" two times, chanting as you write. Choose two children to erase them (using a pointer finger) while the class chants. Next, refer to the poster-board clock and make a letter "**c**" by starting at 2 o'clock and ending at 4 o'clock. Then, write "**c**" six times on the chalkboard lines, chanting as you write. The *chant* for the letter "**c**" might be: "Put your pencil at 2:00. Up to 12:00. Down to 6:00. Back to 4:00. Lift up your pencil." The letter "**c**" is a short 2-o'clock letter because it begins under the dotted line. Select children to chant and erase the letters.

Draw three more horizontal writing lines. Use the same process to teach the letter "**d.**" The *chant:* "Put your pencil at 2:00. Up to 12:00. Down to 6:00. Back to

2:00 and up, up (have your voice go up) to the tall letter line and straight down to the baseline." Because it begins under the dotted line, the letter "**d**" is a short letter with a tall part. A frequent reminder of this can help in avoiding reversals. *Note:* This is the final day that chalkboard erasing will be discussed as a means of teaching letter formation; however, continue using this same technique for all of the other remaining lower-case letters.

Handwriting Paper 4. The format for the handwriting papers should now be familiar: Trace the first half of the line and complete the same letter on the second half of the line. Line 5 is for independent practice. Words may be written on line 5, always using letters that have already been taught. Two words that may be written on Handwriting Paper 4 are "dad" and "add." The children have to learn to leave a "clock space" between words. Placing a Cheerio between words is a "fun" way to learn how much space is needed (see *Suggestion* on page 152).

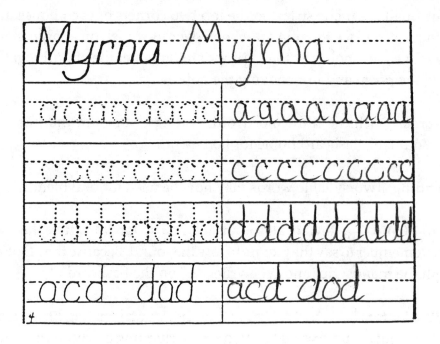

Figure 8.1. Handwriting Paper 4

When writing words, the children need to learn to reverse the "say it fast" technique and "say it slowly." For example, in oral blending the teacher said: "/**d**/ /**ă**/ /**d**/ Say it fast," and the children responded: "dad." To reverse the process, the teacher says "dad" and then asks: "What was the first sound?" Answer: "/**d**/." Teacher: "Write it." (Teacher writes on a transparency.) Teacher: "What is the next sound? /**d**/ /?/ . . . " (Lead the children into the next sound by repeating the preceding sounds.) Answer: "/**ă**/." Teacher: "Write it." (Emphasize the need to have all letters in words close but not touching.) Teacher: "What is the last sound? /d/ /ă/ /?/ . . ." Answer: /d/." Teacher: "Write it."

Teacher Message. Continue to write messages on the chalkboard. An idea for today is: "David and Carol are good listeners." Throughout the day, erase just the names and write two different names in their place.

Class Rules, Chart Stories. Sometime during the day, review reading the class rules and any chart stories.

VIP Chart Story. Teacher tracks and reads own VIP chart story. Read it a second time, encouraging the children to read too. Leave the chart story up so that it can be reread on following days. The children can use it for "reading the walls." *Note:* If this is Friday, then it is time to select the next VIP. Send home the reminder letter (see *VIP Letter* on page 242) along with the class mascot and two journal writing papers (see Figure 13.2 on page 74). The VIP is encouraged to bring a few things to share each day.

Storytime. Suggested books for today have the "orange" theme:

1. *The Big Orange Splot* by Daniel Manus Pinkwater
2. *I Feel Orange Today* by Patricia Godwin and Kitty Macaulay
3. *Pig's Orange House* by Ethel and Leonard Kessler (mixing colors)

Names for Art. This art lesson is good for reading and spelling names:

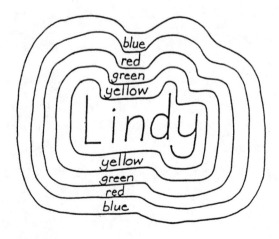

Figure 8.2. Art Names

Using an extra-wide black marking pen, each child needs to have his or her name written (by the teacher) in the center of a piece of 12″ × 18″ white construction paper. Step-by-step instructions to the children are:

1. Choose any color crayon except black.
2. Outline the entire shape of the name—close, but not touching.
3. Use the same color to double the outline, about one inch away.
4. With the same color crayon, color between the two lines.
5. Choose a different color and outline about one inch away.
6. Color in the space with this second color.
7. Keep repeating with different colors until the paper is filled.

Teacher cuts around the final shape and puts the names on a wall in alphabetical order. Choose a wall that could display these names throughout most of the school year. Children can refer to them for spelling names. *Note:* Children can learn a lot from visual exposure. One first grader, while away from school, had written from memory everyone's name in his class in alphabetical order. Each name had been spelled correctly.

Mixing Colors. Sometime during the day, have another science lesson:

yellow + red = orange

9

Day 6

READING AND WRITING OBJECTIVES

1. Review previous lessons.
2. Read color-word "purple."
3. Write the letters "**f**" and "**g**."
4. Learn sounds for **Oo** and **Ss.**
5. Listen to daily poem and stories.
6. Continue oral blending with two-syllable words.
7. Practice reading chart story, "Mary Wore a Red Dress."

BEFORE THE SCHOOL DAY BEGINS, PREPARE THE FOLLOWING:

1. Add "purple" to the bulletin board and have flashcards available.
2. Put up **Oo** and **Ss** and have flashcards available.
3. Select daily poem and stories to read.
4. Plan practice-work and free-time activity.
5. Duplicate Handwriting Paper 5 and transparency.
6. Select ten two-syllable words for oral blending.
7. Remove names from the pocket chart (save).
8. Prepare "Mary Wore a Red Dress" chart (see page 55).
9. Assemble items for color mixing: red + blue = purple.

THE SIXTH SCHOOL DAY BEGINS

A Poem a Day. A suggested poem for today is "Drinking Fountain."

At first just a trickle,   Right smack in my eye:
Two drops splash and tickle.   The fountain must think
And then there's a spurt,   That I need a face-wash
A sudden big squirt,   More than a drink!

—*Ethel Jacobson*

Reading Names. It should no longer be necessary to take attendance by reading the names. However, continue the practice of reading names. *Suggestion:* Occasionally, instead of saying names, hold up the name flashcards that were saved from the first day of school pocket-chart activity.

Color Words. Teach the color-word "purple." Practice all color-word flashcards. Send home the "purple" flashcard for homework.

Sounds. Review all sounds. Use a pointer stick to go over the sounds on the alphabet display, saying the pictures and the sounds. Repeat the process using the flashcards. Change the order of the cards. Also, position yourself at the back of the room, so that the children cannot refer to the alphabet display.

Sounds of Oo and Ss. Introduce the sounds for the letters **Oo** and **Ss.** Remember that **Oo** has three sounds ($/\breve{o}/$ $/\bar{o}/$ $/\ddot{o}/$) and **Ss** has two sounds ($/s/$ $/z/$).

Handwriting Paper 5. This paper teaches the letters "f" and "g." In teaching the "**f**," discuss tall letter 2 o'clock. If children are taught the counter-clockwise direction for writing clocks, the "f" is less likely to be reversed. *Chant:* "Put your pencil at tall letter 2:00. Up to 12:00. Down, down to the baseline. Lift up your pencil. Across on the dotted line." The letter "**g**" begins just like an "**a**" except for the ending: " . . . Back to 2:00. Down, down and make a monkey's tail." *Note:* The "tail" touches the line below the baseline.

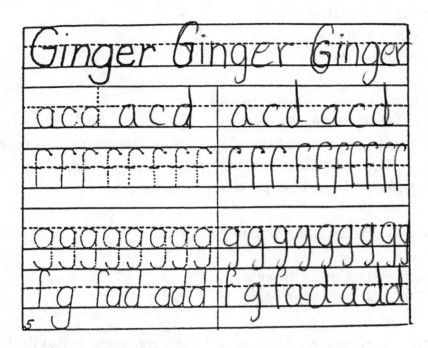

Figure 9.1. Handwriting Paper 5

"Mary Wore a Red Dress" Chart. The folk song "Mary Wore a Red Dress" lends itself to a chart story and the making of a class book. Write this pattern on a large chart paper:

> Mary wore a red dress,
> red dress, red dress.
> Mary wore a red dress
> All day long.

Suggestion: Color code the chart. For example, write the name ("Mary") in red, "wore" in blue, the color ("red") in black, the article of clothing ("dress") in green, and the rest ("a" and "All day long") in purple. "Track" and read the four lines to the children. Practice choral reading it until mastered. Have a child come up and find the word "Mary" wherever it appears. Have another child find all the "red" words. Someone else can find "dress." "All day long" and "a" may also be found.

Using the pattern of the first line, finish the chart paper by writing sentences pertaining to children in the classroom. Use the same color code. Change the color and the article of clothing to fit the student. The additional sentences might read:

> Sally wore a green dress.
> Brian wore a yellow shirt.
> Justin wore blue jeans.

Practice reading these additional sentences.

A class book that patterns this song may be worked on tomorrow. To make the book, the children will draw pictures of themselves wearing particular articles of clothing in specific colors. The teacher will write a sentence under the picture with the same pattern: "Jeri wore a purple skirt all day long."

Teacher Message. The message for today might be:

> Table 1 (Row 1) is ready to begin.
> Table 2 (Row 2) is ready to begin.

Oral Blending. Continue working on oral blending, using two-syllable words. Perhaps today's words may be all of the two-syllable names in the class. This is a good time to introduce the clapping of syllables. The purpose of clapping syllables is to prepare the children for spelling. Later they will be taught to spell by "claps" (syllables).

First, blend the two-syllable words without clapping. Then repeat the list of words with clapping. For example, "Lin-da" would need two claps. Ask: "How many claps did you hear?" Answer: "Two." Repeat the name and let the children clap with you.

Practice-Work Papers. The work today might be to color a picture. Students may only use red, yellow, and blue crayons. Green and orange should appear when the proper colors are combined. Remind them that drawings should be completely colored and that the picture should fill the entire paper.

Mixing Colors. Sometime during the day, have another science lesson:

> red + blue = purple

Storytime. Suggested books for the sixth day of school are:

1. *Harold and the Purple Crayon* by Crockett Johnson
2. *The Purple Coat* by Amy Hest
3. *Lilly's Purple Plastic Purse* by Kevin Henkes

"Show and Tell." There are pros and cons to having the children "Show and Tell" on a regular basis. Developing oral language is one of the "pros." The sharing of "news" may also be used in the teaching of reading. *Suggestions:*

1. Assign one day per week for each child to share.
2. Establish some ground rules: Limit the talk to 3 minutes. If a child brings an object, it should be one that stimulates learning, such as a plant, a rock, or a book (a toy seldom fits this category). There should be no exaggerating and no discussion of private family matters.
3. If a child forgets to bring something, select a topic to talk about: tell about his or her favorite sport, TV show, book, or food.
4. After each child shares, write a sentence about the sharing.
5. Read each sentence as it is written; then have the children read it.
6. At the end of the session, chorally read the entire chart story.
7. Leave each chart up for a week. Replace last week's chart with today's, so there are always five charts up for "reading the walls."
8. Make a copy of the chart and place the copy in a cumulative "Good News" book. *Suggestion:* Use a binder when pages are added on a regular basis to a class book. Binders are also good for the VIP chart stories and the "mascot" journals.

Note: At the beginning of the year, the sentences should be written very simply. Most sentences can be written with the verbs "has," "told," or "went." Later in the year, the sentences should become more complex. The following are two examples of the same "news"; one might have been shared in September and the other in April.

Good News
Today is Monday,
    September 15, _____.
Janice has a black backpack.
Brad told about his trip.
Bonnie has three rocks.
Ashley has a good book.
Jason went to a restaurant.
Travis told about his dog.

Good News
Today is Monday,
    April 11, _____.
Janice brought a new backpack to school.
Brad saw Mickey Mouse at Disneyland.
Bonnie found three rocks in the mountains.
Ashley read a book about a funny clown.
Jason's family ate at a Chinese restaurant.
Travis' dog had four puppies last night!

10

Day 7

READING AND WRITING OBJECTIVES

1. Review previous lessons.
2. Read color-word "black."
3. Write the letters "**o**" and "**s**."
4. Learn sound for **Qu qu**.
5. Listen to daily poem and stories.
6. Practice oral blending to three-syllable words.
7. Illustrate a class book: *Mary Wore a Red Dress*.

BEFORE THE SCHOOL DAY BEGINS, PREPARE THE FOLLOWING:

1. Add "black" to the bulletin board and have flashcards available.
2. Put up **Qu qu** and have flashcard available.
3. Select daily poem and stories to read.
4. Plan practice-work and free-time activity.
5. Duplicate Handwriting Paper 6 and transparency.
6. Select ten three-syllable words for oral blending.
7. Prepare cover and papers for *Mary Wore a Red Dress* book.

Note: Most purchased alphabet sets do not include a "**u**" after the "**q**." To reinforce the idea that a "**u**" always follows the "**q**," it is advisable to insert a "**u**" after the lower-case "**q**" on the alphabet display.

The Seventh School Day Begins

A Poem a Day. A silly poem to follow the introduction of the color-word "purple" is "Mabel Murple." *Suggestion:* For a listening activity, tell the children that they will be asked to draw a picture to go with the poem after listening to it just one time.

> Mabel Murple's house was purple   Mabel Murple's bike was purple
> So was Mabel's hair   So were Mabel's ears
> Mabel Murple's cat was purple   And when Mabel Murple cried
> Purple everywhere.   She cried terrible purple tears.
>
> —*Sheree Fitch*

Suggestion: Later in the day (after the pictures are drawn) reread the poem, pausing to let the children shout "purple" whenever the word is needed.

Sound of Qu qu. Review all sounds. Introduce the sound /**qu**/. Tell the children that the letter "**u**" always follows the letter "**q**" and the sound they make together is /**kw**/.

Teacher Message. Today's chalkboard message might be:

> Stand if you have a red dress.
> Stand if you have blue pants.

Oral Blending. Today's blending activities may be with three-syllable words. Include names of children in the class that have three syllables. Clap the three-syllable words. Ask: "How many claps did you hear?"

Storytime. Suggested books for the seventh day of school have the "black" theme:

1. *Four Black Puppies* by Sally Grindley
2. *Old Black Fly* by Jim Aylesworth
3. *Black Crow, Black Crow* by Ginger Foglesong Guy

Handwriting Paper 6. This paper teaches the letters "**o**" and "**s**." The "**o**" was already taught when learning to make clocks. The letter "**s**" is often reversed; however, if the starting direction is taught as being the same as writing a clock, the "**s**" will be written correctly. *Chant:* "Put your pencil at 2:00. Up to 12:00. Curve down to 6:00 and make a snake's tail."

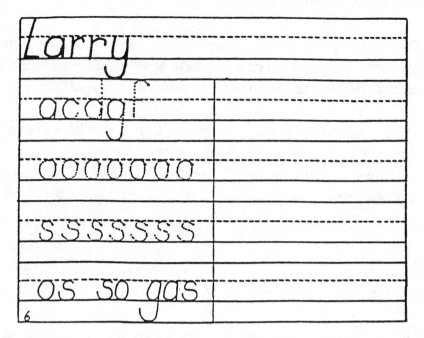

Figure 10.1. Handwriting Paper 6

Color Words. Teach the color-word "black." Review all color-word flashcards. Send home the "black" flashcard for homework. *Note:* Because the flashcard homework assignments are not returned to school, the teacher needs to remind the children what they should be doing for homework (learning to read the words). When reviewing color-word flashcards, individual students may be called on to read all the words. Different children may be called on each day as a means of assessing their reading of the color words. A parent may need to be contacted if a child has apparent difficulties. The difficulty may be because of not doing the homework, or it may be because of a learning disability.

Practice-Work Paper. Another color-mixing paper may be included today: Color a picture using only the red, yellow, and blue crayons. This time green, orange, and purple must appear somewhere in the picture.

"Mary Wore a Red Dress" Book. Once again, read the four lines. Then teach the children to sing the words. (Whenever songs are taught via reading, the children first learn to read it as a poem; then they learn to sing it.) One at a time, read the personal sentences on the chart paper ("Sally wore a green dress." "Brian wore a yellow shirt.") and learn to sing each one, following the four-line pattern. Finally, include other children from the class in this manner: Hold up the flashcard of a child's name. That child stands and quickly comes forward. The teacher points to the article of clothing that will be mentioned. For instance, if the teacher points to a black belt, they will sing:

"_____ wore a black belt, black belt, black belt.
(child's name)

_____ wore a black belt, All day long."
(child's name)

In preparing a class book, it is best to have a directed drawing lesson first, teaching the children how to draw people. Then, as each child works on his or her final picture, the teacher goes around and writes one sentence on each paper. The sentence pattern would be:

"Sally wore a green dress all day long."
"Brian wore a blue shirt all day long."
"Justin wore black shoes all day long."

After assembling the pages into one book, let each child read his or her page to the rest of the class. Then add the book to the class library.

11

Day 8

READING AND WRITING OBJECTIVES

1. Review previous lessons.
2. Read color-word "brown."
3. Write "**qu.**"
4. Listen to daily poem and stories.
5. Practice oral blending with multi-syllable words.
6. Develop patterned sentences: "I see a _____ _____."

BEFORE THE SCHOOL DAY BEGINS, PREPARE THE FOLLOWING:

1. Add "brown" to the bulletin board and have flashcards available.
2. Duplicate Handwriting Paper 7 and transparency.
3. Prepare charts for patterned sentences: "I see a _____ _____." (see page 65).
4. Select daily poem and stories to read.
5. Plan practice-work papers and free-time activity.
6. Select multi-syllable words for oral blending.

THE EIGHTH SCHOOL DAY BEGINS

A Poem a Day. "The Painting Lesson" is about mixing colors to make new colors. Perhaps this poem can be read on the day that painting is introduced to the class.

Red and blue make purple
Yellow and blue make green.
Such a lot of colors
To paint a lovely scene.

Pink and blue make orchid;
Black and white make gray.
Now I'll dry my brushes
Until another day.

—Frances Greenwood

Color Words. Teach "brown." Review all color-word flashcards. Send home the "brown" flashcard. *Note:* This is the last color word to be introduced for awhile. The color-word "white" may be introduced with the phonogram /**wh**/. "Gray" may be added with the phonogram /**ay**/. "Pink" may be introduced when that color word is needed.

Sounds. No new sounds are introduced today. Plan a game for reviewing sounds learned so far. *Suggestion:* Divide the class into two groups. Show Group 1 the flashcard of a letter of the alphabet (perhaps an "**a**"). The teacher says "Get ready," and Group 1 chants only the name of the picture (apple) that goes with the letter. That flashcard ("**a**") is not shown to Group 2. The teacher simply points to the group and says "Get ready." Group 2 chants the sounds (/ă/ /ā/ /ä/). Mix up the flashcards and switch group instructions. Repeat until the children start to tire of the game.

Handwriting Paper 7. This paper teaches the children to write "**qu.**" The "**q**" is the last 2-o'clock letter to be taught. Remind the children that the letter "**u**" always follows the "**q**." (Qantas, a proper name, is one of the very few exceptions.) When writing the "**q,**" the *chant* is the same as for the letter "**a,**" except at the end: " . . . Back to 2:00. Down, down and a line (or curve) pointing to its twin ("**u**")." For the letter "**u**," *chant:* "Put your pencil on the dotted line. Down to the baseline. Curve up and down."

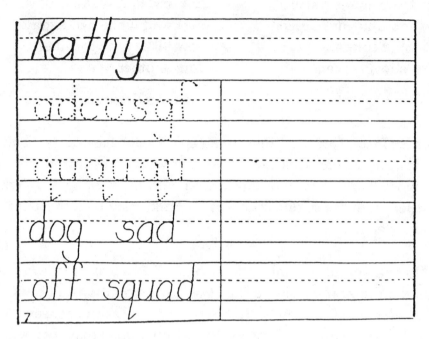

Figure 11.1. Handwriting Paper 7

Alphabet Display. Now is the time to ask if anyone can solve the mystery. Why are there spaces in the alphabet display? *Answer:* Letters put up so far (**a, c, d, f, g, o, q,** and **s**) all begin at 2 o'clock.

Oral Blending. For oral blending, use another list of three-syllable words or a list with an increased number of syllables. Clap the words when saying them the second time. Be sure all multi-syllable names of children have been included. One-syllable names will be used later when each sound is isolated.

Practice-Work Papers. Now that the eight color words have been introduced, two types of pictures may be colored on two separate days. One day the children would use all eight colors to make one complete picture. On the other day, a paper would be folded into eight squares. The children color eight pictures, one per square, using a different color in each square.

Storytime. Book suggestions for the eighth day are:

1. *The Great Blueness* by Arnold Lobel
2. *Brown Bear, Brown Bear, What Do You See?* by Bill Martin Jr.
3. *Brown Cow, Green Grass, Yellow Mellow Sun* by Ellen Jackson
4. *My Many Colored Days* by Dr. Seuss

Note: Brown Bear, Brown Bear, What Do You See? is an excellent book for reading and writing patterned sentences. After reading the book to the children, write the following teacher's message.

Teacher Message. This message is in preparation for the patterned sentences to be written later in the day.

> I see a red ball. (Point to it.)
> I see a brown piano. (Point to it.)

"I see a _____ _____" **Chart.** Today's patterned sentences follow the pattern: "I see a _____ _____." The sentences are written on large chart papers. Each child needs to be included in a sentence. Considering the attention span of many first graders, it might be wise to divide the class into thirds, possibly in alphabetical order. If there are 24 children in the class, one third (8) of the children participate in composing today's sentences. Tomorrow, eight more children participate. The final eight children have their turn on the third day. With this division, there will be three chart papers.

Ask the first child to name something "red" he or she sees in the room. Write the patterned sentence. Let the child sign his or her name after the sentence. Ask the next child to name something "yellow" in the room. Write that patterned sentence. Let the child sign his or her name after the sentence. Continue this procedure, finding different objects in different colors. Be sure that all eight colors are included in a sentence each day. *Suggestion:* Color code each sentence. Alternate writing the sentences with two different colored marking pens, such as red and blue. A third color, perhaps black, may be used for all signatures. The first day's chart may read something like this:

I see a red ball. Kyle	**Color Key**
I see a purple crayon. Nicole	**Bold** = red
I see a brown chair. Luke	*Italics* = blue
I see an orange jacket. Cara	Names = black

When all of the day's sentences have been written, practice choral reading the chart.

12

Day 9

READING AND WRITING OBJECTIVES

1. Review previous lessons.
2. Learn sounds for **Bb** and **Hh.**
3. Write "**b**" and "**h.**"
4. Read the number-words "one" and "two."
5. Continue to develop patterned sentences: "I see a _____ _____."
6. Listen to daily poem and stories.
7. Practice oral blending using words with three single sounds.

BEFORE THE SCHOOL DAY BEGINS, PREPARE THE FOLLOWING:

1. Put up **Bb** and **Hh** and have flashcards available.
2. Put "one" and "two" on the number-word display. Have class and homework flashcards available (see *E. Number Words* on page 18).
3. Duplicate Handwriting Paper 8 and transparency.
4. Select words for oral blending.
5. Select daily poem and stories to read.
6. Plan practice-work papers and free-time activity.

Note: When putting up the number words, leave a space for "zero," which will be added after "ten" is introduced.

THE NINTH SCHOOL DAY BEGINS

A Poem a Day. A suggested poem for today is "Wiggly Tooth."

Once I had a little tooth
That wobbled every day;
When I ate and when I talked,
It wiggled every way.

Then I had some candy—
A sticky taffy roll;
Now where my wiggly tooth was—
Is nothing but a hole!

—Lillie D. Chaffin

Sounds of Bb and Hh. Review the sounds that have been learned so far. Teach the two new sounds: /b/ and /h/.

Oral Blending. The class should be ready for single sounds in oral blending. Select words that have three separate sounds in each word, for instance /c/-/ă/-/t/, /b/-/ŭ/-/g/, and /d/-/ŏ/-/g/. Include any children with names having only three sounds, such as /S/-/ĭ/-/d/, /J/-/ă/-/n/, and /R/-/ĭ/-/ck/.

Handwriting Paper 8. Explain that both the "b" and "h" are tall line letters. They both begin alike, with the tall line going down. The *chant* for "b" is: "Down to the baseline. Up to the dotted line, around and touch the line." The *chant* for the "h" is: "Down to the baseline. Up to the dotted line. Make a hill and go back down to the baseline."

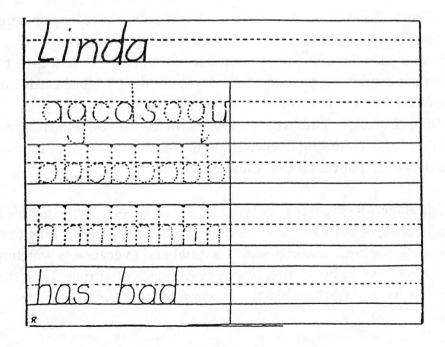

Figure 12.1. Handwriting Paper 8

Reversals. Always refer to the "**b**" as a tall line letter and the "**d**" as a short 2-o'clock letter with a tall part. Keep repeating this concept, because reversing these two letters is very common. *Suggestion:* Prepare and put up a chart to help children in distinguishing between a "**b**" and a "**d**." Leave room so that a "**p**" can be added later. Vertically, divide a heavy piece of paper into thirds. The first third needs a picture of a /**b**/ word, such as a *b*us, with a large letter "**b**" written under it. The middle third needs a picture of a /**d**/ word, such as a *d*inosaur, with a large letter "**d**" written under it. Later, a picture of a /**p**/ word, such as a *p*ig, may be added in the remaining space.

Figure 12.2. b-d-p

Number Words. Teach "one" and "two" just as the color words were taught. First, tap the "one" at the number-word display and say "Get ready." The children respond: "one." Do the same for the number-word "two." Practice the flashcards away from the display. At the end of the day, send the two flashcards home in an envelope (see *F. Homework Flashcards* on page 18).

Suggestion: Correlate math with the reading of the number words. Use manipulatives for the understanding of each number. Teach the writing of the numerals. Plan practice-work papers around these numbers.

Teacher Message. Messages may be written to change behavior, to get the attention of the entire class, or both. At the same time, the children are learning to read. The teacher should continue writing until it is quiet and everyone is watching. Three sentences may have to be written before everyone is attentive. Then the teacher says "Get ready" and tracks while the children read all three sentences:

Mike is working very quietly.
Jane is working very quietly.
Billy is working very quietly.

Storytime. Select books that correspond to the number words being taught. If "one" and "two" are introduced today, then books such as these may be read:

1. *One Hungry Spider* by Jeannie Baker
2. *One Bear With Bees in His Hair* by Jakki Wood
3. *Two Lonely Ducks* by Roger Antoine Duvoisin
4. *Two Bad Ants* by Chris Van Allsburg

"I see a _____ " Chart. Choral read yesterday's patterned sentences. Solicit sentences from the next group of children. Write the sentences on another chart paper, using two different colored marking pens. Let each child write his or her name in black after each sentence. Choral read these new sentences.

13

Day 10

READING AND WRITING OBJECTIVES

1. Review previous lessons.
2. Learn sounds for **Kk** and **Ee.**
3. Write "**k**" and "**e.**"
4. Read the number-words "three" and "four."
5. Practice oral blending, using words with four single sounds.
6. Develop final set of patterned sentences: "I see a _____ _____."
7. Listen to daily poem and stories.

BEFORE THE SCHOOL DAY BEGINS, PREPARE THE FOLLOWING:

1. Put up **Kk** and **Ee** and have flashcards available.
2. Put up "three" and "four" and have flashcards available.
3. Duplicate Handwriting Paper 9 and transparency.
4. Select words for oral blending.
5. Select daily poem and stories to read.
6. Plan practice-work papers and free-time activity.

Note: Because there are not that many activities planned for today, this could be a "catch-up" day. It is important not to get behind in the introduction of new sounds and the corresponding handwriting papers. Other suggested activities are not as critical in timing . . . follow your own time line.

THE TENTH SCHOOL DAY BEGINS

A Poem a Day. A poem for the number-word "one" is "A House for One."

> The turtle children,   Each baby turtle
> Sister and brother,   Is happy alone
> Do not live in one house   In a snug little house
> With their father and mother.   Of his very own.
>
> —*Laura Arlon*

Sounds of Kk and Ee. Review all sounds learned so far. Teach the new sounds: /k/ and /ĕ/ /ē/.

Number Words. Teach the reading of the words "three" and "four." Practice all of the number-word flashcards several times, mixing them up each time. Send home the two new flashcards for homework.

Oral Blending. Continue blending words that have four separate sounds, such as /h/- /ĕ/- /l/- /p/, /j/- /ŭ/- /m/- /p/, and /S/c/- /ŏ/ -/tt/).

"I see a _____ _____ " Chart. Choral read the two completed chart stories with the patterned sentences. Solicit sentences from the final group of children. Write the sentences and let each child sign his or her name. Choral read the new sentences.

Handwriting Paper 9. This paper teaches the tall letter "**k.**" The *chant* is: "Down to the baseline. Pick up your pencil and move out to the dotted line. Slant in. Kiss the line! Slant down." The letter "**e**" is a line letter that starts by going across. The *chant:* "Across. Stop and make a point. Up to 12:00. Down to 6:00. Back to 4:00. Lift up your pencil."

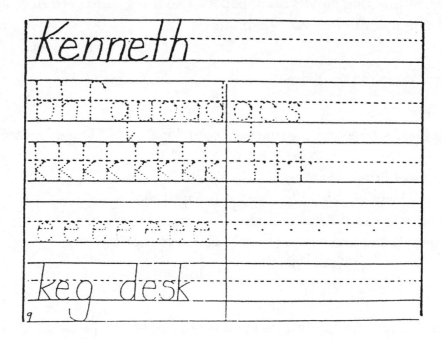

Figure 13.1. Handwriting Paper 9

Teacher Message. Another idea might be:

John has finished his work. Good job, John!
Sharon has finished her work. Good job, Sharon!

VIP Chart Story. Before Friday, the teacher needs to interview the VIP, to gather information for the chart story. All questions are not appropriate for all students. Some suggested questions are: (a) What does your dad do at his job? (b) What do you like to do with him? (c) Same two questions about mom. (d) What does your brother do? (e) What do you like to do with him? (f) Same questions about all siblings. (g) Do you have any pets or collections? (h) What do you like to do at home and at school? (i) Have you ever gone anywhere special? (j) What is your favorite food, game, and TV show?

At the beginning of the year, the teacher first tracks and reads the entire VIP chart story. Then the story is reread, with the children choral reading with the teacher. As the year progresses, the children should be able to read the story the first time without having it read to them. However, the teacher should read with the children during the second reading. This rereading is for those who may not have been able to read it the first time and also for fluency (good expression).

Suggestion: Before the large chart is sent home with the VIP, recopy the story and put it in a class VIP book.

The following is a copy of Kendra Gates's VIP story. The picture that was taken on the first day of school was taped beside the first sentence. Kendra's name was on the picture.

> I am special!
> My mommy works for children who need foster homes.
> My dad works at Jessup Doors, but it is closing down.
> I was adopted right after I was born.
> I'm lucky my parents chose me!
> I ride horses out at Sun Hunter.
> I went to summer camp there.
> I ride in horse shows.
> I belong to the Orland 4-H Club.
> I'm in cooking and arts and crafts.
> I like to read!

In writing these stories, two different colored pens may be used. Change colors with the change of topics (lines 6, 7, and 8 are three sentences, but only one topic). The next topic may begin right after it on the same writing line, but in a different color. Thus, no writing lines are wasted, and the change of color helps the children in their reading.

Mascot. The class mascot gets to stay at home with the VIP for the entire week (Friday to Thursday). Set Thursday as the deadline. If it is forgotten, a phone call or reminder needs to be sent home.

Journal. The journal is an important part of sending the mascot home. The VIP writes about what happened with the mascot during the week. (If the VIP is not yet able to write, the story is dictated to someone in the family.) The journal comes back to school with the mascot on Thursday, and it is read to the class.

Suggestions:

1. Send home two copies (an extra in case of a mistake) of the mascot writing paper. The teacher may write the date on the first line.

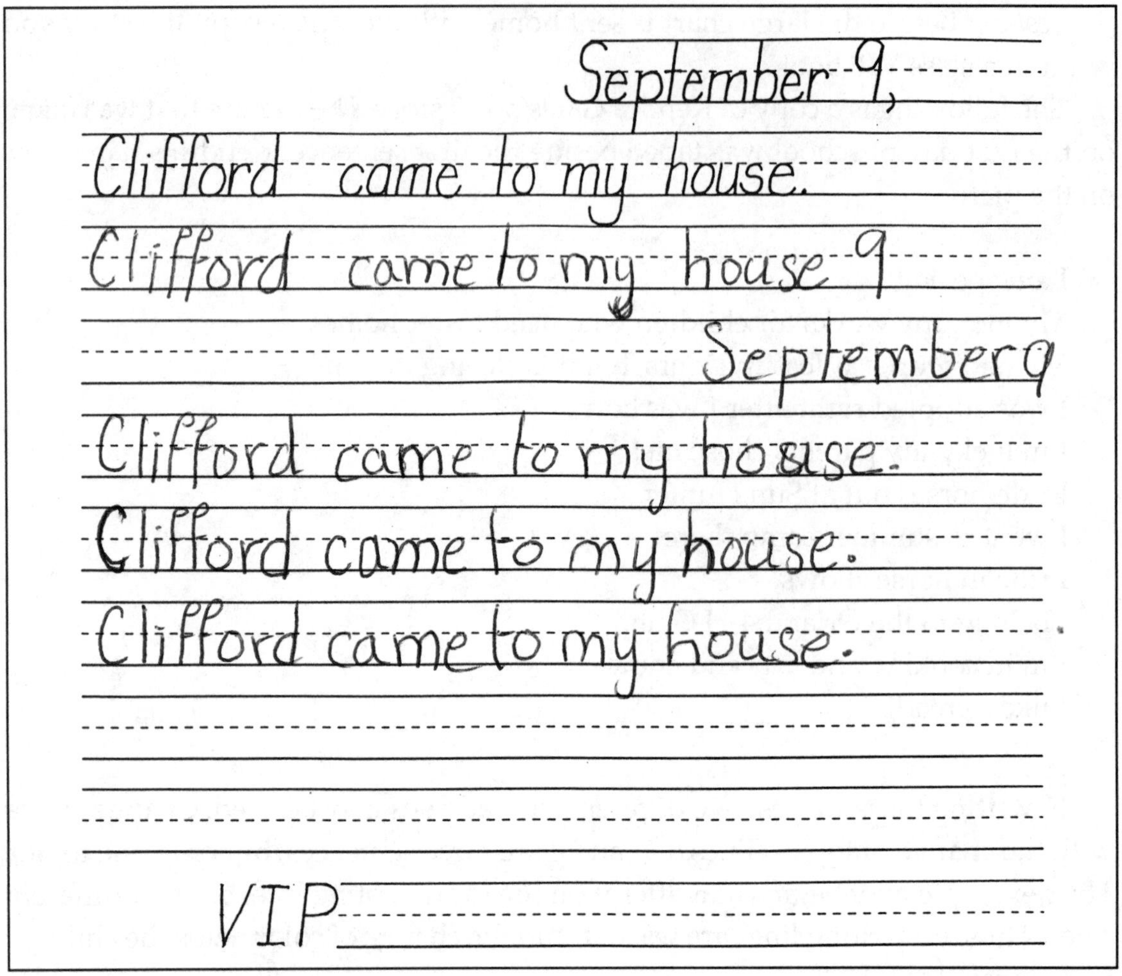

Figure 13.2. Mascot Journal

2. Send papers home in a file folder with side pockets for holding the writing papers. Upon return, the journal is added to a cumulative "mascot" book.
3. Get a canvas bag for carrying the mascot and journal to and from school.

Storytime. Suggested "number" books to read today are:

1. *Goldilocks and the Three Bears* by Jan Brett
2. *Three Blind Mice* by John W. Ivimey
3. *Bea's Four Bears* by Martha Weston
4. *Four Black Puppies* by Sally Grindley

Suggestion: Feature well-known authors and illustrators throughout the year. Plan activities to enhance the study of these distinguished writers and artists.

14

Day 11

READING AND WRITING OBJECTIVES

1. Review previous lessons.
2. Learn sounds for **Ii** and **Jj.**
3. Write "**i**" and "**j.**"
4. Read the number-words "five" and "six."
5. Listen to daily poem and stories.
6. Illustrate and read patterned sentences: "I see a _____ _____."
7. Practice oral blending with five (or more) single sounds.

BEFORE THE SCHOOL DAY BEGINS, PREPARE THE FOLLOWING:

1. Put up **Ii** and **Jj** and have flashcards available.
2. Put up "five" and "six" and have flashcards available.
3. Duplicate Handwriting Paper 10 and transparency.
4. Prepare papers for patterned-sentences: "I see a _____ _____."
5. Select daily poem and stories to read.
6. Plan practice-work papers and free-time activity.
7. Select final words for oral blending.

THE ELEVENTH SCHOOL DAY BEGINS

A Poem a Day. A poem for today might be "Old King Cole" with his fiddlers three. This Mother Goose rhyme has been set to music.

Old King Cole	Every fiddler, he had a fiddle,
Was a merry old soul	And a very fine fiddle had he;
And a merry old soul was he.	Twee tweedle dee, tweedle dee,
He called for his pipe	Went the fiddlers.
And he called for his bowl	Oh, there's none so rare
And he called for his fiddlers three.	As can compare
	With King Cole and his fiddlers three.

Number Words. Teach the number words "five" and "six." Now there are six number words to practice. Send home the "five" and "six" flashcards for homework.

Oral Blending. This will be the last time that oral blending will be planned for the entire class. Most of the children have undoubtedly perfected this skill. Those children needing more practice will get it again in the smaller reading groups.

Sounds. Teach the new sounds: /ĭ/, /ī/, and /j/. It is important that the children continue to review all sounds learned so far. Two distinctly different skills need to be developed. The first skill is for reading, and the second skill is for spelling.

Skill 1: Ability to say the sound when shown the letter. Show flashcards and let the children chant the sounds.

Skill 2: Ability to write the letter when told the sound. Say the sounds without showing the flashcards and have the children write the letters. If there's an aide, practicing this skill works well in small groups. Children may write on individual chalkboards. The aide can readily see whether each child knows how to write the correct letter. *Note:* Individual chalkboards for all students are great to have in a primary classroom. The chalkboards may be kept in children's desks along with chalk and a sock for an eraser. The children may be assigned tasks during practice-work time, such as writing words or practicing letter and number formations. Chalkboards may also be a choice during free time.

If there is no aide in the classroom, the teacher can do the following: Subdivide the back side of each handwriting paper into numbered boxes (see Form 14.1 at end of chapter) and dictate the sounds after completing the front side. *Suggestion:*

Because a teacher cannot keep watch over the entire class during a Skill 2 dictation lesson, the following teaching technique is a possibility:

Make a transparency of the numbered, sectioned, lined paper. Dictate a sound for the children to write in the first box. Allow enough time for the children to write the letter. Then the teacher writes the letter in the first box on the transparency, using an overhead projector. The children must write the letter again, in the same box, beside the one already written.

Writing it correctly is important! If they make an error, they may not erase it. Keep watch to see that no one waits and writes both letters at once! Continue this process for all letters being reviewed: one letter per box with each letter being written two times. When correcting this dictation lesson, the teacher can readily see those who know the letters and those who need help.

Handwriting Paper 10. This paper teaches the letters "i" and "j." They are both short line letters. The *chant* for the "i" is: "Down to the baseline. And a dot on top." The letter "j" begins the same: "Down to the baseline. Down, down and make a monkey's tail. Then a dot on top."

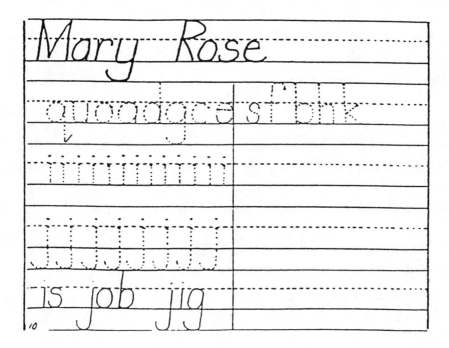

Figure 14.1. Handwriting Paper 10

Teacher Message. When the children come in from recess, a chalkboard message is an excellent means of getting them quiet and settled for the next activity. The message might say:

> Everyone at Table 3 came in and quietly sat down. Good job!
> Everyone at Table 1 came in and quietly sat down. Good job!

Write until all tables are quiet. Then, choral read the messages.

Practice-Work Papers. Today, each child can illustrate his or her sentence from the three previous chart stories. The teacher needs to have prepared the papers beforehand by writing each sentence for each child.

The format can be changed just a little. On the chart, the sentences read:

> I see a red ball. Kyle
> I have a blue car. Allison
> I want a purple shirt. Nicole

The practice-work sentences may be changed to:

> Kyle sees a red ball.
> Allison has a blue car.
> Nicole wants a purple shirt.

Remind the children to add more to their pictures. Assemble all of the papers into a book, perhaps titled *What Do We See?* Read the book to the children. Perhaps the children could read their own pages! Add the book to the class library.

Storytime. Suggested number-word books to read today are:

1. *Five Silly Fishermen* by Roberta Edwards
2. *Five Little Monkeys Sitting in a Tree* by Eileen Christelow
3. *Six Little Ducks* by Chris Conover
4. *Six Foolish Fishermen* by Benjamin Elkin

Form 14.1

15

Day 12

READING AND WRITING OBJECTIVES

1. Review previous lessons.
2. Learn sounds for **Ll** and **Uu.**
3. Write "l" and "**u.**"
4. Read the number-words "seven" and "eight."
5. Practice reading poem "Quack! Quack! Quack!"
6. Listen to daily poem and stories.
7. Learn to play the game "I'm Thinking of a Sound."
8. Begin testing for reading and writing skills.

BEFORE THE SCHOOL DAY BEGINS, PREPARE THE FOLLOWING:

1. Put up **Ll** and **Uu** and have flashcards available.
2. Put up "seven" and "eight" and have flashcards available.
3. Duplicate Handwriting Paper 11 and transparency.
4. Select daily poem and stories to read.
5. Write chart: "Quack! Quack! Quack!" (see today's poem).
6. Plan practice-work papers and free-time activity.
7. Divide children into three groups for testing.
8. Plan testing activities.

THE TWELFTH SCHOOL DAY BEGINS

A Poem a Day. After introducing the number-word "six," the traditional poem/song "Quack! Quack! Quack!" is ideal to read.

> Six little ducks that I once knew,
> Big ones, little ones, skinny ones, too.
> (*Refrain*) *But the one little duck with the*
> *Feather on his back,*
> *All he could do was, "Quack! Quack! Quack!"*
> *All he could do was, "Quack! Quack! Quack!"*
> Down to the river they would go,
> Waddling, waddling, to and fro.
> (*Refrain*)
> Up from the river they would come.
> Ho, ho, ho, ho, hum, hum, hum.
> (*Refrain*)

Suggestion: Because the last four lines of each verse (*refrain*) are the same, write these four lines on a chart paper. Then, the teacher could recite the first two lines of each verse and the children could read the last four lines.

"I'm Thinking of a Sound." Introduce a new game. Mix up the letter flashcards. Place them into a pocket chart. The teacher thinks of one of the letters (perhaps "**s**") and says "I'm thinking of a sound. What sound am I thinking of?" The first child in order might guess: "/ŏ/ /ō/ /ö/." Because that guess is incorrect, keep soliciting guesses until a child says the correct sounds . . . /s/ /z/. That child comes up and takes that flashcard. The teacher thinks of a new sound and continues the game with the next child in order. The game ends when all of the flashcards have been selected. Collect all the flashcards.

Handwriting Paper 11. The new sounds for today are /l/ and /ŭ/ /ū/ /ü/. In writing the letters, the "**l**" is simply a tall line letter. The *chant* is: "Down to the baseline." The letter "**u**" is a short line letter. It was previously taught with the letter "**q**." The *chant* is: "Put your pencil on the dotted line. Down to the baseline. Curve up and down."

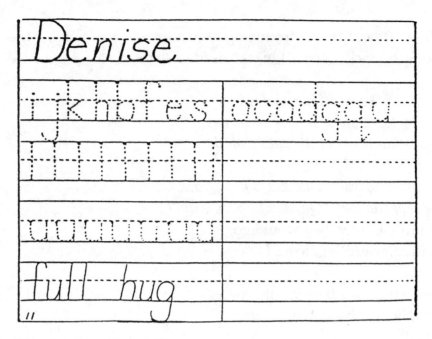

Figure 15.1. Handwriting Paper 11

Number Words. Teach the number words "seven" and "eight." Review all number words. Send home the two new flashcards for homework.

Practice-Work Papers. There are many books available on ideas for practice-work. Because the children have not yet been instructed in writing all of the letters, select writing activities with care. Bad habits are hard to break! At this point, the children should be able to work independently on activities that reinforce beginning sounds, color words, and number words.

Teacher Message. The messages do not always have to be in praise of good behavior. Learning to read the message is also an important goal. The following message could be written when you feel your class is ready for it:

> This morning I found a red box on my desk.
> I opened the box. Can you guess what was in the box?

Choral read the message before calling on children to guess. Be creative as to what is in that box! (new storybook? jump ropes? cookies?)

Working With Reading Groups. This is a good time to begin working with three groups, rather than total-class instruction. The purpose of these groups is to begin testing in order later to establish ability reading groups. Plan for three 20-minute time periods. While the teacher works with one group at the reading table, another group is doing practice-work at their desks, and the third group is with an aide at another table. If there is no aide, then the third group has "controlled" free time (teacher-planned), away from their desks. Possible schedule:

	Practice-Work	**Teacher**	**Aide/Free Time**
First 20 minutes	Group 1	Group 3	Group 2
Second 20 minutes	Group 2	Group 1	Group 3
Third 20 minutes	Group 3	Group 2	Group 1

Note: It is easiest for the teacher to call a group *from* practice-work. Then the teacher sends the group *to* the aide (or free time).

Aide. The aide could work on reviewing and testing the writing of sounds, formation of letters, and name writing. Each child in the group has a lined chalkboard, a chalk pencil, and an eraser. When testing for sounds, the aide says "Write an /ă/ /ā/ /ä/." In small groups, the aide can see who is able to write the sounds (not letter names) without assistance. This skill is important for spelling.

Free Time. Without an aide, "controlled" free time is a good alternative. "Controlled" means that the free-time activities are assigned. Because one group will be at their desks with practice-work, it is important that these free-time activities are not disruptive.

Plan 1. All children do the same free-time activity (e.g., Unifix cubes) at five different locations in the classroom. Two children may work together. The activity is changed each day (e.g., pattern blocks on the second day, clay on the third day).

Plan 2. Set up five different activities at five different locations. The children work in pairs. Each child goes to only one center a day. It takes five days to complete the five centers. Suggested centers are: (1) Unifix cubes, (2) easy art, (3) pattern blocks, (4) jigsaw puzzles, (5) clay.

If any children finish practice-work or free time early, their only choice is to read a book. They may sit on the floor near the class library.

Teacher. At the reading table, the teacher begins testing. Areas for testing are sounds, color words, number words, names, oral blending, chart stories, and reading comprehension. Rather than completely testing each child separately, move from child to child to eliminate long periods of waiting. For instance, in testing color words, ask the first child to read the first color-word flashcard. The next child gets the next word, the third child gets the next word, and so forth. Eventually, each child will get every word. Don't allow too much waiting time. The children should know the skill being tested rather quickly. Individual testing will later be needed for those who made errors.

To test reading comprehension, plan to read the same short story to each of the three groups. It is best to choose stories without pictures, or not to show the pictures until after testing is completed. After reading the story, ask each child one recall question to test for comprehension (see *2. Recall Questions* on page 193).

Storytime. Suggested books to read today:

1. *Seven Blind Mice* by Ed Young
2. *Seven Little Rabbits* by John Leonard Becker
3. *Seven Froggies Went to School* by Kate Duke
4. *What Do I Do at 8 O'Clock* (Pop-up book) by Carla Dijs

16

Day 13

READING AND WRITING OBJECTIVES

1. Review previous lessons.
2. Learn sounds for **Mm** and **Nn.**
3. Write "**m**" and "**n.**"
4. Read the number words "nine" and "ten."
5. Practice reading nursery rhyme: "One, Two, Three, Four, Five."
6. Illustrate sentence strips: "I see a _____ looking at me."
7. Listen to daily poem and stories.
8. Continue testing for reading and writing skills.

BEFORE THE SCHOOL DAY BEGINS, PREPARE THE FOLLOWING:

1. Put up **Mm** and **Nn** and have flashcards available.
2. Put up "nine" and "ten" and have flashcards available.
3. Duplicate Handwriting Paper 12 and transparency.
4. Write chart for nursery rhyme: "One, Two, Three, Four, Five" (see page 88).
5. Select daily poem and stories to read.
6. Prepare sentence strips: "I see a _____ looking at me."
7. Plan aide or center activities.
8. Plan testing activities.

THE THIRTEENTH SCHOOL DAY BEGINS

A Poem a Day. A suggested poem for today is "The Silent One."

He never makes a sound   Although he may not mind
To tell when he's around;   Being the silent kind,
Can't sing when he feels sunny   I wish that a giraffe
Or laugh when something's funny; Could laugh.

—*Margaret E. Singleton*

Handwriting Paper 12. Review all sounds and then teach the two new sounds: /**m**/ and /**n**/. When writing, both are short line letters. This writing paper teaches the "**n**" first. Explain that an "**n**" is like an "**h**" except that it begins with a short line. *Chant:* "Put your pencil on the dotted line. Down to the baseline. Up to the dotted line. Make a hill and back down to the baseline." The letter "**m**" is exactly the same chant, except at the end add: "Make another hill and back down to the baseline."

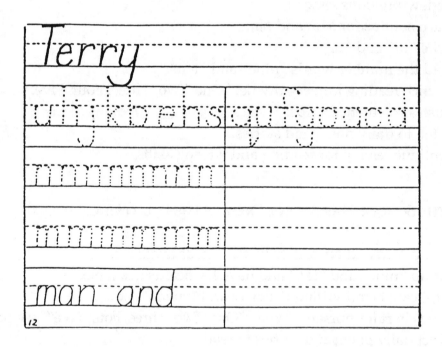

Figure 16.1. Handwriting Paper 12

Number Words. Teach the next two number words, "nine" and "ten." Review all number words (only "zero" is left!). Send home the two new flashcards for homework.

black spider

green and yellow snake

brown hat

red flower

blue balloon

orange and purple fish

Storytime. Suggested books to read for today are:

1. *Nine Ducks Nine* by Sarah Hayes
2. *Comet's Nine Lives* by Jan Brett
3. *Ten Old Pails* by Nicholas Heller
4. *Ten, Nine, Eight* by M. Band

Sentence Strip Fun. Beginning readers enjoy creating individual sentence strips. In introducing this activity for the first time, the teacher should write one sentence strip for each child. For example, each sentence strip might say: "I see a [leave a 5-inch space] looking at me."

Duplicate one set of the "red flower" paper for each child (see Form 16.1 on page 87). Each child needs to draw and color these six pictures. Each set will need to be cut apart and put into a single pile, and then stapled, one on top of the other, onto the 5-inch space left on each prepared sentence strip. Be sure that the order is the same for each child, so that they will be able to choral read them together.

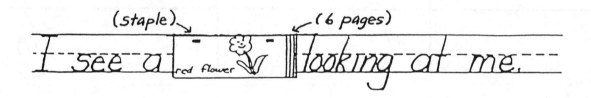

Figure 16.2. "I see a _____ looking at me."

As the year progresses, the children should be able to write their own sentences onto the sentence strips. The sentences need to include "flip" pictures that are stapled in place. In one sentence, there may even be two or three different spaces for these "flip" pictures. These pictures need to be much narrower. Some sentence suggestions are:

1. Halloween night I saw a (leave a space for "flip" pictures).
2. I am thankful for (. . . space . . .).
3. I wish I could give my mother (. . . space . . .).
4. A (. . . space . . .) is a house for a (. . . space . . .).
5. A (. . . space . . .) can (. . . space . . .). It cannot (. . . space . . .).

Figure 16.3. "A _____ is a house for a _____."

Reading Groups. Continue with the same groups for three 20-minute periods (teacher, practice-work, and aide/free time). The *teacher* continues testing in these areas: reading comprehension (read another short story), color words, names, oral blending, chart stories, sounds, and number words. Although all number words and sounds have not yet been taught, enough have been to determine the capabilities of the students.

The *aide* continues dictating sounds for children to write on individual chalkboards. Sounds may be dictated that actually form words, such as /m/ /ē/ or /r/ /ă/ /n/. *Note:* If there is no aide, the children work at one of the planned centers.

"One, Two, Three, Four, Five" Chart. Nursery rhymes are a wonderful source for teaching reading. A suggestion for today ("ten" day) is:

One, two, three, four, five,	*Why did you let it go?*
Once I caught a fish alive,	Because it bit my finger so.
Six, seven, eight, nine, ten,	*Which finger did it bite?*
Then I let it go again.	The little finger on the right.

Write the words on large chart paper. Write lines 1 and 3 (**bold** = number words) in one color; write the other lines in another color. The children read the number words; the teacher reads the other lines of the poem. More capable readers may even replace the teacher! Another possibility is to have some children read the questions (*italics* = lines 5 and 7) and other children read the answers (underlined = lines 6 and 8).

Teacher Message. Another idea for a chalkboard message is:

Today is a special day for Bob. It is his birthday. He is six years old. What can we do to make Bob happy?
(Sing "Happy Birthday.")

17

Day 14

READING AND WRITING OBJECTIVES

1. Review previous lessons.
2. Learn to distinguish between vowels and consonants.
3. Write vowels and consonants that have been introduced.
4. Read the number word "zero."
5. Read sentence strips: "I see a _____ looking at me."
6. Listen to daily poem and stories.
7. Continue testing for reading and writing skills.

BEFORE THE SCHOOL DAY BEGINS, PREPARE THE FOLLOWING:

1. Separate flashcards into vowels and consonants.
2. Put up "zero" and have flashcard available.
3. Duplicate Handwriting Paper 13 and transparency.
4. Assemble individual "I see a _____ looking at me" sentence strips.
5. Plan practice-work papers and aide/free-time activities.
6. Select daily poem and stories to read.
7. Plan testing activities.

THE FOURTEENTH SCHOOL DAY BEGINS

A Poem a Day. A suggested poem for today is "School of Minnows."

Down in the brook where the water runs cool—
That's where the minnows are going to school!
Why do they study, I wonder, and then,
When do they get to go home again?
Schools for the fish aren't like mine, I guess—
No teachers or blackboards or books—just recess!
When Daddy says, "Look! School of minnows there, Son!"
It sure looks to me like they're just having fun!

—*Jane Keefer Frey*

Sounds. Review the consonant sounds; then review the vowel sounds. Write the five vowels (**a, e, i, o, u**) on the chalkboard ("**y**" is not yet discussed as a vowel). Discuss that vowels are special. Every word and syllable (clap) must have a vowel. Talk about the fact that all vowels have more than one sound ("**a**," "**o**," and "**u**" have three sounds each; "**e**" and "**i**" have two sounds each).

Handwriting Paper 13. This paper simply separates the vowels from the consonants. Review the formation of the letters by tracing them. On line 3, change the order when dictating the vowels. On line 5, dictate the consonants in a different order than that presented on line 4.

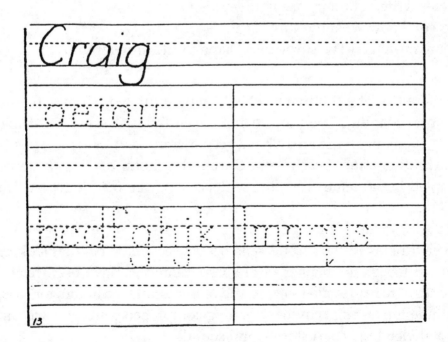

Figure 17.1. Handwriting Paper 13

Storytime. Suggested books to read today are:

1. *Ten Little Mice* by Joyce Dunbar
2. *Ten Little Rabbits* by Virginia Grossman and Sylvia Long
3. *My Crayons Talk* by Patricia Hubbard

Number Word. "Zero" is the final number word taught at this time. It is saved until last because the concept of "zero" (an empty set) should be developed after the teaching of the other numbers. However, "zero" is placed in proper order on the display (before the "one"). Teach "zero" and review all of the number-word flashcards. Send this final number flashcard for homework.

Nursery Rhyme. Practice reading "One, two, three, four, five."

Teacher Message.

After lunch, we will have a surprise.
Do you know what the surprise will be? (3 children guess)
(Later write:) The surprise is little and brown.
Now can you guess what the surprise will be? (2 guesses)
(Later write:) The surprise is alive.
Do you know what the surprise is? (1 guess)
(Final message:) The surprise is Diane's little brown puppy!

Reading Groups. The children need to be taught to use their own pointer fingers when choral reading. The pattern for the individual sentence strips (I see a _____ looking at me.) may have been memorized; therefore, it is important that the children "track" each word during the choral reading. If the six papers were stapled in the same order, the sentences may be read together. The teacher says "Get ready," and the children track and read the first sentence: "I see a red flower looking at me." Then the teacher says "Turn the page" (pause) "Get ready," and the children read the second sentence: "I see a blue balloon looking at me." Continue in this same manner until all six sentences have been read. Save the sentence strips to read again tomorrow in preparation for a homework assignment.

Continue the testing activities: reading comprehension, color words, number words, oral blending, chart stories, and sounds.

18

Day 15

READING AND WRITING OBJECTIVES

1. Review previous lessons.
2. Learn sounds for **Pp** and **Rr**.
3. Write "**p**" and "**r**."
4. Learn vowel code markings for "**a**."
5. Learn code marking for silent letters.
6. Begin reading words with /ă/ /ā/ /ä/.
7. Listen to daily poem and stories.
8. Read individual "I see a _____ looking at me" sentence strips.
9. Practice reading next VIP's chart story.
10. Listen to VIP's journal entry about mascot's visit home.
11. Continue testing for reading and writing skills.

BEFORE THE SCHOOL DAY BEGINS, PREPARE THE FOLLOWING:

1. Put up **Pp** and **Rr** and have flashcards available.
2. Duplicate Handwriting Paper 14 and transparency.
3. Put up the vowel code poster for the letter "**a**" (see *J. Vowel Code Posters* on page 19 and Resources on page 245).
4. Prepare long arrow on tagboard (see example on page 96).

5. Prepare chart with /ă/ /ā/ /ä/ words for blending (see *Suggested Words* on page 97).
6. Select daily poem and stories to read.
7. Plan practice-work papers and aide/free-time activities.
8. Plan reading group activities.
9. Write VIP's chart story.
10. Duplicate *Homework Letter 2* and *Signature Form* (see pages 238 and 215).
11. Prepare large homework envelopes (see *G. Homework Letter and Envelope* on page 18).

THE FIFTEENTH SCHOOL DAY BEGINS

A Poem a Day. "The Smile" is a delightful poem to read and demonstrate.

A scowl and a smile
      Met each other one day;
But somehow the scowl
      Was not able to stay.
Facing the smile,
      It just melted away.

—*Winifred J. Mott*

Handwriting Paper 14. Teach the two new consonant sounds: /p/ and /r/. Both are short line letters. The paper teaches the "r" first. Tell the children that its formation is similar to an "**n.**" *Chant:* "Put your pencil on the dotted line. Down to the baseline. Up to the dotted line. Make a hill but stop at 2:00." The *chant* for writing a "**p**" would be: "Put your pencil on the dotted line. Down, down, and back to the dotted line. Around and make a ball."

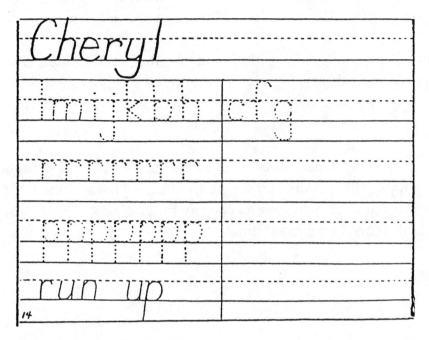

Figure 18.1. Handwriting Paper 14

Poster With b-d-p. Add a picture of a /**p**/ word, such as a pig, to the final third of the "b-d-p poster" (see Figure 12.2 on page 68). Write a large "**p**" under it.

Reversals. The letters "**p**" and "**r**" are not as likely to be reversed if the short lines are written first; then the hills are made in the direction we always move when reading or writing (to the right). When writing words, the next letter should always be "close but not touching" the previous letter. If the "**p**" or "**r**" begins with a line and is close to the previous letter, then there is only one direction to go to finish the letter properly . . . to the right. *Suggestion:* Plan activities and games that emphasize moving from left to right.

Teacher Message. The message for today might be:

> Did someone have a special smile for you today? Raise your hand and tell me who it was. I'll write their name in this big "smiling face."

Note: Draw a big "smiling face" on the chalkboard. Leave message to be reread throughout the day. If a name is repeated, put a star (*) after the name.

VIP Chart Story. Track and read the VIP story to the children. Say "Get ready" and chorally read it again. Also read the VIP's mascot journal paper.

Vowel Code. Review consonant sounds and then the vowel sounds. Discuss codes, such as the Morse Code and Sign Language. Tell the children that they are going to learn a code that their parents might not even know. They will have to teach their parents the code!

ă
ā
ä

Display this *Vowel Code Poster* for the letter "**a.**" Teach this code by first tapping the picture and saying the name of the picture: "Apple." Then move under each letter as you say the sounds "/ă/ /ā/ /ä/." Repeat this procedure several times.

Reading Groups. The following are suggestions for today's reading group activities (no testing!):

1. Practice tracking and choral reading the "I see a _____ looking at me" sentence strips. The sentence needs to be read six times, once for each colored picture. Let each child track and read one sentence alone. Explain that this sentence strip will be their homework tonight. They will need to read all six pages to an adult. The sentence strip stays home, but the signature paper needs to be returned tomorrow. (Do not plan this for a Friday.) Let each child put his or her sentence strip, Homework Letter #2, and the signature form into the new homework envelope.

2. Introduce the large arrow (drawn on a 5" × 11" piece of tagboard, using a black permanent marking pen).

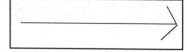

   This arrow teaches the direction for reading and writing . . . from left to right. Demonstrate the direction by putting your pointer finger on the dot and moving right to the tip of the arrow.

   Let the children all have a turn moving their own pointer fingers on the arrow.

3. Teach another code: silent letters have a little "x" over them (e.g., name, ball, and walk).

4. Begin blending sounds in the reading of words with /ă/ /ā/ /ä/. Write "căt" (mark the "a" with the vowel code) on the chalkboard with an arrow under the word. Then say:

Teacher: **"My turn. /c/ /ă/ /t/**
Say it fast."
Children: **"cat"**

Continue the same procedure with these words: **ănd, dăd, ăt, măn, săd.** *Note:* The teacher moves a pointer finger along the arrow under each letter as it is being sounded out. When the children "say it fast," the finger moves "fast" on the arrow. The children may have turns sounding with the teacher, then without the teacher, and then individually.

5. Prepare a chart with "a" words for blending by dividing a large chart paper vertically into thirds. This paper will be used for all three "a" sounds: /ă/ /ā/ /ä/. On the top writing line of the first third, write an "ă" as the heading. The middle third needs "ā" as the heading. The final third needs an "ä." List six words with all the markings under each heading.

Note: Because words do not always fit the desired pattern, do not solicit words from the students. For instance, "sleigh" has the /ā/ sound with the /eigh/ phonogram. Also, /ä/ and /ŏ/ both have the same sound (ball, not boll; yet doll, not dall). Bewildering!

Suggested words:

"ă"	căt	ănd	dăd	ăt	măn	săd
"ā"	āte	nāme	gāte	māde	wāve	plāne
"ä"	äll	bäll	wälk	tälk	wänt	hähä

Note: Save the extra lines for additional words to be added later.

Teaching Procedure. The teacher sounds out and reads each list of words. Tell the children that tomorrow they will get to sound out and read with you at the reading table. (Enough for one day . . . something to look forward to!)

Storytime. Suggested books to read today:

1. *Over in the Meadow* illustrated by Paul Galdone
2. *Rooster's Off to See the World* by Eric Carle
3. *How Many Snails . . . A Counting Book* by Paul Giganti Jr.
4. *This Old Man* by Kontz, Adams, and Jones

19

Day 16

1. Review previous lessons.
2. Learn sounds for **Tt** and **Xx.**
3. Write "**t**" and "**x.**"
4. Read words on /ă/ /ā/ /ä/ chart.
5. Learn vowel code markings for "**e.**"
6. Begin reading words with /ĕ/ /ē/.
7. Read homework paper: "I see (<u>classmate</u>) looking at me."
8. Learn to play game: "I'm Thinking of a Word."
9. Listen to daily poem and stories.
10. Continue testing for reading and writing skills.

BEFORE THE SCHOOL DAY BEGINS, PREPARE THE FOLLOWING:

1. Put up **Tt** and **Xx** and have flashcards available.
2. Duplicate Handwriting Paper 15 and transparency.
3. Put up the vowel code poster for the letter "**e.**"
4. Prepare chart with /ĕ/ /ē/ words.
5. Prepare "I see (<u>classmate</u>) looking at me" homework (see Figure 19.1 on page 100).
6. Select daily poem and stories to read.
7. Plan seatwork and aide/free-time activities.
8. Plan testing activities.

THE SIXTEENTH SCHOOL DAY BEGINS

A Poem a Day. Today's suggestion is great to use after the introduction of the sound of "**p.**" It is the tongue-twister "Peter Piper" by Mother Goose.

> Peter Piper picked a peck of pickled peppers.
> A peck of pickled peppers Peter Piper picked.
> If Peter Piper picked a peck of pickled peppers,
> Where's the peck of pickled peppers Peter Piper picked?

Suggestion: Write this poem on chart paper for the children to read and say.

Teacher Message. Another type of message could be:

> Today is a red letter day! No one is absent.
> No one was late. Give yourselves a pat on the back.

"I See (<u>classmate</u>) Looking at Me" Homework. The objective of the homework assignments for the next two or three days is to practice reading the names of the children in the classroom (teacher's name too!).

Preparation. Photocopy the pictures that were taken of the children on the first day of school, one picture per child. Cut each picture so that just the face is showing (about one inch square). Place the pictures on the left side of a blank 8½" × 11" piece of paper. Beside each picture write the same patterned sentence: "I see _____ looking at me." In the blank space, write the child's name, corresponding with the picture to the left. Example:

Figure 19.1. "I see (_____) looking at me."

There will be more than one page, depending on the size of the class. For homework, assign one page per day. The children are to read the page to an adult. Practice choral reading today's homework page. Send the paper home in the homework envelope. Tell the children that after completing the reading of the homework, the paper must be signed on the back by the adult. *Note:* These pages can be assembled into a class book titled: *Who Do I See?* It will undoubtedly be a favorite to read during "free time."

Handwriting Paper 15. Review all sounds, separating consonants and vowels. Teach the two new consonant sounds: "**Tt**" and "**Xx.**" The sound for "**x**" is /**ks**/. For handwriting, the letter "**t**" is a tall line letter. The *chant* is: "Down to the baseline. Lift up your pencil. Across on the dotted line." The letter "**x**" is a short slanted-line letter. The *chant* is: "Put your pencil at the dotted line. Slant down. Lift up your pencil. Go straight up to the dotted line. Slant down in the opposite direction."

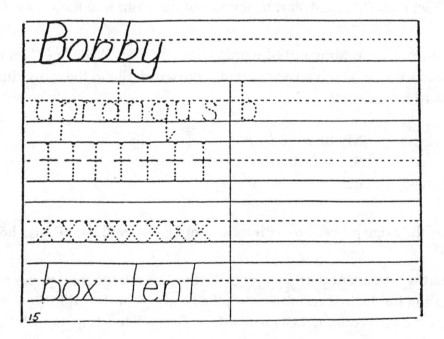

Figure 19.2. Handwriting Paper 15

Vowel Code. Review the arrow by letting a few children come up and trace it with a pointer finger, moving from left to right. Review the "**a**" vowel code.

ĕ
ē

Display the *Vowel Code Poster* for the letter "e." Teach this code by first tapping the picture and saying the name of the picture. Then move under both vowel code letters as you say the sounds: "/ĕ/ /ē/."

Reading Groups. The reading group activities may include:

1. Together, sound out and read yesterday's /ă/ /ā/ /ä/ words. Just read them through once; mastery is not yet expected. The teacher can develop a steady rhythm by saying "Get ready" with only the first word in each column. Move the pointer finger under each letter in the first word (c-ă-t) and then move "fast" under the word as the word is said "fast." Move down to the next word (ă-n-d) without saying "Get ready" . . . just start to sound out the word and then "say it fast."

2. Introduce the sounding out of words with /ĕ/ /ē/. Write "gĕt" on the chalkboard (mark the "e") with an arrow under the word. Blend the individual sounds into a word in this way:

Teacher:	**"My turn. /g/ /ĕ/ /t/**
	Say it fast."
Children:	**"get"**

Continue the same procedure with these words: **tĕn, rĕd, bē, hē,** and **hērĕ.**

3. Prepare a permanent chart by vertically dividing a large chart paper into thirds. The heading for the first column is "ĕ"; the heading for the middle column is "ē." Cut away the final column. List six words under each heading. Put a little "**x**" over the silent letters.
   Suggested words:

"ĕ"	gĕt	tĕn	rĕd	wĕnt	yĕs	ĕgg (x over gg)
"ē"	bē	hē	mē	wē	hēre (x)	Pēte (x)

Chorally sound out and read both lists of words. One time is enough.

4. Continue with individual testing.

5. Play a variation on the "I'm Thinking of a Sound" game. Put some name flashcards in the pocket chart. Say: "I'm thinking of a name." Proceed with the game (see *I'm Thinking of a Word* on page 187).

Storytime. Suggested books to read today are alphabet (ABC) books:

1. *C Is for Curious . . . An ABC Book of Feeling* by Woodleigh Hubbard
2. *From Apple to Zipper* by Nora Cohen
3. *A Helpful Alphabet of Friendly Objects* by John Updike and David Updike

20

Day 17

READING AND WRITING OBJECTIVES

1. Review previous lessons.
2. Learn sounds for **Vv** and **Ww.**
3. Write "**v**" and "**w.**"
4. Learn vowel code markings for "**i.**"
5. Begin reading words with /ĭ/ /ī/.
6. Practice reading: "One, Two, Buckle My Shoe."
7. Listen to daily poem and stories.
8. Continue testing for reading and writing skills.

BEFORE THE SCHOOL DAY BEGINS, PREPARE THE FOLLOWING:

1. Put up **Vv** and **Ww** and have flashcards available.
2. Duplicate Handwriting Paper 16 and transparency.
3. Put up the vowel code poster for the letter "**i.**"
4. Prepare chart with /ĭ/ /ī/ words.
5. Prepare chart paper: "One, Two, Buckle My Shoe" (see page 106).
6. Select daily poem and stories to read.
7. Plan practice-work papers and aide/free-time activities.
8. Plan testing activities.

THE SEVENTEENTH SCHOOL DAY BEGINS

A Poem a Day. A suggested poem for today is "Exactly Right."

They say that I'm too young
To cross the street to play,
That I'm too old to cry
When I don't get my way,
That I am much too big
To swing on the garden gate,

But very much too small
To stay up after eight.
I'm young, I'm old, I'm big, I'm small . . .
Do you think, in age and height,
I will ever grow to be
Just exactly right?

—*Laura Arlon*

Handwriting Paper 16. Review all consonant and vowel sounds. Then teach the new consonant sounds: /**v**/ and /**w**/. For writing, both are short slanted-line letters. The *chant* for "**v**" is: "Put your pencil on the dotted line. Slant down. Slant up." The "**w**" is just two "**vs**" put together, so add another: "Slant down. Slant up."

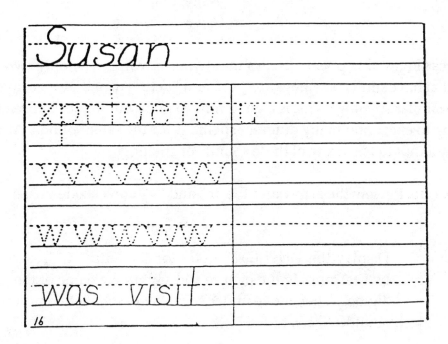

Figure 20.1. Handwriting Paper 16

Teacher Message. When the children are restless, a chalkboard message might be:

Stand up. (pause) Jump two times. (pause)
Turn around. (pause) Clap five times. (pause)
Smile at me. (pause) *Quietly* sit down.

"One, Two, Buckle My Shoe" Chart. The nursery rhyme "One, Two, Buckle My Shoe" is another excellent poem to read with the study of number words. Use two different colored pens when writing the poem: One color is used for all of the number words (**bold**); the other color is used for the remaining words (*italics*).

One, two,
Buckle my shoe.

Three, four,
Shut the door.

Five, six,
Pick up sticks.

Seven, eight,
Lay them straight.

Nine, ten,
A big, fat hen.

In the reading of this poem, discuss the rhyming words. The only two rhyming words that have similar spellings are "ten" and "hen." All of the other rhymes have very dissimilar spellings. This is a good time to point out to the children that they are going to encounter many different spellings for the same sounds. At this time, do not attempt to teach any of these sounds or spellings.

Vowel Code. Review the arrow and the "**a**" and "**e**" vowel code posters.

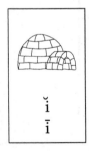

Display the *Vowel Code Poster* for the letter "**i.**" Teach this code by first tapping the picture and saying the name of the picture: "igloo." Then move under each vowel code letter as you say the sounds: "/ĭ/ /ī/."

Reading Groups. Suggested activities for today are:

1. Review the sounding out and reading of words from both the "**a**" and "**e**" charts. *Suggestion:* When reviewing, don't read all of the words every time. Instead, select

two words from each column. When reviewing on the next day, select two different words from each column, and so forth.

2. Introduce the sounding out of words with /ĭ/ /ī/. Write "lĭttle" on the chalkboard.

Teacher:	"**My turn.** /l/ /ĭ/ /t/ /l/
	Say it fast."
Children:	"little"

Note: No sounds are made when the teacher moves the pointer finger under the two silent letters (the second "**t**" and the "**e**"). The two silent letters should still be written on the chalkboard, however.

3. Use the same procedure in preparing the chart: two columns with two headings, "**ĭ**" and "**ī.**" List six words with all the markings under each heading. Sound out and read all of the words.

Suggested words:

| "ĭ" | ĭt | wĭll | dĭd | hĭm | trĭp | lĭttle |
| "ī" | fīve | nīne | līke | kīte | mīle | fīnd |

4. Have each child individually "track" and read a sentence from today's homework assignment (the second page of "I see (<u>classmate</u>) looking at me.").

5. Continue any needed testing. All testing should be completed by Day 19.

Storytime. Suggestions for today are more ABC books:

1. *Alphabears: An ABC Book* by Kathleen Hague
2. *A, My Name Is Alice* by Jane Bayer
3. *A to Z Animals Around the World* by Alexandra E. Fischer

Reminder: Day 20 is approaching. If parent-aides are to be used on a regular basis, the work schedule (day and time) will need to be completed. The aides should be trained as to what they will be doing in the classroom and the procedures and rules that will need to be followed.

21

Day 18

READING AND WRITING OBJECTIVES

1. Review previous lessons.
2. Learn sounds for **Yy** and **Zz.**
3. Write "**y**" and "**z.**"
4. Learn vowel code markings for "**o.**"
5. Begin reading words with /ŏ/ /ō/ /ö/.
6. Practice reading number-word song: "Ten Little Children in a Row."
7. Listen to daily poem and stories.
8. Continue testing for reading and writing skills.

BEFORE THE SCHOOL DAY BEGINS, PREPARE THE FOLLOWING:

1. Put up **Yy** and **Zz** and have flashcards available.
2. Duplicate Handwriting Paper 17 and transparency.
3. Put up vowel code poster for the letter "**o.**"
4. Prepare chart with /ŏ/ /ō/ /ö/ words.
5. Duplicate "One, Two, Buckle My Shoe" (see Form 21.1 at end of chapter).
6. Write "Ten Little Children in a Row" on chart paper (see page 110).
7. Select daily poem and stories to read.
8. Plan practice-work papers and aide/free-time activities.
9. Plan testing activities.

THE EIGHTEENTH SCHOOL DAY BEGINS

A Poem a Day. A suggested poem for today is "Vacuum Cleaner."

> The vacuum cleaner
> Goes vvv, vvv, vvvv.
> It vacuums the rugs,
> The sofas and chairs,
> Beneath the piano,
> And up the stairs.
> Vvv, vvv, vvvv
> Around the TV.
> If I don't move
> It might vacuum me!
> Vvv, vvvv, vvvvv!

—*Ethel Jacobson*

Teacher Message. After the poem, write on the chalkboard:

> Raise your hand if you see something special that has happened since
>   yesterday. (Read the message out loud and wait for responses. When
>   the correct answer is given, add):
> Yes, the alphabet letters are all up!

Sounds of Yy. Review all sounds. Then teach the sounds for "y" and "z." The "y" has three sounds: /y/ /ē/ /ī/. The first sound is its consonant sound: /y/ as in "yellow." This sound only comes at the beginning of a word or syllable, such as "yes" and "be-yond." The other two sounds are vowel sounds: /ē/ as in "funny" and /ī/ as in "my." The /ē/ sound for the letter "y" is at the end of a word consisting of two or more syllables. The /ī/ sound is at the end of a one-syllable word. There are a few exceptions to these rules (see *Vowel "y"* on page 9). At this time it is not advisable to explain these exceptions. Simply teach the "y" sound, after identifying the picture, as: "(picture) /y/ /ē/ /ī/."

Handwriting Paper 17. Writing the letter "y" is a combination of writing a "u" and a "g." It is a short line letter. *Chant:* "Put your pencil on the dotted line. Down to the baseline. Curve up. Then come down, down and make a monkey's tail." The "z" is also a short letter and is the only letter that begins by going across on the

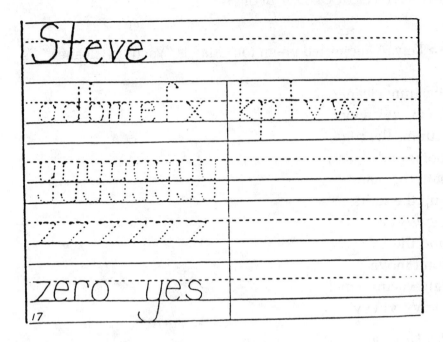

Figure 21.1. Handwriting Paper 17

dotted line. *Chant:* "Put your pencil on the dotted line. Across in the direction we write. Slant down. Across on the baseline."

Storytime. Suggested books to read today are:

1. *Math in the Bath* by Sara Atherlay
2. *Little Pig and the Blue-Green Sea* by Tannis Vernon
3. *The Rainbow Fish* by Marcus Pfister

"Ten Little Children in a Row." Introduce the number-word song "Ten Little Children in a Row." The song is sung to the tune of "Ten Little Indians." Use four different colors when preparing the chart for the song.

One <u>little</u>, *two* <u>little</u>,
Three <u>little</u> **children**,
Four <u>little</u>, *five* <u>little</u>,
Six <u>little</u> **children**,
Seven <u>little</u>, *eight* <u>little</u>,
Nine <u>little</u> **children**,
Ten <u>little</u> **children** in a row.

Color Key
Italics = red
Bold = blue
<u>Underlined</u> = black
. . . in a row = purple

Point to and read the number words in order. Point to and read "little" each time it appears. Do the same for "children." Read the ending ("in a row"). Now go back and choral read (don't sing!) the entire chart.

Vowel Code. Review the "**a,**" "**e,**" and "**i**" vowel code posters.

ŏ
ō
ö

Display the *Vowel Code Poster* for the letter "**o.**" Teach this code by first tapping the picture and saying the name of the picture: "octopus." Then move under each vowel code letter as you say the sounds: " /ŏ/ /ō/ /ö/."

Reading Groups. Today's reading group activities may include:

1. Choral read two words from each column of the "**a,**" "**e,**" and "**i**" charts. Words from the first two charts may no longer need to be sounded out.

2. Using the same format as in previous lessons, begin blending words that have /ŏ/ /ō/ /ö/. Prepare the chart: three vertical columns with three headings, "ŏ," "ō," and "ö." List six words with all markings under each heading.

Suggested words:

"ŏ"	nŏt	dŏg	ŏff	dŏll	hŏp	Tŏm
"ō"	nō	gō	sō	cōne	jōke	mōst
"ö"	tö	twö	dö	möve	löse	whö

3. Pass out "One, two, buckle my shoe" to each child. Let each child "track" and read the rhyme. Ask the children to find specific words in no particular order such as *sticks*, *shut*, and *big*. Reading this paper is tonight's homework. It needs to be signed and returned.

One, two,
Buckle my shoe.
Three, four,
Shut the door.
Five, six,
Pick up sticks.
Seven, eight,
Lay them straight.
Nine, ten,
A big, fat hen.

Sign and return:

Form 21.1

22

Day 19

READING AND WRITING OBJECTIVES

1. Review previous lessons.
2. Review sounds for all letters.
3. Review writing all lower-case letters.
4. Learn "imagination" for remembering letters.
5. Learn vowel code markings for "**u.**"
6. Begin reading words with /ŭ/ /ū/ /ü/.
7. Practice reading and singing: "Ten Little Children in a Row."
8. Listen to daily poem and stories.
9. Finalize testing for reading skills.

BEFORE THE SCHOOL DAY BEGINS, PREPARE THE FOLLOWING:

1. Duplicate Handwriting Paper 18.
2. Put up vowel code poster for the letter "**u.**"
3. Prepare chart with /ŭ/ /ū/ /ü/ words.
4. Duplicate "Ten Little Children in a Row" (see Form 22.1 at end of chapter).
5. Combine color- and number-word flashcards.
6. Plan final testing activities.
7. Select daily poem and stories to read.
8. Plan practice-work papers and aide/free-time activities.

THE NINETEENTH SCHOOL DAY BEGINS

A Poem a Day. Begin the day by reading "Now That I Can Read."

I used to need somebody
To sit and read to me.
I'd look at every page they read
And listen carefully.

But now that I am in first grade,
I'm filling up a shelf
With stories, poems, and other books
That I can read myself.

—*Ruth Etkin*

Imagination for Letters. Now that all of the alphabet letters have been introduced, it's time to present an idea that helps some children in remembering letters and their sounds. The physical appearance of each letter stimulates an imaginative picture of something that begins with that letter sound. These imaginative pictures can be "far-out." The more unusual the image, the easier it may be to remember. The following are ideas to discuss for each letter of the alphabet:

a   looks like a candied *a*pple on a stick (manuscript—ɑ)
b   looks like a *b*ook on a shelf with a *b*all for a bookend
c   looks like an old bent *c*arrot
d   looks like a *d*ish with a spoon beside it
e   looks like the trunk of an *e*lephant ready to hold a peanut
f   looks like a hand ready to throw a *f*ootball
g   looks like a one-horned *g*oat with its head down (manuscript—ɡ)
h   looks like a *h*ouse with a chimney
i   looks like an *i*ce cream cone with one scoop of ice cream
j   looks like a *j*ack-in-the-box ready to jump up
k   looks like a *k*ey
l   looks like a *l*amp without a shade
m   looks like a *m*itten that would fit over two fingers
n   looks like a *n*est that fell out of a tree and the eggs fell out
o   looks like an *o*ctopus without any of its eight arms
p   looks like a *p*ole hitting a ball
qu   looks like the *qu*een's twins, the prince and the princess (two letters)
r   looks like an upside-down *r*ake
s   looks like a *s*nake
t   looks like the center pole that holds up a *t*ent
u   looks like an *u*mbrella that went upside-down in a windstorm
v   looks like a *v*ase without any flowers

w	looks like two *witches'* hats that fell upside-down on the sidewalk
x	looks like an "*x*"
y	looks like the string on a *yo-yo*
z	looks like a zipper

Handwriting Paper 18. This paper is for reviewing the formation of all the letters and putting them in alphabetical order. After tracing the letters, dictate the letters in a different order. Perhaps the order could be by letters with similar writing formations such as:

2:00 letters: a, c, d, f, g, o, q, s
Tall line letters: b, h, k, l, t
Short line letters: i, j, m, n, p, r, u, y
Slanted letters: v, w, x
Letters that begin by going across: e, z

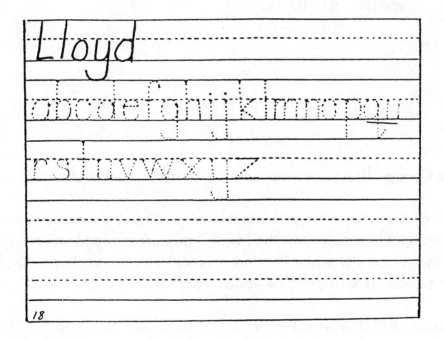

Figure 22.1. Handwriting Paper 18

Teacher Message. An idea for today is:

I see one little, two little, three little children.

I see _____, _____, and _____.

Read the message out loud. Have the children close their eyes. Write three names in the blanks. Children open their eyes. Teacher says "Get ready," and the children read the entire message. Repeat this message until all children have been chosen. This activity may take more than one day.

"Ten Little Children in a Row" Chart. This may be a good time to let students come up and "track" with a pointer stick as everyone else reads. Then teach the children to sing the words to the tune of "Ten Little Indians." If the teacher plays the piano or a guitar while the children sing, then a capable child can "track" while everyone sings.

Vowel Code. Review all previous vowel code posters.

Display the *Vowel Code Poster* for the letter "**u**." Teach this code by first tapping the picture and saying the name of the picture: "umbrella." Then move under each vowel code letter as you say the sounds: /ŭ/ /ū̄/ /ü/."

Reading Groups. Reading group activities for today may include:

1. Combine the color-word and number-word flashcards and practice reading them. Some children may know the words if they are grouped separately but need to look more carefully when they are mixed. Using these flashcards, teach the "clapping game" (see *Clapping Game* on page 188).

2. Pass out today's homework paper: "Ten Little Children in a Row." The children need to "track" and choral read the paper. Ask them to find specific words in no particular order. Tell them that for homework they are to "track" and read in the same way to an adult. *Suggestion:* During the practice-work period, have the students draw and color the faces of the "ten little children" on the homework paper. Encourage them to make each face different.

3. Review reading some of the "**a**," "**e**," and "**i**" words. Sound out and read six of the "**o**" words, two from each column.

4. Using the same format as in previous lessons, begin blending words that have /ŭ/ /ū/ /ü/. Prepare the chart: three vertical columns with three headings, "ŭ," "ū," and "ü." List six words with all markings under each heading.

Suggested words:

"ŭ"	ŭp	cŭt	rŭn	ŭs	fŭn	jŭmp
"ū"	cūte˟	ūse˟	rūle˟	tūne˟	mu̱le˟	Jūne˟
"ü"	püt	pü˟ll	fü˟ll	wöü˟ld	cöü˟ld (five words for now)

Storytime. Books listed below are "pattern books." They should not all be read on the same day. Select one to read and repeat reading it for a few days so that the children become very familiar with the patterns. *Suggestion:* Write the patterns on chart paper and practice reading them. Make a copy of the patterns for each child. Have them "track" and read them together and individually. Look for specific words out of order. Reading these papers may be homework assignments.

1. *I Know an Old Lady* illustrated by G. Brian Karas
2. *Four Fur Feet* by Margaret Wise Brown
3. *Five Little Monkeys Jumping on the Bed* by Eileen Christelow
4. *My Friends* by Taro Gomi

One little, two little,
Three little children,
Four little, five little,
Six little children,
Seven little, eight little,
Nine little children,
Ten little children in a row.

Sign and return:

_____

Form 22.1

23

Day 20

READING AND WRITING OBJECTIVES

1. Review previous lessons.
2. Practice "sounds" paper for homework.
3. Practice reading teacher-composed story.
4. Begin writing upper-case letters.
5. Listen to daily poem and stories.
6. Practice reading next VIP's chart story.
7. Listen to VIP's journal entry about mascot's visit home.

BEFORE THE SCHOOL DAY BEGINS, PREPARE THE FOLLOWING:

1. Duplicate the "sounds" paper (see Form 23.1, *Homework,* at end of chapter).
2. Write teacher-composed story on chart paper (see page 123).
3. Duplicate first upper-case writing paper (see *H.W. 19* on page 270).
4. Divide children into homogeneous (similar ability) reading groups.
5. Select daily poem and stories to read.
6. Plan practice-work papers, aide, and learning center activities.

Note: Today will be a day for changes. The reading groups are changed from "mixed" to "similar ability." The schedule may be somewhat changed. It is hoped that at least five parents (one for each day of the week) have responded to your request to participate in the class (see *Volunteer-Aide Letter* on page 241). If so, this is the day that parents will begin working with the children on a regular basis. The children need to be prepared for working with different adults. Rules and expectations need to be reinforced for both the parents and the students. Perhaps it's a good day to change seating. Where children sit may affect work habits and classroom behavior. *Suggestion:* Change seating for everyone about once a month.

Schedule for Reading Groups. The following schedule is for four reading groups and at least one classroom aide. With only one aide, the children need to be more independent. The majority of the students must be able to do the "practice-work papers" with little or no help. They must also be able to work on their own at the learning centers. These learning centers may include computers, easel painting, art, math manipulatives, and listening to tape-recorded books. With two aides, the extra aide may help with the learning centers and the "practice-work papers," so the activities may be more complex. Each time period is for 30 minutes. The reading groups may be given color names (red, yellow, blue, and green).

	Teacher	Aide	Learning Centers	Practice-Work
Time 1	Red	Green	Blue	Yellow
Time 2	Yellow	Red	Green	Blue
Time 3	Blue	Yellow	Red	Green
Time 4	Green	Blue	Yellow	Red

Note: It works well to have practice-work follow learning centers. As soon as the children finish their learning center activities, they go back to their desks and begin their practice-work papers. They do not need to wait for the precise time that groups change.

Schedule for Learning Centers. Five learning centers need to be planned, one for each day of the week. All five centers are going on at the same time; however, each child does only one center per day. Thus, it takes five days for a child to complete the five learning centers. Only one group is at centers at a time. The following is an example of the Blue Group's learning center schedule for one week, with eight children in the group:

	Day 1	**Day 2**	**Day 3**	**Day 4**	**Day 5**
Computer	Jill Kim	Betty	Ray George	Ann Louise	Craig
Easel Painting (or Science)	Craig	Jill Kim	Betty	Ray George	Ann Louise
Art	Ann Louise	Craig	Jill Kim	Betty	Ray George
Listening (tapes)	Ray George	Ann Louise	Craig	Jill Kim	Betty
Math (manipulatives)	Betty	Ray George	Ann Louise	Craig	Jill Kim

THE TWENTIETH SCHOOL DAY BEGINS

A Poem a Day. After a month of school, "Learning" is a good poem to read.

> Last year when I was little
>   I could only count to three.
> And never could remember
>   What the next number should be!
> But now that I've grown bigger
>   I know more than I did then,
> For I have been in school a month—
>   And I can count to ten!

—*M. Lucille Ford*

Teacher Message. As the year progresses, more difficult words may be used in the messages written on the chalkboard. Words may be marked to help in sounding them out. The markings in this message are for the sounds that the children have been introduced to so far.

Măny diffĕrent thǐngs are gōǐng to hăppĕn tödāy.

At the ĕnd o̲f̲ the day, you will tell me what was different and I will wrīte it.

Be a go̲o̲d dĕtēctǐve!

VIP Chart Story. Sometime during the day, read the VIP chart story. Read the story twice, the second time for choral reading. If your class has a mascot, read the VIP's mascot journal to the children.

Upper-Case Letters. During the "aide" group time, the children may begin writing upper-case letters (see *H.W. 19-24* on pages 270 to 275). Four letters are taught with each paper. The letters are arranged by similarity in writing. The procedure for teaching upper-case letters is similar to teaching the lower-case letters. The children first trace the letters and then write on their own. Plan out the chanting instructions if volunteer aides teach the letters, so that the chants are consistent. *Suggestions for chants:*

> N = "Tall stick. Tall stick. Go back to where you started and slant down."
>   (This helps to avoid reversals.)
> M = "Tall stick. Tall stick. Put a 'V' in the middle."
> Y = "Make a 'v' at the top. Go back to the point. Then go straight down."

Reading Groups. Activities with the teacher may include the following:

1. Review all of the vowel code posters. Read six words from the "**a,**" "**e,**" "**i,**" and "**o**" charts, two per column. Sound out and read all of the "**u**" words.

2. Review "imagination" for remembering the letter sounds.

3. Pass out the "sounds" homework paper. Practice saying the sounds, such as: "apple /ă/ /ā/ /ä/." The children need to track from letter to letter. Explain that this is tonight's homework. An adult will listen to them say the sounds. If the sound is known, the adult will put a "+" in the square. *Suggestion:* Send home a paper with the homework, detailing all of the sounds. Include an explanation about saying the "picture-word" before saying the sound. Give examples of words for each sound that the child is to say. For example: **a** = "apple . . . /ă/ (ăm) . . . /ā/ (āte) . . . /ä/ (wänt)."

4. Introduce on chart paper the teacher-composed story, which can be tomorrow's homework (see Form 23.2 at end of chapter). *Note:* Children illustrate their own papers.

> A man sees a little yellow cat.
> The cat is looking at him.
> It looks sad.
> It needs help.
> Will the man help the cat?
> Will the man keep it?

Suggestion: Teacher-composed stories are a good technique when teaching beginning reading. The teacher knows what words have been taught phonetically and by "sight" and can incorporate them into stories. It is a good idea to have the children occasionally read stories that have no illustrations. They need to learn to read "words" and not "pictures." Teacher-composed stories are particularly beneficial to use with the lower reading group students whose lessons may need to be individualized, especially if there are not enough books to be read at this lower level (see *teacher-composed stories* on pages 134 and 185).

Storytime. This final suggestion for books to read includes three more "pattern books":

1. *Let's Count It Out, Jesse Bear* by Nancy White Carlstrom
2. *Today Is Monday* by Eric Carle
3. *Five Little Ducks: Songs to Read* by Raffi
4. *The Wolf's Chicken Stew* by Keiko Kasza (Great for the 100th day of school!)

Note: Remember to feature well-known children's authors throughout the year. *Suggestions:* Frank Asch, Jan Brett, Eric Carle, Don Freeman, Paul Galdone, Thacher Hurd, Leo Lionni, Bill Peet, and Maurice Sendak.

Homework

All of the individual letter
sounds have been introduced.
Homework is to say the sounds
(not the letter names).

a	b	c	d	e	f	g
	j	k				
				m	n	o
q u	r	s	t	u	v	w
y	z					

Parents: Write a + in the square if your child
knew the sound. For example:

Signature: _____

124

Form 23.1

A man sees a little yellow cat.
The cat is looking at him.
It looks sad.
It needs help.
Will the man help the cat?
Will the man keep it?

Sign and return:

_____

24

Lessons After Day 20

What Next?

The first 20 days set the stage for the reading, writing, and spelling to follow. The remaining chapters will not provide additional daily lesson plans. It is important to have a sequential plan and time line for continuing to teach the necessary reading, writing, and spelling skills. This plan must include all of the grade level objectives for the language arts. Pacing should be determined by the capabilities of the students.

The teacher may use ideas from these remaining chapters concurrently to develop future lesson plans. For example, the plans for one given day may include: (a) teaching a new phonogram—Chapter 25; (b) spelling dictation centered around that phonogram—Chapter 26; (c) two reading groups working in a basal reader—Chapter 27; (d) a slower group still working at the readiness level—Chapter 28; (e) a vocabulary game in one of the reading groups—Chapter 29; and (f) children reading at home—Chapter 31.

Letter Sounds

Continue practicing the letter sounds in the reading groups. The lower groups probably need to practice each day. The higher groups need to practice less often. "Practice" means to have the children say the sounds when shown the letters (reading skill) and also to write the sounds without being shown the letters (spelling skill). When saying the sounds, use a variety of games (see *Chapter 29, "Vocabulary Flashcard Activities"*). When writing the sounds, words can be spelled. First, select words that have no phonograms or silent letters, such as sun, pet, find, hand, post, and belt. Add words with phonograms as they are introduced. Include silent letters when teaching specific rules.

Upper-Case Letters

Upper-case letters need to be taught before the students can begin writing sentences on their own. This instruction may be in small groups with an aide or as a total-class activity. Four letters are taught with each upper-case writing paper (see *Resources . . . H.W. 19-24* on pages 270 through 275). For total-class writing instruction, use transparencies and the overhead projector. It takes approximately six days to complete these papers. *Note:* The upper-case "**R**" may be written either by lifting or not lifting the pencil for the first slanted line. It is preferable not to lift, similar to the "**K.**"

Writing Last Names

As the upper-case letters are taught, the children should begin to learn to write their own last names. It may be difficult to find time to work with each child individually. An alternative is to prepare homework for each child and to get the family involved in teaching the spelling and writing of their child's last name. An explanation of this assignment should be included (see *Homework Letter 3* on page 240).

Because this is an extra homework assignment, it need not be returned until completed. Children take the assignment home on different days, depending on when their upper-case letter is taught. Most children anticipate and are excited about the arrival of "their day."

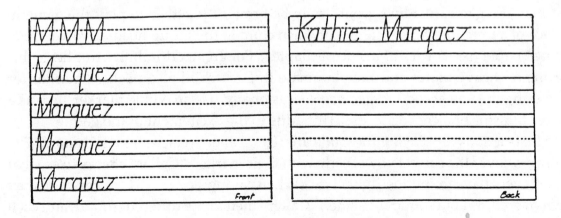

Figure 24.1. Last-Name Homework Paper

The last-name homework paper is two-sided. The front side is for practicing the upper-case letter and writing the last name. The back side is for writing both the first and last name, leaving a space between the two names. Once a child has completed this assignment, both names should be written on all writing papers. *Note:* Placing a Cheerio between words is a great way to teach spacing (see *Suggestion* on page 152). At home, a nickel may be used instead of a Cheerio.

Vowel Code

Continue reviewing the different vowel sounds in the reading groups. Make 13 flashcards, one for each vowel in the code. First practice the flashcards in the order taught: /ă/ /ā/ /ä/ /ĕ/ /ē/ /ĭ/ /ī/ /ŏ/ /ō/ /ö/ /ŭ/ /ū/ /ü/. When the reading group seems ready to move on, change the order within each letter, for example, /ä/ /ă/ /ā/ /ē/ /ĕ/ /ī/ /ĭ/ /ō/ /ŏ/ /ö/ /ŭ/ /ü/ /ū/. Next, completely mix up the flashcards, for example, /ē/ /ö/ /ĭ/ /ā/ /ŏ/ /ū/ /ä/ /ī/ /ĕ/ /ŭ/ /ō/ /ă/ /ü/. Continue practicing these flashcards with the children as a group and individually until they are mastered. Knowing the different sounds that vowels can make is important!

The five vowel code posters that were originally displayed take up quite a bit of space. These five posters may be replaced by one single vowel code chart (see *Vowel Code Posters* on page 245). It is advisable to display two of these smaller charts, one near the reading table and one at the front of the classroom.

Vowel Code Bingo

This is a great game for learning the vowel code. It is best to play the game with small groups so that it can be monitored. Volunteer aides may be instructed how to play the game. Reading groups may be brought together to play the game in place of a practice-work assignment. Each child in the group needs a Vowel Code Bingo paper (see Form 24.1 at end of chapter). For greater durability, duplicate this game on heavy paper and then laminate it. Each child also needs a marker for covering the vowel code. *Suggestion:* Occasionally, use an edible marker such as a box of raisins or a chocolate kiss. This adds to the excitement of the game.

Instructions for playing the game are: The "caller" (teacher) says a sound. The players cover the correct vowel code with their marker. "Caller" checks to see that all players have found the right code. (When calling /ŏ/ or /ä/, either code may be covered, as both sound the same.) "Caller" then says a different sound, and each player picks up his or her marker and moves it to the new vowel code. Unlike "real" Bingo, there are no winners. With only one marker, rows are never completely covered. The game is over when all of the sounds have been called at least once.

Vowel Dictation

The teacher dictates vowel sounds. Children write a vowel for each of the given sounds. As a total-class lesson, these letters may be written on individual chalkboards. The chalkboards may be held up on a given signal for correcting (see *Show Me Game* on page 162). If working with a reading group, the children may write at the same time on the classroom chalkboard. They may write the sounds in a vertical row. The teacher can easily monitor for correct writing.

Vowels in Words

When children are reading independently and come to words they do not know, they can be taught to try each of the vowel sounds in order. After phonograms have been introduced, the children can be taught to see if the vowel is part of a phonogram before trying the individual vowel code sounds (e.g., th<u>ey</u>, sh<u>ou</u>t, and fr<u>ui</u>t). They need to know that vowels other than the "u" can say /ŭ/, such as w<u>a</u>s, <u>a</u>bout, and c<u>o</u>me. Readers should also be taught that if there is a single "e" at the end of the word, that "e" is usually silent. *Exceptions:* be, he, me, we, and she.

Children need to practice trying the different vowel sounds when sounding out a word in order to become accomplished in using the skill. When a reading group is ready, the teacher selects a few words each day for them to practice together. They may need to sound each word three or four times, depending on how many sounds there are for the vowel that is in the word. Three examples for using this technique are prŏve, prōve, pröve; mŏnth, mōnth, mönth, month; mŏst, mōst.

Word Detectives

Playing "word detectives" is an excellent use of those few extra minutes that sometimes occur, such as before the recess bell rings. The teacher writes a word on the chalkboard and then says "Get ready." The teacher "tracks" under the word as the children attempt to sound it out. If the children have difficulty, the teacher may separate the word into syllables and mark letters to help in the sounding. *Suggestion:* If the word is sounded out with no further help from the teacher, devise an instant reward, such as they pat themselves on the back or the teacher rings a small bell. The teacher needs to have lists of words available for playing "word detectives." Try to select words that have not been used before, but can be sounded out. A word list containing no phonograms may be: *Monopoly, emblem, closet,* and *hippopotamus.* If /**th**/ is the first phonogram introduced, then the word list may be: *themselves, thimble, throne,* and *mathematics.*

Letter "y"

The letter "**y**" is usually a vowel. If the following saying is taught, it should be taught as: "The vowels are '**a**,' '**e**,' '**i**,' '**o**,' '**u**' and *usually* (not *sometimes*) '**y**.' " The only time "**y**" is not a vowel is at the beginning of a word or syllable. It is considered to be a vowel in these phonograms: /**ay**/, /**oy**/, /**ey**/. Throughout the year, special attention needs to be focused on this "tricky" letter.

Suggestion: Prepare charts with lists of words for the different uses of the letter "**y**." Add to the lists as words are discovered. Examples of different headings and lists are:

Consonant	/ē/ (end of word)	/ī/ (end of word)	/ĭ/ (middle of word)	/ī/ (middle of word)
yellow	happy	my	bicycle	style
yes	Billy	cry	mystery	type
beyond	candy	sky	Plymouth	analyze

ay	oy	ey
play	boy	key
maybe	Corduroy	monkey
today	enjoy	they

Instant Word List

Work on mastering a list of approximately 100 words, such as the Dolch words, the Fry word list, or any similar type of word list. For the more capable students, 100 words may be divided into four separate lists of 25 words each. Slower students may need to have the lists separated into even smaller segments. Flashcards can be made of these words for use in a reading group. Use the words in chalkboard messages. Mastering these words may be homework assignments (see Forms 24.2, 24.3, 24.4, and 24.5 at end of chapter).

Once children have mastered a list of 100 instant words, they are on their way to being independent readers. Some may not be ready to master all of the words until second grade. Setting individual goals can be a good motivation for many students. *Suggestion:* Do not use class charts with stars or stickers. Such charts often discourage the slower students. Instead, devise ways to motivate individually.

Caution: Do not limit reading group time to "sounds" and word lists! Other reading activities that emphasize reading comprehension are essential.

Basal Readers and/or Individual Books

After the 20th day, it is time to begin a traditional reading program utilizing books as a regular part of the daily schedule. Books need to be selected that are appropriate to the different reading levels of the reading groups. There is a difference between instructional reading level and recreational reading level. For instruction, the reading level should challenge, yet not frustrate, the reader. Obviously, each child within a group has his or her own reading level. However, if the children are put together into a reading group, a reading level needs to be established that is appropriate for all.

One benefit of using basal readers is that they are arranged into reading levels. Previous criticisms of the basal readers are no longer valid. Now, the stories in most basal readers are well written and beautifully illustrated. The teacher's manuals are helpful, particularly for those new to the teaching of reading. The teaching of skills is included in the manuals. Teachers may pick and choose what to teach, according to the needs of the students. Teachers may incorporate their own teaching strategies into the reading of the stories within the basal readers.

In addition to the basal readers, individual books also have a place in a beginning reading program. With a reading group, they may be interspersed with basal readers as instructional tools. The decision does not have to be whether to use basal readers *or* individual books. Basal readers and individual books can be used together effectively. When combining basal readers and individual books into a reading program, there needs to be some sort of continuity. Complete all of the planned activities for one story or book before beginning another. *Note:* Basal readers need to be used almost daily in order to successfully complete the books that are recommended for each grade level. Individual books can be used with the total class during "storytime" and then expanded upon at the various "learning centers," such as listening, writing, and art.

Poems and Songs

Continue to use poems and songs for the teaching of reading throughout the school year. The resources are unlimited! This activity is also appropriate for second and third graders. Write the poems and songs on chart papers or sentence strips. Color code them whenever appropriate. Make copies to be placed in a cumulative class book/binder. Keep this *Poems and Songs* book in the class library.

Because of its repetitious pattern, the Mother Goose rhyme "Here We Go Round the Mulberry Bush" is an excellent poem to teach beginning readers. The first two verses can be written with color coding on sentence strips. The second verse may be changed to make many different verses. The children may compose their own changes.

Verse 1:

> <u>Here we go round</u> *the mulberry bush,*
> *The mulberry bush, the mulberry bush,*
> <u>Here we go round</u> *the mulberry bush*
> **So early in the morning.**

Verse 2:

> <u>This is the way</u> *we brush our teeth,*
> *Brush our teeth, brush our teeth,*
> <u>This is the way</u> *we brush our teeth*
> **So early in the morning.**

Color-coding key: <u>underlined</u> = black; *italics* = green; **bold** = orange.

To change Verse 2, rewrite the italics on other sentence strips. Place these revisions right over the original italics. One such revision might read:

<u>This is the way</u> *we go to school,*
Go to school, go to school,
<u>This is the way</u> *we go to school*
So early in the morning.

Suggestions for other poems and songs to write on charts for reading are:

1. Do You Know the Muffin Man?
2. Where Has My Little Dog Gone?
3. Jack and Jill
4. Humpty Dumpty
5. Teddy Bear, Teddy Bear
6. The Swing
7. The Little Turtle
8. Over the River and Through the Woods
9. It's a Small, Small World
10. Jingle Bells
11. Take Me Out to the Ballgame
12. This Land Is Your Land
13. Old McDonald Had a Farm
14. She'll Be Coming 'Round the Mountain

Teacher-Composed Stories

As discussed in Chapter 23, stories composed by the teacher are a good technique for teaching beginning reading. These stories can be written to be used with the total class, with reading groups, or with individual students. A story may be written on chart paper for its initial introduction, and then duplicated for reading individually and for homework. The children may illustrate their own copies of the stories. Stories written for the total class are great to leave up on the walls so that the children can read them when they are "reading the walls."

The following example of a teacher-composed story was introduced near St. Patrick's Day and coincided with the teaching of four phonograms: /**ch**/ /**ee**/ /**er**/ and /**th**/. The story was first introduced by reading it from a chart paper. The children had the opportunity to find and circle these phonograms on the chart paper. Later, they had their own copies of the story. They illustrated their own copies and then used them for a homework assignment.

Is <u>th</u>at a w<u>ee</u> little lepre<u>ch</u>aun?
<u>Th</u>ere he is, und<u>er</u> the <u>ch</u>air!
He is small<u>er</u> <u>th</u>an my fa<u>ther</u>'s <u>th</u>umb.
Do you s<u>ee</u> his gr<u>ee</u>n clo<u>th</u>es?
F<u>ee</u>l <u>th</u>ose gr<u>ee</u>n shoes on his f<u>ee</u>t.
We bett<u>er</u> play with him!

Write the word "clo<u>th</u>." *Explain:* "clo<u>th</u>es" are made out of "clo<u>th</u>." For additional examples, see Chapter 28.

Drama

Putting on plays should be a frequent activity in the early primary grades. Plays are a "fun" culmination to a reading lesson and an excellent opportunity for children to develop verbal skills. The plays should not be big productions, and perfection should not be expected.

The plays may be planned around stories being read in the reading groups. Most stories can be adapted to involve the entire reading group. The rest of the class can be the audience for these plays. Outsiders need not be invited except for special plays that involve the entire class.

Memorizing parts is not always necessary. It depends on the play. If several children are choral reading, parts can be written out for them to read. Individual children may say their parts in their own words. Sometimes the teacher may need to prompt the children to remind them what to say. Keep a collection of costumes and masks in a large box (see *W. Costumes* on page 22). A parent or grandparent may be able to sew costumes that can be used year after year.

Dialogue, props, and movements can be planned and practiced by the reading group at the reading table. Because perfection is not expected, there does not need to be a lot of rehearsing. The children will be on "stage" (some convenient place in the classroom) for the first time during the actual performance. More rehearsing and preparation are required when it is a total-class play and outsiders, such as another class or parents, are invited. The teacher will be very involved throughout the play. The cast needs to be introduced, and the performers may need to be reminded as to what they should be doing and saying. There will be explanations to the audience, such as the passing of time or something that needs to be imagined. At the end, the cast should line up and bow. The audience must learn to be attentive and clap at the end (no whistling or shouting). A play should be a total learning experience.

Some well-known stories that make good plays are "Little Red Hen," "Chicken Little," "Bremen-Town Musicians," "Gingerbread Boy," "Three Little Pigs," "Are You My Mother?" and "The Big Turnip" (or Carrot). "Over in the Meadow" (see page 193) can be dramatized by the entire class. The more capable readers may recite the verses while the "mothers" and the "little ones" act out their respective parts. Simple masks may be made for all the animals.

Children are good at using their imaginations, so keep props to a minimum. The top of a reading table can be the robbers' house in the "Bremen-Town Musicians"; the Gingerbread Boy can come out from under the same table when coming out of the oven.

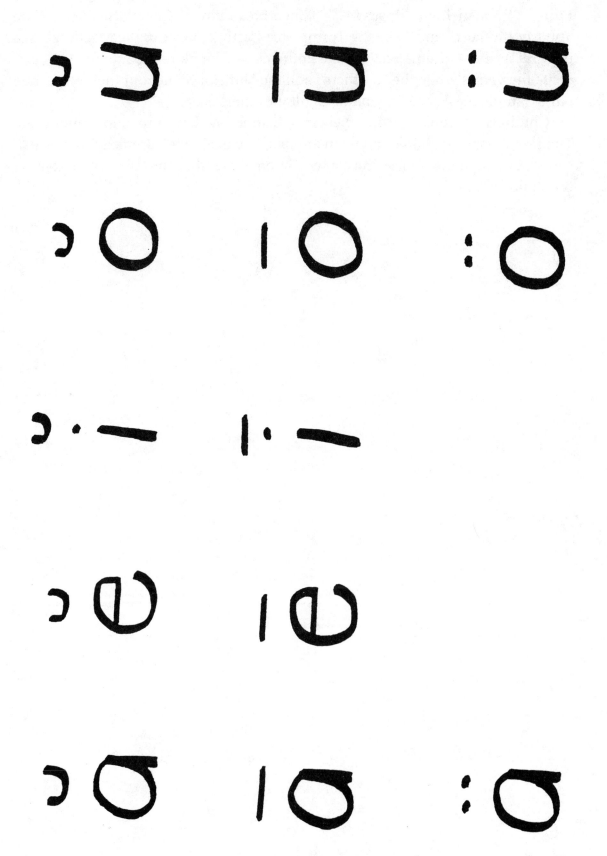

Instant Words List 1		is
a	he	by
go	like	job
see	and	I
into	up	do
him	get	not
be	on	yes
the	can	at
no	it	has

Homework: Read these words. Read in different directions (down, up, and across). Work for instant mastery (no sounding out).

Sign and return:

Mastered: Yes No (Circle)

_____

Instant Words List 2		down
you	run	look
have	all	time
one	king	make
box	with	some
she	want	long
come	for	her
two	quick	ball
clock	this	zoo

<u>Homework</u>: Read these words. Read in different directions (down, up, and across). Work for instant mastery (no sounding out).

Sign and return:

Mastered: Yes No (Circle)

_____

Form 24.3

Instant Words List 3		may
read	from	was
now	your	are
there	more	over
boy	today	saw
find	were	first
of	join	new
mother	when	train
said	put	here

<u>Homework:</u> Read these words. Read in different directions (down, up, and across). Work for instant mastery (no sounding out).

Sign and return:

Mastered: Yes No (Circle)

_____

Instant Words List 4		word
each	ready	know
what	could	out
people	learn	very
use	draw	picture
night	write	been
every	father	they
where	party	about
color	many	who

Homework: Read these words. Read in different directions (down, up, and across). Work for instant mastery (no sounding out).

Sign and return:

Mastered: Yes No (Circle)

_____

Form 24.5

25

Teaching the Special Sounds of Phonograms

General Information

As soon as all of the consonant sounds and the vowel code sounds have been taught, it is time to begin teaching phonograms (also known as digraphs). Phonograms were discussed in Chapter 2, "What You Need to Know About Phonics" (see *Phonograms* on pages 10 through 12). The phonograms are all listed along with words to help in deciphering the different sounds. Teachers and aides should use Chapter 2 as a reference guide whenever needed.

This chapter contains detailed methods and techniques for teaching the phonograms. Included are: (a) phonogram display and flashcards; (b) chants that help in remembering the different sounds; (c) phonogram dictionary; (d) phonogram hunt; and (e) phonogram stories.

Although there is no specific order for teaching phonograms, certain ones should be introduced before others because of their frequency in beginning reading materials. Some phonograms need to be taught early because the sounds cannot be determined by looking at the individual letters. Such phonograms are /sh/, /th/, /ch/, /ow/, /oo/, /oy/, and /oi/.

In first grade, it is best to teach no more than one phonogram a day. Pacing depends on the class, the reading group, and the difficulty of the phonogram being taught. Introducing and mastering phonograms may not be completed until the end of the third grade. Second- and third-grade teachers should continue to teach and review the phonograms, but the pacing can be accelerated. Certain phonograms can be paired together, such as /**ow**/ and /**ou**/; /**oy**/ and /**oi**/; /**ai**/ and /**ay**/.

As phonograms are being taught, students may be assigned phonogram-flash-card homework papers (see Form 25.1 at end of chapter). The slower students should take home only one phonogram at a time. For these students, send home a letter of explanation with the first flashcard and an envelope for keeping the phonograms together.

With the introduction of phonograms, it is time to begin dictated spelling lessons. Spelling tests are not necessary in the first grade. Instead, the children should be taught to spell words that are dictated and then to put these words into sentences. Practice is the way for beginners to learn. The dictation technique may be used throughout the elementary grades. Spelling books are not needed. Instead, word lists need to be compiled and spelling rules need to be repeated frequently. Correct spelling needs to be taught and not left to chance! *Note:* Spelling dictation, which is explained in detail in the next chapter, should be used simultaneously with this chapter.

Phonogram Display and Flashcards

There needs to be a permanent spot in the classroom for displaying the phonograms as they are introduced. *Suggestion:* Prepare a phonogram train. The train cars are numbered in order. The phonograms are written on colored 3″ × 5″ file cards and placed into the cars as they are introduced (see following illustration). Each train car should have only one of each color. This is ideal for finding phonograms on the display: /**sh**/ is on a pink card in Car 1, /**ou**/ is on a yellow card in Car 2, /**ai**/ is on a green card in Car 5, and so forth.

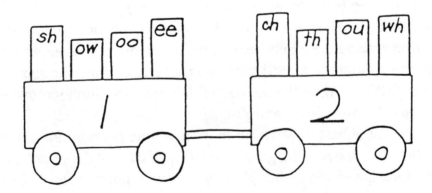

Figure 25.1. Phonogram Train

File card colors: **sh** = pink; **ow** = green; **oo** = yellow; **ee** = blue
ch = pink; **th** = green; **ou** = yellow; **wh** = blue

The procedure for teaching and displaying the phonograms is similar to the way letters, color words, and number words were taught. Do not put them all up at once, but add them one at a time as they are introduced. This procedure should be followed in the second and third grades, but at a faster pace, even if the phonograms are just being reviewed. Flashcards need to be prepared for all of the phonograms. On the back of each flashcard, write a reminder of the phonogram sound(s). Go through the flashcards one time each day until they are mastered.

Phonogram Hunts

"Phonogram hunts" are effective for recognizing and mastering these special sounds. The children enjoy being "detectives." As each phonogram is introduced, let the children find it on any charts that are already displayed in the classroom. If the charts are to be saved for future use, the children can make imaginary circles around the phonograms. Prepare "phonogram hunt" practice-work papers with sentences containing phonograms (see Form 25.2 at end of the chapter).

Detailed Teaching Procedures

Body language, vocal intonations, and chants can help in mastering the phonograms. Most important, they can make practicing flashcards fun. *Suggestions:*

/**th**/   The only sound in which the tongue comes out between the teeth. It is either voiced (<u>th</u>is) or voiceless (<u>th</u>ing).

/**sh**/   Put a pointer finger over the lips for this "quiet" sound, "shhhh."

/**ow**/   "Prick" the inside of an arm with the pointer finger of the opposite hand and say, "Ow!" Then, quietly say, "$\overline{o}$w" (sn<u>ow</u>).

/**oo**/   These are ghost eyes. Say "Oooooo" like a ghost. Finish with a quick "/$\ddot{o}o$/" (l<u>oo</u>k).

/**ch**/   Point to the chin and say "chin." Then point to a cheek and say "cheek." Then say the sounds: "/**ch**/" (<u>ch</u>in), "/**k**/" (s<u>ch</u>ool).
Note: When it comes up, explain "/**sh**/" (ma<u>ch</u>ine).

/**ee**/   Chant: "/$\overline{e}$/ the double-letter 'e.' "

/wh/   Chant: "/w/ as in <u>wh</u>ite."

/ou/   Chant: "/ou/ as in <u>ou</u>t." *Note:* Second graders can be taught all five sounds from the beginning. Put up five fingers and point to each finger as the sounds are recited: "/ou/" (<u>ou</u>t), "/$\bar{\text{o}}$u/" (th<u>ou</u>gh), "/$\ddot{\text{o}}$u/" (s<u>ou</u>p), "/$\breve{\text{u}}$u/" (fam<u>ou</u>s), "/$\ddot{\text{u}}$u/" (c<u>ou</u>ld).

/ar/   Chant: "/ar/, /$\bar{\text{a}}$r/ begins with an 'a' " (c<u>ar</u> and c<u>ar</u>rot).

/or/   Chant: "/or/ as in <u>or</u>ange."

/ck/   Chant: "/k/ the two-letter /k/ after a short vowel" (bl<u>ă</u>c<u>k</u>, d<u>ě</u>c<u>k</u>, s<u>ĭ</u>c<u>k</u>, cl<u>ŏ</u>c<u>k</u>, tr<u>ŭ</u>c<u>k</u>). *Note:* This phonogram is always at the end of a syllable or a word.

/ay/   Chant: "/$\bar{\text{a}}$/ as in s<u>ay</u> at the end of a word or syllable."

/ai/   Chant: "/$\bar{\text{a}}$/ as in w<u>ai</u>t at the beginning or middle of a word."

/ea/   Chant: "/$\bar{\text{e}}$/ /$\breve{\text{e}}$/ <u>ea</u>t br<u>ea</u>d" and pretend you are eating bread. Later, the /$\bar{\text{a}}$/ sound can be added (gr<u>ea</u>t st<u>ea</u>k).

/oy/   Chant: "/oy/ as in b<u>oy</u> at the end of a word or syllable."

/oi/   Chant: "/oi/ as in <u>oi</u>l at the beginning or middle of a word."

/er/   Chant: "/er/ /$\bar{\text{a}}$r/ begins with an 'e' " (h<u>er</u> and v<u>er</u>y).

/ir/   Chant: "/ir/ as in f<u>ir</u>st begins with an 'i.' "

/ur/   Chant: /ur/ as in f<u>ur</u> begins with a 'u.' "

/ear/   Chant: "/ear/ the three-letter /ear/ (<u>ear</u>ly). *Note:* Distinguish the phonogram /ear/ from the word "ear" (/$\bar{\text{e}}$a/ + /r/).

/wor/   Chant: "/wor/ as in <u>wor</u>k."

/oa/   Chant: "/oa/ as in g<u>oa</u>t."

/ing/   Chant: "/ing/ as in r<u>ing</u>" and look at an imaginary or real ring on your hand.

/ed/   Chant: "/<u>ĕ</u>d/ (paint<u>ed</u>) /d/ (color<u>ed</u>) /t/ (look<u>ed</u>) puts a word in the past." Discuss the meaning of past tense. Explain that this phonogram is added to a "doing-word" (verb).

/gh/   Chant: "/g/ /f/ 'silent' (finger over the lips)." Examples of words using the three "sounds" of this phonogram are:

           /g/ = <u>gh</u>ost, <u>gh</u>astly, <u>gh</u>etto
           /f/ = lau<u>gh</u>, cou<u>gh</u>, enou<u>gh</u>
           "silent" = hi<u>gh</u>, ni<u>gh</u>t, wei<u>gh</u>t

         Note: Instead of saying the word *silent,* the children are silent with their pointer finger over their lips. Be sure that this "silence" is not confused with the /sh/ phonogram.

/igh/   Put up three fingers and chant: "/$\bar{\text{i}}$/ the three-letter /$\bar{\text{i}}$/."

/**eigh**/ Put up four fingers and chant: "/$\overline{a}$/ the four-letter /$\overline{a}$/."

/**ph**/ Chant: "/f/ the silly /f/." Christmas is a good time to introduce this phonogram, using the word Rudolph."

/**ew**/ Chant: "/ew/ as in n<u>ew</u>, begins with an 'e.'"

/**ue**/ Chant:"/ue/ as in bl<u>ue</u>, ends with an 'e.'"

/**ui**/ Chant: "/ui/ as in fr<u>ui</u>t, and there is no 'e.'"

/**aw**/ Chant: "/aw/ with a 'w' as in s<u>aw</u>."

/**au**/ Chant: "/au/ with a 'u' at the beginning or middle of a word."

/**ey**/ Chant: "/$\overline{e}$/ /$\overline{a}$/ monk<u>ey</u>, th<u>ey</u> (point to imaginary monkeys).

/**dge**/ Put up three fingers and chant: "/j/ the three-letter /j/."

/**kn**/ Chant: "/n/ with a 'k' as in <u>kn</u>ee." (Point to a knee.)

/**wr**/ Chant: "/r/ with a 'w' as in <u>wr</u>ist." (Point to a wrist.)

/**gn**/ Chant: "/n/ with a 'g' as in <u>gn</u>at." (Swat at an imaginary gnat.)

/**ps**/ Chant: "/s/ with a 'p' as in <u>ps</u>alm."

/**ei**/ Chant: "/$\overline{e}$/ /$\overline{a}$/ but it's spelled 'e' 'i'."
        Suggestion: Imagine receiving r<u>ei</u>ndeer as a gift.

/**ie**/ Chant: "/$\overline{i}$/ /$\overline{e}$/ and it's spelled 'i' 'e'."
        Suggestion: Imagine a f<u>ie</u>ld of p<u>ie</u>s.

/**tion**/ Chant: "shun with a 't.'"

/**sion**/ Chant: "shun with an 's.'"

/**cial**/ Chant: "shul with a 'c.'"

/**tial**/ Chant: "shul with a 't.'"

/**cious/** Chant: "shus with a 'c' as in deli<u>cious</u>."

/**tious**/ Chant: "shus with a 't' as in cau<u>tious</u>."

/**tient**/ Chant: "shent with a 't' as in pa<u>tient</u>."

/**ought**/Chant: "ot, the five-letter 'ot' with an 'o.'"

/**aught**/Chant: "ot, the five-letter 'ot' with an 'a.'"

Phonogram Dictionary

Before beginning the study of phonograms, a phonogram dictionary may be prepared for each child. The teacher prepares duplicating masters, two phonograms per page (see Form 25.3 at end of chapter). The pages are cut in half and assembled into books in the order the phonograms are to be taught. *Suggestion:* Use only the common phonograms, such as the phonograms used in the stories in the next section.

As each phonogram is introduced, the children draw and color a picture on the page that corresponds to that specific phonogram. (A directed drawing lesson does help to ensure recognizable pictures!) Frequently allow for time to "choral read" these books, chanting the sound and the word as each page is turned.

Stories to Reinforce Phonograms

Stories are another way to reinforce the study of phonograms. The teacher writes each story on chart paper with the phonograms highlighted by using different colors. After a story is mastered, the children may be given a copy to illustrate. The papers may be saved and put together into individual phonogram-story books. Save an extra copy for a class book. Following are sample phonogram stories.

/**ee**/ I see a yellow bee.
It is a queen bee.
It is by a tree.
Oh, my! The bee stung me!

/**ch**/ I went in the church.
I found a big chest.
What was in the chest?
Lots of chocolates!

/**sh**/ Shelly is on the sand.
She gets little shells.
She puts them in a dish.
Then Shelly sees a big ship.
And she sees a shiny fish.

/**ck**/ Jack has a black dog.
Mack is his dog.
Jack and Mack like to run.
Mack will lick Jack.
Jack will pick Mack up
and hug him.

/**ur**/ It is Thursday.
Burt got a surprise.
It was in a purple box.
Hurry, Burt!
Open the surprise!

/**th**/ That is a big cat.
The cat is black.
It was with them.
Then it got lost.

/**oy**/ A boy is full of joy.
His name is Roy.
Roy has a toy.
It is a bear named Corduroy.

/**wh**/ What is that?
When did it get here?
Why is it here?
Where did it come from?
Oh, it is just a little white cat.

/**ing**/ The king sat on a swing.
He had a big ring.
He started to sing.
What did he sing?
(Old King Cole)
Suggestion: Learn to sing this song.

/**ight**/ My Christmas tree shines at night.
The red lights blink big and bright.
The yellow lights blink big and bright.
The blue lights blink big and bright.
Together they all blink in the night.

/**ou**/ I went <u>ou</u>t of the h<u>ou</u>se.
I went to the s<u>ou</u>th.
Was that a sh<u>ou</u>t?
What was it ab<u>ou</u>t?
Was Santa ab<u>ou</u>t?
Were his reindeer <u>ou</u>t?

/**ay**/ Yesterd<u>ay</u> was Sund<u>ay</u>.
Tod<u>ay</u> is Monday.
It is a gr<u>ay</u> d<u>ay</u>.
It m<u>ay</u> rain tod<u>ay</u>.
F<u>ay</u> wants to pl<u>ay</u> with R<u>ay</u>.
But R<u>ay</u> ran aw<u>ay</u>.

/**ow**/ A man was in the deep sn<u>ow</u>.
He had to walk sl<u>ow</u>ly.
He had on a yell<u>ow</u> hat.
The wind began to bl<u>ow</u>.
The hat fell in the sn<u>ow</u>.
The man lost his yell<u>ow</u> hat.

/**ow**/ A br<u>ow</u>n <u>ow</u>l is in a tree.
It sees a cl<u>ow</u>n with a fr<u>ow</u>n.
N<u>ow</u> it sees a man with a cr<u>ow</u>n.
The man has a fl<u>ow</u>er in his hand.
The <u>ow</u>l flies d<u>ow</u>n to the t<u>ow</u>n.
Good-by <u>ow</u>l!

/**ph**/ I had a <u>ph</u>one call.
It was from my ne<u>ph</u>ew.
He has a new <u>ph</u>oto album.
He has a <u>ph</u>oto of an ele<u>ph</u>ant.
And a <u>ph</u>oto of a <u>ph</u>easant.
And a <u>ph</u>oto of two dol<u>ph</u>ins.
His best <u>ph</u>oto is of Rudol<u>ph</u>!

/**ar**/ The man lives on a f<u>ar</u>m.
The f<u>ar</u>m is by a p<u>ar</u>k.
A dog b<u>ar</u>ks in the y<u>ar</u>d.
A l<u>ar</u>ge b<u>ar</u>n is on the f<u>ar</u>m.
A c<u>ar</u> is in the b<u>ar</u>n.
The c<u>ar</u> is d<u>ar</u>k green.

/**oo**/ L<u>oo</u>k at this!
I have a g<u>oo</u>d b<u>oo</u>k.
It is a z<u>oo</u> book.
A kangar<u>oo</u> is in a z<u>oo</u>.
Is a m<u>oo</u>se in a z<u>oo</u>?
If a m<u>oo</u>se is l<u>oo</u>se,
Do not sh<u>oo</u>t it!

/**or**/ C<u>or</u>y went to the st<u>or</u>e.
He left in the m<u>or</u>ning.
He w<u>or</u>e an <u>or</u>ange shirt.
He went n<u>or</u>th for f<u>or</u>ty miles.
He went f<u>or</u> more c<u>or</u>n.
And he went to get a h<u>or</u>n.

/**oa**/ A hungry g<u>oa</u>t ate a c<u>oa</u>t.
Then the g<u>oa</u>t began to m<u>oa</u>n.
The g<u>oa</u>t got in a b<u>oa</u>t.
A frog was in that b<u>oa</u>t.
The frog began to cr<u>oa</u>k.
And the b<u>oa</u>t began to fl<u>oa</u>t.

/**ir**/ K<u>ir</u>k and Sh<u>ir</u>ley played in the d<u>ir</u>t.
Sh<u>ir</u>ley is f<u>ir</u>st in line.
She has a d<u>ir</u>ty sk<u>ir</u>t.
She is hot and th<u>ir</u>sty.
K<u>ir</u>k is th<u>ir</u>d in line.
He has a d<u>ir</u>ty sh<u>ir</u>t.
He is hot and th<u>ir</u>sty too.

HOMEWORK

Phonograms are when two or more letters go
together to make a special sound. These
phonograms need to be mastered. The word
(or words) includes the sound (or sounds) of
that phonogram. Master the phonogram
sound and words.

sh _she_	**th** _this_
ow _now_ _snow_	**ou** _out_
oo _soon_ _book_	**ch** _chin_
ee _see_	**wh** _when_

Check one:

____Needed help

____No help (mastered)

Sign and return:

_____

Form 25.1

Name _____

Phonogram Hunt

Circle all of these phonograms: **sh, th, ow** and **oo.**

1. She is good at throwing the ball.

2. This book is too short.

3. How does the moon shine?

4. That shadow is a spooky thing.

5. Look at those groovy shoes!

6. Shannon pushed Beth too hard.

7. Ruth threw a snowball at Shelly.

8. They saw three brown cows.

9. The clown had yellow flowers on his shirt.

10. Then show me a thin and thick slice of brown bread.

How many phonograms did you find?

sh _____   **ow** _____

th _____   **oo** _____

ar

car

_____

sh

shoe

150   Form 25.3

26

Teaching Spelling Through Dictation

The children should already be familiar with the dictation format. It was used in learning individual sounds and in writing simple words at the end of each handwriting lesson. Once you begin to use phonograms, the students need to practice using them in reading and writing. Writing sentences also needs to begin. Upper-case letters need to be taught prior to the starting of sentence writing.

Sample Lessons

Although there is no set sequence for teaching spelling through dictation, each lesson (one per day) must build upon the previous lessons. To demonstrate this progression, the following four sample lessons begin with the introduction of the phonograms /**sh**/, /**th**/, and /**ow**/.

Lesson 1: / sh /   *Teacher's Key: 1-<u>sh</u>*

Put the /**sh**/ card up on the phonogram display (see *phonogram train* on page 142). Teach the sound (see /**sh**/ on page 143). If this is the first phonogram introduced, discuss with the children that sounds are different in phonograms. In this phonogram, the sounds are no longer /**s** / and /**h** /. Instead, there is a new sound, /**sh**/.

Practice saying the sound with the flashcard. Find /**sh**/ words in charts that are already around the room and begin a list of /**sh**/ words. Pass out writing paper that has been vertically folded in half. The teacher needs a transparency of the writing paper to be used on an overhead projector. The folding line needs to be on the transparency.

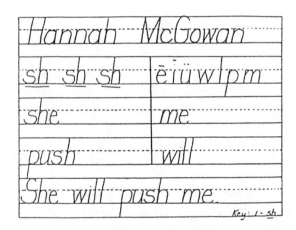

Figure 26.1. Key 1—<u>sh</u>

The children write their own names on the first writing line. Most children should be able to write both their first and last names. The teacher needs to demonstrate spacing between words by writing a first and last name on the transparency. Do not teach the technique of placing a finger after a word in order to make a space because this is difficult for left-handed writers. *Suggestion:* Give each child one or more Cheerios. A Cheerio represents a "clock space." Place a Cheerio after the last letter of a word (close but not touching). The next word begins after the Cheerio, close but not touching. The children can move and place the Cheerio after each word before writing the next. This tactile technique can stop when the children are automatically able to leave correct spacing between words.

After the names have been written, the teacher says the phonogram "/**sh**/." When dictating a phonogram, the teacher holds up the number of fingers that represent the number of letters that need to be written for that phonogram. Have the fingers touching. Thus, when the phonogram /**sh**/ is to be written, two fingers should be held up and touching each other. For the phonogram /**ing**/, three fingers need to be raised and touching each other.

The teacher now writes <u>sh</u> on the second writing line. Underline the phonogram when writing it as a sound, but do not underline it in words. The children write on their papers after each teacher demonstration. Place a Cheerio (clock space) on the transparency after the /**sh**/ before saying and writing <u>sh</u> two more times. On the same writing line, after the fold, separately say and write each letter that appears on the teacher's key. For example, the teacher says "/ē/" and then writes the letter "ē" with the code over it. Complete the line in this manner. Notice that this dictation practices all the sounds that will be in the words that follow.

Next comes dictating the four words that will be written in the sentence. The children need to develop the skill of saying the word and then breaking it down into its individual sounds, in other words, "say it slowly." This is the reverse of "say it fast."

The teacher says "she"; then the children say "she." The teacher asks, "What sound do you hear first?" . . . (/**sh**/). The teacher holds up two fingers to represent the number of letters in the /**sh**/ sound. The teacher and the children write **sh.** The teacher repeats the word and asks: "What is the next sound? . . . /**sh**/ /?/" Answer: /ē/. Everyone writes the "**e**" (without the code marking) to complete the word.

Continue in this same manner to write "push," "me," and "will." When adding the second "**l**," state the rule that an "**l**" is doubled after a short or two-dot vowel (w<u>i</u>ll, d<u>o</u>ll, and f<u>a</u>ll). In the future, repeat this rule whenever it comes up. Eventually the children can recite and use the rule without being reminded. *Note:* The second "**l**" is dropped in all, full, and till when these words are added to another syllable, such as al-ways, hope-ful, and un-til.

Now it is time to begin the sentence dictation. The teacher says the sentence, "She will push me" and asks for the first word . . . "she." Tell the children that all sentences must begin with an upper-case letter and then demonstrate by writing "She" on the next writing line. The children also write the word. Leave a clock space (Cheerio) and write the next word, "will." Say the sounds as the word is being written (/**w**/ /ĭ/ /l/). Repeat the double "**l**" rule. Use the same process in sounding and writing "push" and "me." Then explain that this is a "telling" sentence, so it needs a period after the last word. A period is like a stop sign. Our voice needs to stop. Read the entire sentence together. Read with expression, not word for word.

The dictation lesson is now over. If this lesson is prior to practice-work time, the children may turn the paper over for a practice-work assignment. The practice-work activity would be to write the sentence again on the back in their "best" handwriting. For easier copying, the sentence should be written on the chalkboard. Have the children draw a picture about the sentence to denote comprehension. More capable students may add another sentence or two to make a story.

Suggestion: Although any primary writing paper can be used for dictation, special writing paper does make for a better finished product. For the dictation lessons, duplicate the six-lined writing paper (see *Additional Resources*, page 251). The extra line can accommodate longer sentences. On the back of the paper, at the bottom, duplicate two lines (see *Additional Resources*, page 247) for rewriting the sentence during practice-work time.

Lesson 2: / th /   *Teacher's Key: 2-th*

Review yesterday's phonogram: /**sh**/. Introduce the new phonogram, /**th**/, in the same manner. Say just the "voiced" sound when practicing with the flashcard. Find /**th**/ words on charts around the room, and begin a chart list of /**th**/ words. Follow the dictation technique in Lesson 1 for writing the sounds, words, and sentence. The teacher writes on the same lined transparency that was erased at the

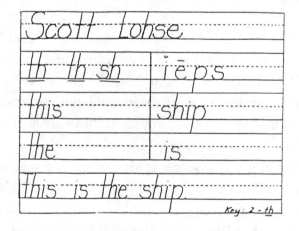

Figure 26.2. Key 2—<u>th</u>

conclusion of Lesson 1.

To teach the spelling of the word "the," tell the children that we say "th**ē**" for spelling. Tell them that any vowel can say /ŭ/, and in this word the letter "**e**" says the /ŭ/ sound. Notice that the word "<u>sh</u>ip" can be used in the sentence because the phonogram /**sh**/ has already been taught. This is what is meant by "lessons building upon previous lessons." For practice-work, the sentence may be rewritten and a picture drawn as in Lesson 1.

Lesson 3: /ow/   *Teacher's Key: 3-**ow***

Teach this new phonogram with its two sounds, /**ow**/ /**ōw**/. This phonogram is seldom found at the beginning of a word. It is usually in the middle or at the end of a word. Exceptions: <u>owl</u>, <u>owe</u>, and <u>own</u>. Find words on the charts around the room. Two word lists may be started, one for each sound. There are now three phonogram flashcards to practice.

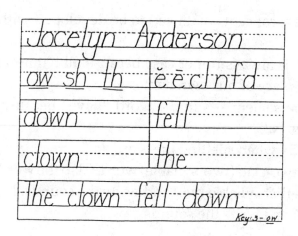

Figure 26.3. Key 3—<u>ow</u>

Lesson 3 dictation uses only the first sound of the phonogram, /**ow**/. Repeat the double "l" rule when writing the word "fell." Remind the children that we say "thē" when spelling. Assign writing and drawing a picture for practice-work as in the previous lessons.

Lesson 4: /ow/   *Teacher's Key: 4-**ow***

There are no new phonograms in Lesson 4; however, the dictation lesson features the second sound of the phonogram, /**ōw**/.

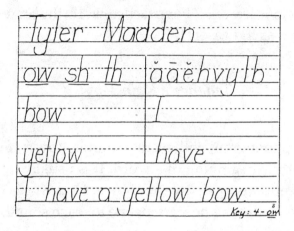

Figure 26.4. Key 2—o̅w

There are four new concepts that need to be developed with this lesson:

1. The word "I" is always upper case because all names are capitalized and we use "I" in place of our own names.
2. There must be a silent "**e**" in the word "have" because no word can end with the letter "**v.**"
3. We can say /$\bar{a}$/ when spelling the word "a."
4. "Yellow" is a two-clap (two-syllable) word. Clap the word with the children. Then, say the first syllable (yel) and write the sounds. Next, say the second syllable (low) and write the sounds.

Remember to put up two fingers, touching, to show the /o̅w/ sound. Notice that "**l**" is written in both syllables. *Rule:* Syllables always divide between doubled consonants.

Suggestion: The following Mother Goose rhyme is especially appropriate to read with the introduction of the /**ow**/, /**ar**/, /**ai**/, /**ck**/, and /**ou**/ phonograms:

Sl<u>ow</u>ly, sl<u>ow</u>ly, very sl<u>ow</u>ly	Qui<u>ck</u>ly, qui<u>ck</u>ly, very qui<u>ck</u>ly
Goes the g<u>ar</u>den sn<u>ai</u>l,	Runs the little m<u>ou</u>se,
Sl<u>ow</u>ly, sl<u>ow</u>ly, very sl<u>ow</u>ly	Qui<u>ck</u>ly, qui<u>ck</u>ly, very qui<u>ck</u>ly
Up the g<u>ar</u>den r<u>ai</u>l.	To his little h<u>ou</u>se.

Write the entire poem on eight sentence strips. Place these in a pocket chart. The children practice by reading the first verse "slowly" and the second verse "quickly." Reread the entire poem, perhaps having half of the students read lines 1, 3, 5, and 7 and the other half of the students read the other lines.

Subsequent Dictation Lessons

The preceding four spelling dictation lessons are only the beginning. Further lessons need to be developed according to the phonogram sequence used in the classroom. If you follow the phonogram order in this book, you may develop your next lessons from the sentences that follow (see *Spelling Dictation Sentences* on pages 157-159). Spelling rules and spelling hints are listed under the sentences. Included are the seven rules for putting a silent "**e**" at the end of a word. If rules are repeated, they eventually become second nature.

Silent "e" Rules

These seven rules help to explain why a silent "**e**" is added to some words:

1. To make the vowel in the same syllable, say the long sound:
    made   complete   ride   hope   cute
2. No word can end with a "**v**":
    have   live   love   give   shove
3. To make the letter "**c**," say the /**s**/ sound:
    dance   face   voice   piece   fence
4. To make the letter "**g**," say the /**j**/ sound:
    large   revenge   badge   fringe   baggage
5. No word can end with a single "**s**" after a phonogram or a single consonant:
    house   please   loose   intense   sense
6. Every syllable needs a vowel:
    pur ple   lit tle   pad dle   gen tle   cra dle
7. Some words end with a silent "**e**" for no reason:
    come   more   are   there   were

Spelling Dictation Sentences

The following 20 sentences are sequential. Each sentence builds on what was introduced in the previous lessons. Under each sentence are rules and reminders to continually reinforce when dictating sentences and teaching spelling.

1. /**sh**/: *She will push me.*
    wil*l*—double the "**l**" after a short or two-dot vowel

2. /**th**/: *This is the ship.*
    th*e*—for spelling, say "th$\overline{\text{e}}$"

3. /**ow**/: *The clown fell down.*
    fel*l*—double the "**l**" after a short or two-dot vowel

4. /**ow**/: *I have a yellow bow.*
    I—always written upper case because it represents our name
    hav*e*—a silent "**e**" because no word can end with a "**v**"
    a—for spelling, say /$\overline{\text{a}}$/
    yellow—divide syllables between doubled consonants (**l l**)

5. /**oo**/: *The moon will soon shine.*
    shin*e*—a silent "**e**" makes the vowel in that syllable long (/$\overline{\text{i}}$/)

6. /**oo**/: *He gave me a good book.*
    gav*e*—a silent "**e**" makes the vowel in that syllable long (/$\overline{\text{a}}$/) and
        no word can end with a "**v**"
    boo*k*—usually when you hear /**k**/ at the end of a word, it is spelled
        with a "**k**." Exceptions: magic, gigantic, Titanic

7. /**ch**/: *Bob and I chose a brown chest.*
    I—always written upper case
    chos*e*—a silent "**e**" makes the vowel in that syllable long (/$\overline{\text{o}}$/)

8. /**ee**/: *I see a kite in the green tree.*
    kit*e*—a silent "**e**" makes the vowel in that syllable long (/$\overline{\text{i}}$/)

9. /**wh**/: *What is red, white, and purple?*
    what—for spelling, say "wh$\breve{\text{a}}$t"
    whit*e*—a silent "**e**" makes the vowel in that syllable long (/$\overline{\text{i}}$/)
    purpl*e*—a silent "**e**" because every syllable needs a vowel (pl*e*)

10. /**ou**/: *The mouse has come out of its hole.*
    mous*e*—a silent "**e**" because words cannot end with a single "**s**"
        after a phonogram
    com*e*—a silent "**e**" for no reason
    hol*e*—a silent "**e**" makes the vowel in that syllable long (/$\overline{\text{o}}$/)
    of—for spelling, say " '**o**' '**f**' spells 'of.' "

11. /**ar**/: *My car is dark green.*
    dar*k*—usually when you hear /**k**/ at the end of a word, it is spelled
        with a "**k**"
    m*y*—the /$\overline{\text{i}}$/ sound at the end of a one-syllable word is spelled with
        a "**y**"

12. /**ar**/: *Mary has a large parrot.*
     large—the silent "**e**" makes the "**g**" say /**j**/
     parrot—divide syllables between double consonants (**r r**)
13. /**ck**/: *Jack found a nice black dog.*
     nice—the silent "**e**" makes the "**c**" say /**s**/ and the vowel long (/**ī**/)
     Jăck, black—"**ck**" is written only after a short vowel
14. /**ay**/: *Kay and I see a gray cat.*
     I—always written upper case because it represents our own name
     Kay, gray—"**ay**" is written at the end of a word or syllable
15. /**or**/: *The orange ball is for me.*
     orange—the silent "**e**" makes the "**g**" say /**j**/
16. /**oy**/: *The boy lost his toy mice.*
     mice—the silent "**e**" makes the "**c**" say /**s**/ and the vowel long (/**ī**/)
     boy, toy—"**oy**" is written at the end of a word or syllable
17. /**ea**/: *The bread was ready to eat.*
     ready—the /**ē**/ sound at the end of a two-syllable word is spelled
          with a "**y**"
     was—for spelling, say "wăs"
18. /**ai**/: *Rain fell on the passenger train.*
     rain, train—"**ai**" at the beginning or middle of a word
     passenger—clap and then spell the three syllables (pas sen ger)
          divide syllables between double consonants (**s s**)
          an "**e**" after a "**g**" makes it say /**j**/
          second "**e**" because every syllable needs a vowel (g**e**r)
19. /**oi**/: *Lots of oil will spoil the clean beach.*
     of—for spelling, say " '**o**' '**f**' spells 'of' "
     oil, spoil—"**oi**" at the beginning or middle of a word
20. /**oa**/: *One little goat is on the road.*
     one—for spelling, say " 'on' with an '**e**.' "
     little—divide syllables between double consonants (**t t**)
          final "**e**" because every syllable needs a vowel (tl**e**)

Working With Two Spelling Groups

So far, spelling lessons have been a total-class activity because at the beginning of the year it is more productive to work with the entire class at one time. In first grade, beginning skills are presented to everyone. In second and third grades, the spelling review at the beginning of the year should also be a total-class activity.

There may come a time when it is more beneficial to instruct in two separate groups. Slower students need a longer time to absorb what has been taught and the pacing needs to be slower. In first grade, this split may occur about mid-year. If there is an aide in the classroom, the teacher and the aide may alternate between working with the two groups. Without an aide, the teacher may alternate between groups, assigning independent work to the group that is not being instructed at that time.

Suggestion: If there is no aide in the classroom, the teacher may first work with the slower group. The independent assignment that follows this dictation may be to rewrite the sentence on the back of the paper and draw, then color, an illustration. Meanwhile, the faster group may be assigned the same activity, except that they will be rewriting the previous day's lesson. Children who have any free time should be allowed only to read a book. The time for spelling ends with the completion of the faster group's dictation.

There comes a point in time when the teacher should no longer write on a transparency during dictation lessons. The children gradually need to become independent spellers. However, they should know at the conclusion of the dictation whether they have spelled their words correctly. *Suggestion:* All pencils are put away. Children take turns coming up and writing each segment of the dictation on an overhead transparency. Writing on a transparency is a treat, so only choose those who are good "watchers."

Spelling Games

The following games help to make spelling fun:

Hangman. This is an excellent spelling game (see *Hangman* on page 189). A variation of this game can emphasize specific phonograms. The phonogram may be put in its place in the word and lines added for the other letters. For example, if the word is "children," the teacher writes on the chalkboard: ch __ __ __ __ __ __.

Scrabble. Another good spelling game is Scrabble. Duplicate a supply of 1-inch graph paper to be used to make the Scrabble "tiles." Prepare the tiles by writing letters in the squares.

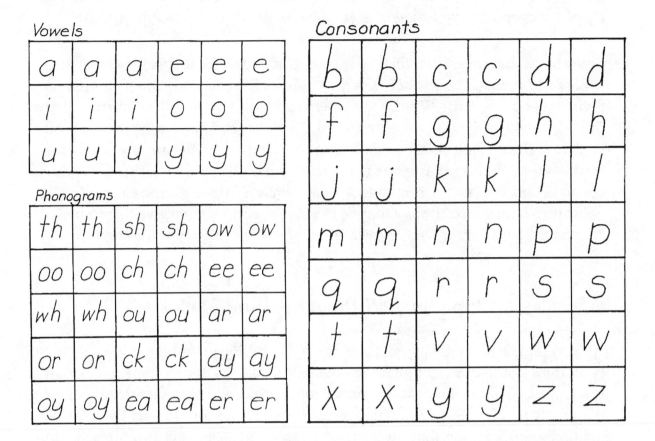

Figure 26.5. Scrabble Tiles

Duplicate these on construction paper, each with a different color. For instance, the consonants may be blue; vowels may be yellow; phonograms may be pink. (As more phonograms are taught, other "pink" papers will need to be prepared.) This color-coding will help to find needed letters more easily. Each child will need a set of tiles consisting of two papers of each color. Laminate the papers for durability and have an adult cut the tiles and place a complete set in a clear, resealable storage bag for each child. Make a few extra sets to allow for lost tiles. When playing Scrabble, the teacher dictates a word, and the children find the letters and arrange them to spell the word correctly. Separating the letters into three piles according to colors will help in finding the letters. Placing the assembled words on a piece of black construction paper makes a good work space. Leave each word that is spelled on the black paper until the game is over. The teacher should pre-plan the words to be dictated so that there are enough letters for all of the words. At the end of the game, the children could get a Cheerio for every correctly spelled word!

Suggestion: Have the children sit on the floor for this game; this eliminates the chance of dropping and losing tiles. Scrabble is also a good free-time activity.

Show Me Game. Individual chalkboards are an excellent tool to use for a total-class "Show Me" game. The teacher asks the students to write something specific on their chalkboards, such as writing a letter representing a sound, writing a word from dictation, or writing a spelling word. Then the teacher says "Show me." All students hold up their chalkboards to show the teacher. If there are any errors, the teacher writes the correct answer on the classroom chalkboard for all to see. If there are no errors, the teacher responds with a "winners" reward: rings a small bell, holds up a happy face, drops a marble in a jar, or has everyone give themselves a "pat on the back." *Note:* The "Show Me" game is excellent to use for math.

"Spelling" Without Spelling Books

Spelling can be taught without spelling books! Filling in the blanks in a spelling book does not in any way guarantee success in the teaching of spelling. Good spellers either have photographic minds, or they have a good understanding of the structure of English words. Because teachers have no control over the creation of photographic minds, the only option for success in spelling is for the teacher to teach, and the students to learn, the structure of English words. Proper spelling needs to be emphasized from the beginning.

Spelling Rules. Rules and their exceptions need to be taught and reviewed throughout the grades. Some of the basic spelling rules that have not been mentioned are:

1. Take off the "**e**" before adding "**ing.**" (hav*e*—having)
2. Double the consonant after a short vowel before adding "**ed**" or "**ing.**" (pl*a*n—planned; beg*i*n—beginning)
3. Change the "**f**" or "**fe**" to a "**v**"; then add "**es.**" (lea*f*—leaves; kni*fe*—knives)
4. After a consonant, change the "**y**" to "**i**"; then add "**es.**" (hur*ry*—hurries)
5. After a vowel, simply add an "**s**" after the "**y.**" (pl*a*y—plays)
6. An apostrophe is only used for a possessive or for a contraction, *not* for forming plurals. (Karen's doll; cannot—can't; two books—*not* two book's)
7. "It is" is written as a contraction (*It's* mine). "Its" is a possessive written without an apostrophe (The tree lost *its* leaves).

8. Words may sound alike but be spelled differently (homonyms). Learn correct spellings for the different meanings. (some or sum; to, two, or too; stare or stair; eight or ate)

Spelling Objectives. The spelling dictation lesson plans for beginning spellers have already been discussed. After all of the phonograms have been introduced, the format may change somewhat, but the dictation approach continues. Isolated sounds no longer need to be dictated, but words and sentences are still a part of the dictation format. School districts should establish specific spelling objectives for each grade level so teachers can compile word lists and dictation sentences that will teach to these objectives. These word lists and sentences should contain words that provide frequent review of previous spelling rules that have been taught. *Note:* If a school district does not have specific spelling objectives, then a school or a grade level should establish its own. As a last resort, a teacher should establish spelling objectives for his or her own class.

Advanced Spelling Format

The format of the lessons already discussed (see *Lessons 1-4* on pages 152 through 157) may continue throughout first grade. Even second grade students may need to continue with the same format until the teacher determines they are ready to move on. The following is an example of an advanced spelling format. Lessons are presented for five days of the school week. Spelling words in the following example were selected in order to review consonants, vowels, and the /**sh**/ /**th**/ /**ow**/ /**ee**/ phonograms.

Day 1. The teacher dictates and the students write 20 words. This is a pretest to determine which sounds and spelling rules are not yet mastered by the individual students. Suggested words are:

(1) **green**	(2) **shells**	(3) **brown**	(4) **five**	(5) **three**
(6) **shelf**	(7) **of**	(8) **yellow**	(9) **huge**	(10) **put**
(11) **gave**	(12) **fish**	(13) **tall**	(14) **swam**	(15) **dishes**
(16) **sitting**	(17) **next**	(18) **them**	(19) **pond**	(20) **by**

After the words have all been written, the students need to have immediate feedback as to whether they spelled the words correctly. The teacher writes the words on chart paper (in two columns) as the students slowly sound them out. Rules and special sounds are discussed whenever appropriate. For example:

Teacher:	**have**
Students:	*/h/ /ă/ /v/*
Teacher:	**What do we write at the end of the word?**
Students:	**A silent "e"**
Teacher:	**Why?**
Students:	**Because no word can end in a "v."**

If a child misspells a word, that child immediately writes it correctly beside the misspelled word. (No erasing!) The teacher collects and reviews the papers. The papers will be returned to the students on Day 3.

Day 2. To assess individual proficiency in the writing of sentences, the teacher dictates and the students write five sentences that incorporate the words from Day 1. *Note:* When dictating a sentence, first say the entire sentence. Then repeat slowly so that each word may be written. Specific rules (*italics*) that need to be reviewed are written under the sentences. These rules are not discussed during the pretest. They are discussed afterward.

1. The green frog is sit*t*ing on a brown log.
   Double the consonant after a short vowel before adding "ing."
2. An old man sees a yel*l*ow bee by the tal*l* tree.
   Double the "l" after a short or two-dot vowel.
3. Put thes*e* shell*s* up on the next shelf.
   Silent "e" to make the vowel long.
   Add an "s" to form the plural.
4. She gav*e* three of the dish*es* to them.
   Silent "e" because no word can end in a "v."
   Add "es" to form the plural when the number of syllables increases.
5. Five hug*e* fish swam in that pond.
   Silent "e" to make the "g" say /j/.

The students read the sentences as the teacher writes them on a chart paper. With each sentence, the teacher asks: "How do we start a sentence?" and "What do we need at the end of a sentence?" Now is the time to review the appropriate spelling rules. If words are misspelled, the teacher waits at the end of each sentence for the students to cross out the error and write it correctly above the misspelling. *Note:* It is essential that students correct their own errors if they are to remember the correct spelling of words. The papers are collected to assess individual proficiency and returned on Day 3. *Suggestion:* Slower students may be required to learn to spell the words from only one or two of the sentences.

Day 3. The papers from Day 1 (spelling words) are returned to the students. Their assignment is to write each of the words in their own dictionary (see *Spelling Dictionaries* on pages 220-221). As the children finish their dictionary assignment, their five-sentence paper is returned to them. Now the assignment is to rewrite correctly on the back any sentences that had mistakes in them. Depending on the number of mistakes, some sentences may need to be written for practice more than once. (Cover up a sentence before writing it again.) Students who made no errors may write five sentences of their own. Tell them to think of a sentence that could follow each of the sentences as if they were writing a story. For example: A follow-up for the first sentence might be: "The green frog is looking for bugs to eat."

Day 4. Select a game for practicing the spelling words (see pages 160 through 162).

Day 5. The final test is today. Dictate the 20 words from Day 1 and the five sentences from Day 2. After the test, plan an activity in which the students work independently at their own desks. The teacher then can go around and correct the tests. If there are errors, the students correct them. They also take out their dictionaries and put check marks after the words that were misspelled. *Suggestion:* To ensure that all words are mastered, the students need to continue studying. Periodically, the students can pair up and test each other on their own misspelled words (any word with a check after it). If a word is spelled correctly in the test, the check may be crossed out. *Caution:* The teacher needs to be assured that all students are "fair" when testing each other.

Spelling Throughout the Grades

This same five-day format may be used in all of the grades:

Day 1: Give a pretest on all of the words. The words should be selected to fit the spelling objectives for the week.

Day 2: Give a pretest for the writing of sentences that incorporate words from Day 1 and words that review spelling rules.

Day 3:   Write all words from Day 1 in individual dictionaries. Also, practice sentences from Day 2 or write own sentences.

Day 4:   Play a variety of spelling games.

Day 5:   Give the final test . . . words and sentences. Put a check mark in the dictionary after words that were misspelled.

Suggestion: If students make spelling errors when writing on their own, the words should be put in their dictionaries with check marks for future testing.

27

Using Basal Readers and Other Books

Schools and school districts vary as to the types of books available to be used in the instruction of reading. One choice is the use of basal readers. This choice need not limit reading instruction to the basals; individual books may also be incorporated into the reading program. Basal readers are an excellent source for the "whole language" approach. They offer opportunities for growth in thinking, reading, writing, listening, and speaking.

There are many fine basal reading series being published today. These readers offer children a great variety of stories by well-known authors and illustrators. At the beginning reading level, it is often difficult to find a variety in reading materials.

If basal readers are used in a first-grade reading program, their actual use begins about Day 20 with the formation of homogeneous groups. By then, most reading groups should be ready to begin a formal reading program. If a reading group is still at the readiness level, the group should not begin the first book of a series until ready (see *Chapter 28, "Promoting Reading Readiness"*).

Generally, all reading groups begin with the same first story in the first book of the series. If only one or two students in the top reading group are proficient readers, it is better to adjust the pacing according to the majority. It is not usually advisable for a group to consist of only one or two students. They need to have the discussions and activities that can only happen in larger groups. Some readers in the top group who gain their proficiency at a later time may surpass the early proficient readers. These early readers may be challenged with supplementary reading assignments during their practice-work time or for homework. *Note:* Team teaching with other teachers is another possibility for handling different reading abilities. Participating teachers need to have similar teaching philosophies and coordinate scheduling so that there is a maximum use of instructional time.

The teacher's editions for all of the basal reading series are very explicit in how to use their series. The detailed lesson plans may be extensively followed; however, activities, techniques, and pacing should vary according to the needs of each reading group.

At the beginning level, the methods and techniques for teaching reading, whether in a basal reader or any other book, should be the same. In this chapter, this teaching process is divided into seven steps. These seven steps are the following:

Step 1 (Prereading)

During prereading, the students should not have access to the book being read so as to avoid reading ahead. Predictions and interest in the stories are greater if stories have not been seen beforehand. *Note:* An exception to this suggestion is when students reread previously read stories during "sustained silent reading" (see *Sustained Silent Reading* on page 197).

The teacher goes through the prereading strategies that are used when reading any story or book to children (see *Reading to Children* on pages 191-193). These strategies include: (a) Predict what the story will be about by reading the title and looking at the first illustration. (b) "Think" and discuss what might happen in the story. (c) Discuss the meanings of any words that may need to be defined prior to the reading of the story. *Note:* Some words are best defined during the reading.

Step 2 (Teacher Reads)

The teacher reads the entire story to the reading group, just as any library book would be read. If appropriate, ask the children to predict what is going to happen before turning to the next page. Ask questions for comprehension and encourage the children to react to the story. (What did they like? What would they change?) *Note:* When a reading group begins the first "hardback" book, the teacher should no longer read the story to the group. Instead, the teacher should guide the group through a silent reading of the story (see *Guided Silent Reading* on pages 195-196).

Step 3 (Sentence Strips)

The teacher composes sentences that contain the ten new words (underlined) in the story. These five separate sentences are written on sentence strips.

> A frog is <u>bragging</u> to a <u>grasshopper.</u>
> I can jump <u>over</u> a <u>pond.</u>
> I can jump to the <u>other</u> side of a <u>river.</u>
> I am not <u>afraid</u> to jump to the <u>moon.</u>
> His <u>friends</u> just <u>laughed</u> at him.

The sentence strips are placed into a pocket chart, and the teacher tracks while the children read each sentence. If no one in the group knows a word, then the teacher guides them in figuring it out, using the four strategies—phonics, reread, skip, and guess (see *Deciphering Words* on pages 193-194). The sentence strips should be reread, practicing good reading expression. Children should learn not to read word for word. Such reading may indicate lack of comprehension.

Step 4 (Vocabulary)

Show the flashcards, one at a time, for all of the new words in the story. The ten new words in this story ("The Frog") are: *afraid, bragging, friends, moon, grasshopper, over, laughed, river, other,* and *pond.* Discuss the phonetic principles that will help in remembering the words. As each word is discussed, it may be written on the chalkboard with the appropriate markings and an arrow to show the direction for sounding out the word. At this level, the appropriate markings are:

brăgging	friĕnds	oth er	grăsshŏpper	ōver
lăughed	riv er	afraid	pŏnd	mōon

Practice the flashcards several times on the first day, changing the order each time. Flashcards from previous stories need to be reviewed until mastered by most of the children in the reading group. Vary the way the flashcards are reviewed (see *Chapter 29, "Vocabulary Flashcard Activities"*). *Note:* Steps 1 through 4 will probably be more than enough for one day's lesson.

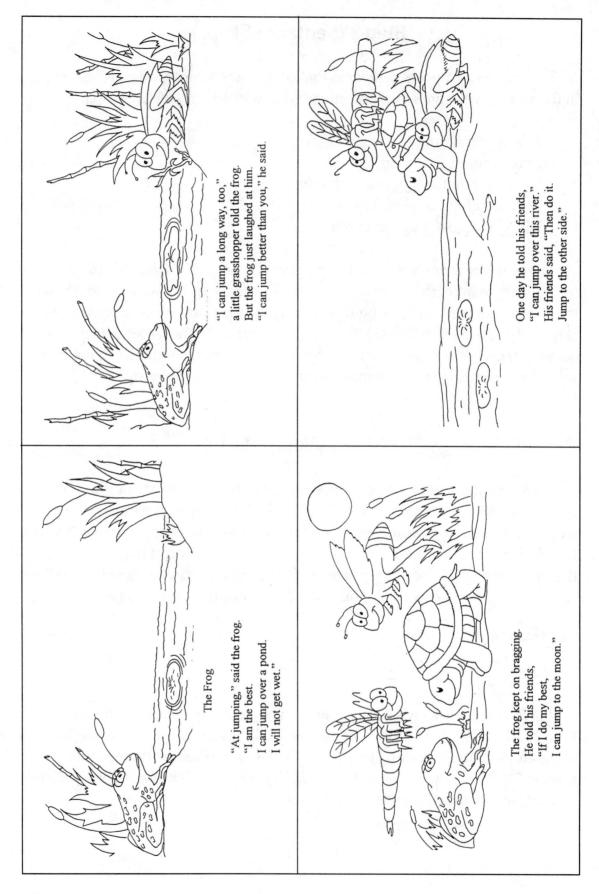

The Frog

"At jumping," said the frog.
"I am the best.
I can jump over a pond.
I will not get wet."

"I can jump a long way, too,"
a little grasshopper told the frog.
But the frog just laughed at him.
"I can jump better than you," he said.

One day he told his friends,
"I can jump over this river."
His friends said, "Then do it.
Jump to the other side."

The frog kept on bragging.
He told his friends,
"If I do my best,
I can jump to the moon."

170

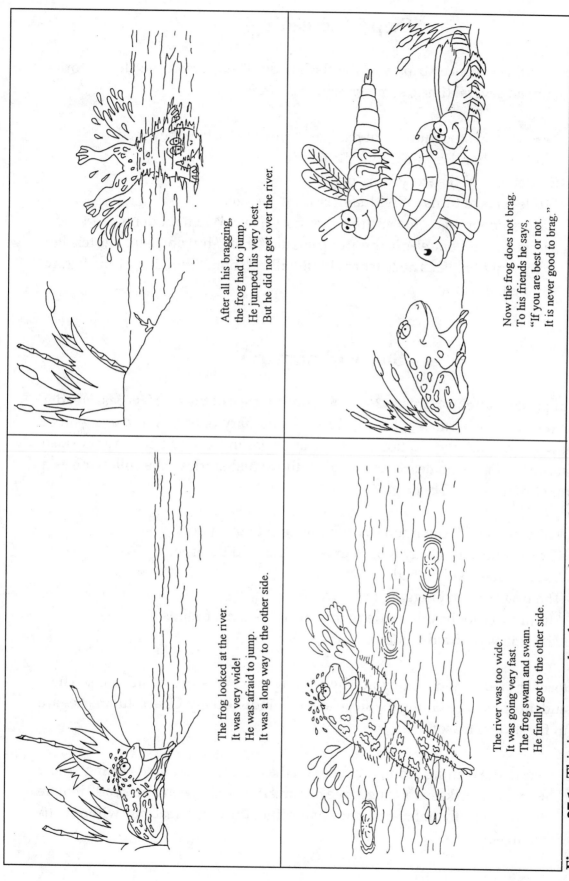

The frog looked at the river.
It was very wide!
He was afraid to jump.
It was a long way to the other side.

After all his bragging,
the frog had to jump.
He jumped his very best.
But he did not get over the river.

The river was too wide.
It was going very fast.
The frog swam and swam.
He finally got to the other side.

Now the frog does not brag.
To his friends he says,
"If you are best or not.
It is never good to brag."

Figure 27.1. This is an example of a story that could be in a beginning basal reading book and is included here for a basis to explain how to proceed with Steps 3 – 7.

Step 5 (Rereading)

Review the sentence strips and the flashcards. Then reread the story. Stories may be reread several times, somewhat in this order:

1. Teacher and students choral read, all "tracking" while they read.
2. Students choral read without the teacher.
3. Students read the story as a "play."
4. Students take turns individually reading a page.
5. Each student reads the entire short story. *Note:* When students read individually, everyone else in the group should "track" but not help. The teacher is the only helper. The teacher should allow some "thinking" time before saying the word.

Step 6 (Summary)

Purchase small chart tablets (24" × 16"), one for each of the first few basal reader books (not for the hardcover books). Write a summary of each story, using all of the new words and punctuation marks. The stories in the first book are short, so the summaries may be nearly identical to the actual stories. The following is a summary of the story *The Frog:*

The frog said, "I can jump over a pond and to the moon."
"I can jump a long way too," a grasshopper told the frog.
But the frog just laughed.
The frog kept on bragging to his friends.
"Jump over to the other side of this river," said his friends.
The frog was afraid to jump.

The teacher models good expression by reading the chart story to the group. Then, the students practice reading the story together individually. Chart summaries are useful for several reasons:

1. The entire reading group can focus on the words, rather than "losing" some students who keep looking at the pictures. Some children can "read" if there are pictures for reference but have difficulty when reading without the pictures.

2. Short stories are great for working on fluency in reading.

3. Summaries are excellent for reviewing stories. Reviewing a summary takes less time than rereading the actual story in the book. Beginning readers should reread stories in order to strengthen vocabulary skills.

Step 7 (Follow-up)

Write the new words on the flashcard homework form (see Form 27.1, *Homework*, at end of chapter). There are ten new words in "The Frog." That leaves two spaces to add two more new words from the next story.

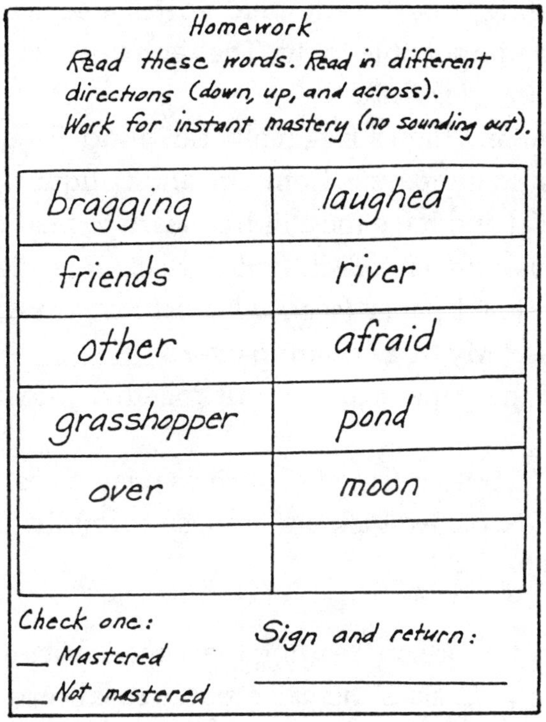

Homework
Read these words. Read in different directions (down, up, and across).
Work for instant mastery (no sounding out).

bragging	laughed
friends	river
other	afraid
grasshopper	pond
over	moon

Check one:
__ Mastered
__ Not mastered

Sign and return:
_____

Figure 27.2. Homework

When a form is filled, duplicate one copy for each child in the reading group. Practice reading the words in different directions. Reading these words becomes a homework assignment.

Prepare and duplicate a reading homework paper of the story summary that was written in the chart tablet (see example in Form 27.2 at end of chapter). One or two illustrations from the story may be added to this paper to help stimulate a discussion with the parents. There needs to be a place at the bottom of the paper for a parent's signature (Sign and return:).

Practice reading the homework paper the day it is being sent home. Be sure that all children "track" as they read. Remind them that they are to "track" when reading at home. Ask the children to point to a few words out of order.

If needed, again send home the letter that tells parents how to work with their children on this type of reading material (see *Homework Letter 2* on page 238). Perhaps the paragraph from the letter beginning with "Some children . . . " and ending with: "5. . . . find these words" may be highlighted.

Suggestions for follow-up activities for the story *The Frog* are:

1. Create a "bragging" book. Each child writes a sentence or two, bragging about something impossible to do. The sentences are illustrated and compiled into *Our Bragging Book.*
2. Find out how far and high a frog really can jump. Each child writes a list of things a frog could jump over. Compare and critique the lists. Combine the ideas into one list and have the children learn to read this list.
3. Practice-work assignment: Each child selects one idea from the list and writes on three-lined paper (see *Additional Resources*, page 248) a pattern sentence such as: "My frog can jump over a _____." They illustrate their sentences, and the papers can be put together into a book entitled *Our Jumping Frogs.*
4. Play "jumping" games during PE, such as relay races and leapfrog.
5. Assign workbook pages. Pick and choose carefully. Do not assign pages simply as "busywork"!

Because all reading groups are not reading the same stories at the same time, it is not always possible to plan class themes around basal reader stories. However, most basal readers do have some sections that can be incorporated into total-class activities. Possible total-class activities may be:

1. **Art:** Many basal readers have art projects to read and do.
2. **Music:** The lyrics of songs are sometimes used as stories in the basal readers. Write the words on a chart paper and have the entire class learn to read and sing this new song.
3. **Cooking:** Some basal readers have cooking projects to read and do.
4. **Science:** Science projects may also be a basal reader story.

5. **Poetry:** Write a chart of each poem in the reader when the first reading group gets to it. Succeeding groups enjoy recognizing the poems when they get to them. Read these poems at the beginning of the school day. The reading group may have a copy for homework.

6. **Familiar Stories:** Some basal readers rewrite familiar stories, such as *Jack and the Beanstalk,* into an easier reading level.

Extended Reading. The teacher may read different versions of the same story to the class. Compare the different versions. Then the children may dictate sentences sequencing the story that the teacher writes on a large chart paper. This story may be duplicated and sent home to be read for homework (see Form 27.3, *Jack and the Beanstalk,* at end of chapter).

Drama. (see *Drama* on pages 134 to 135).

Writing. Make copies of four actual illustrations from a story in a book. Put these illustrations in sequential order on writing paper. (See Forms 27.4 and 27.5, *The Gingerbread Man,* at the end of this chapter.) Duplicate copies of this paper. Capable students can write their own sentences on the writing lines beside each picture, describing the illustrations. (See *Goldilocks,* page 222.) Less capable students may need to dictate the sentences to the teacher or an aide. A reading group may collaborate in dictating a single story, with the adult writing the sentences on the chalkboard. If an individual is dictating, then the sentences may be written by the adult on a separate piece of writing paper. The students then copy the dictated sentences onto their own illustrated writing papers.

HOMEWORK

Read these words. Read in different
directions (down, up, and across).
Work for instant mastery (no sounding out).

Check one:

Sign and return:

____ Mastered

____ Not mastered

_____

Form 27.1

The frog said, "I can jump
over a pond and to the moon."
"I can jump a long way, too,"
a grasshopper told the frog.
But the frog just laughed.
The frog kept on bragging
to his friends.
"Jump over to the other side
of this river," said his friends.
The frog was afraid to jump.

Sign and return:

_____

Jack and the Beanstalk

Jack is trading the cow for five beans.
Jack gave the beans to his mother.
Mother threw them out of the window.
Jack is climbing the tall beanstalk.
Jack is talking to the giant's wife.
The giant's wife hid Jack from the giant.
The giant is counting his gold.
Jack took the gold and gave it to his mother.
Jack took the hen that lays the golden eggs.
Jack took the golden harp that sings.
The giant is coming down!
Jack chops down the beanstalk.

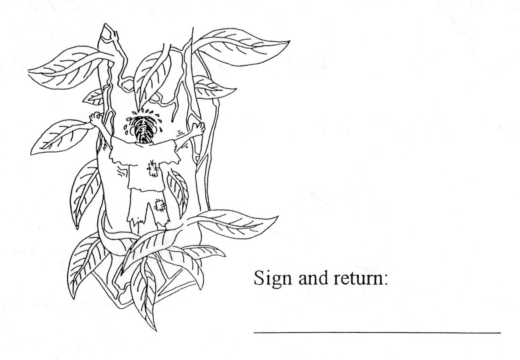

Sign and return:

_____

Form 27.3

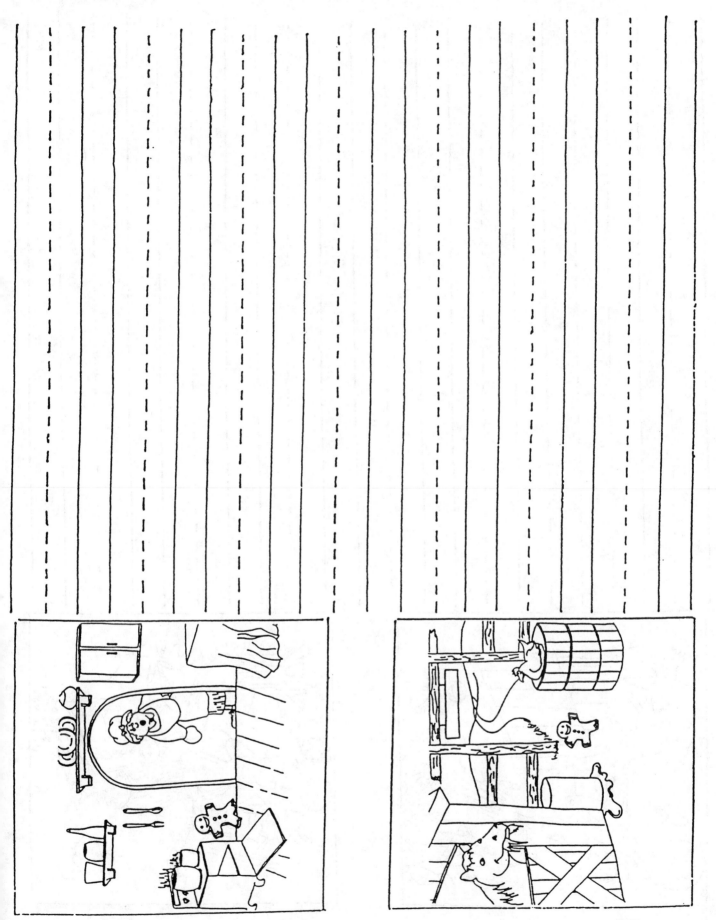

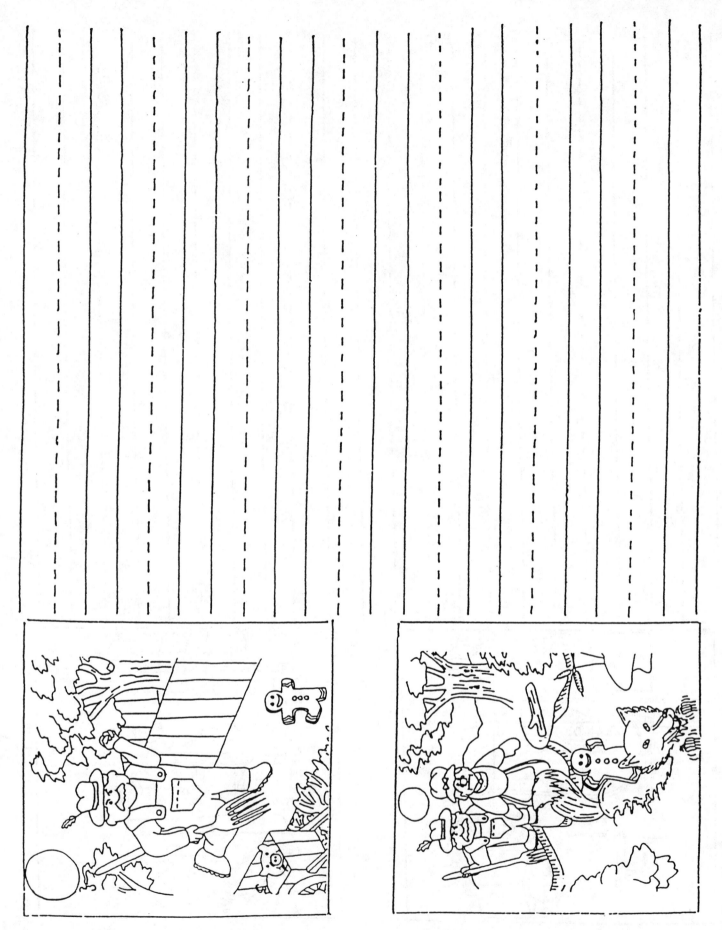

Form 27.5

28

Promoting Reading Readiness

After the first 20 days of first grade, some children are still not ready to begin formal reading. These children need to spend more time at the readiness level. Unfortunately, children are often rushed through this readiness stage and then are labeled as "problem readers." The following are ways to work with first graders who are still in the readiness stage. *Note:* Some of the activities can be used in kindergarten and with students in Special Education.

Read Books

The teacher should often read a short story to this small group. Emphasis should be on good listening, vocabulary development, and comprehension skills.

Daily Phonics

Do some phonics work each day. Use the same lessons from the first 20 days of school. Simply start over and slow down the pace. Phonics activities would include:

1. Oral Blending: Start with compound words, then multi-syllable words, and finally blend individual sounds into words.
2. Consonants: Start with any five consonant sounds and slowly add to them until all of the sounds are mastered. Make lists of words that begin with each consonant. Find specific consonants within words. Assign practice-work activities around the consonant sounds. For this readiness group, homework may be flashcards with consonant sounds, one new sound per day.
3. Vowel Code: Learn the vowel code, one vowel at a time.
4. Dictation: Dictate individual sounds for children to write on small chalkboards.
5. Read Words: Read words by blending the sounds.
6. Spell Words: Spell words by using magnetic letters on individual metal cookie sheets.

Patterned Sentences

Let the children come up with ideas for simple patterned sentences. Make charts of all the ideas. Read and reread the charts together. Make copies of the charts for reading homework. During practice-work time, the children may copy and illustrate the sentences. Ideas for patterned sentences are:

I see a red _____.

I see a blue _____.

This is a yellow _____.

This is a green _____.

A clown can _____.

A clown can _____.

A clown can not _____.

Bob has one red _____.

Sara has two brown _____.

Bill likes to _____.

Ted likes to _____.

Judy likes to _____.

Bears were _____.

Bears have _____.

Cut-Apart Sentences

Write simple sentences on sentence strips. Cut the words apart and put them in a pocket chart out of order. Let the children take turns in putting the words in the correct order. For a practice-work follow-up activity, duplicate copies of a scrambled sentence (see *Scrambled Sentences* on page 218). The children cut the words apart, paste them into the right order, and then draw a picture to go with the sentence.

Labeling

Paste a suitable picture in the center of a large piece of butcher paper. Draw lines to the objects in the picture and label them. The labels may be a single word (*door*) or a word-cluster (*yellow door*). The children learn to read the words. For practice-work, they may be given drawing paper that has been folded into four squares. They will need to write a word (or word-cluster) from the picture in each square and illustrate accordingly.

Stories

Display a picture and have the children think of a simple story to go with the picture. Duplicate copies of the story and have the children practice reading it. Be sure that the children "track" as they read. Ask them to find specific words. For practice-work, the story may be illustrated and then assigned to be read for homework.

Individual Illustrations

Have each child color a picture around a theme, such as "pets." The child then dictates, and the teacher writes, one or two sentences about the child's illustration. Let the children read their sentences to others. *Suggestion:* Fold under approximately two inches across the bottom of the coloring paper. Each child colors a picture on the top portion. The bottom is unfolded for writing the dictated sentence(s).

Nursery Rhymes

Memorizing nursery rhymes is another beginning step to learning to read. After the rhymes are memorized, the words are written and "tracked" in order to see what the words look like. *Suggestion:* Write the nursery rhymes on sentence strips. Place the strips in order in a pocket chart. Let the children take turns "tracking" the words on each of the strips while everyone learns to read them. Then rearrange the strips out of order and use the same reading procedure. Next, cut the words apart, one sentence at a time, and let the children put them into the correct order. Finally, make copies of the nursery rhymes for homework and/or assemble them into individual books.

Rewrite Known Stories

The teacher first reads a known story, such as *The Three Little Pigs,* and then rewrites the story in eight (or fewer) short sentences. For example:

The three pigs said "Bye" to their mother.
The three pigs started to build their houses.
The wolf went to the house of straw.
The wolf went to the house of sticks.
The wolf went to the house of bricks.
The wolf went down the chimney!

The children practice reading the sentences. Next, the teacher writes each sentence on a sentence strip and changes the order before putting them into a pocket chart. The children need to rearrange the sentences into the correct order. For a practice-work activity, duplicate the same sentences, out of order. The children will have to cut the sentences apart and then paste them into the correct order.

Teacher-Composed Stories

As discussed earlier in Chapters 23 and 24, the teacher knows what has been taught in the way of phonics and sight words. So, the teacher can write stories using words that are already known, with very few new words added each time. For children still at the readiness level, these stories may be personalized by using names of the children. Everyone should have a turn to be featured. For students who need to be individualized (they cannot keep up with the lowest reading group), personal stories about the students may be written. With experience, these stories may be written while actually working with the individual child. Two examples are:

1	2
Andrew sees a cat.	Julie sees a fish.
The cat is black.	It is yellow and orange.
It cannot run.	Now she sees a cat.
It cannot see.	The cat sees the fish.
Poor cat!	Will the cat eat the fish?
	No!

Sight Words

Use flashcards for learning specific words on sight without "sounding out." Do not introduce too many words at one time. Let the children suggest ways for remembering the words. Prepare sets of flashcards for each child in the group. Teach the more advanced readers how to help these students individually to practice their flashcards (see *Five-Star Words* and *Say It Fast* on page 190). Reading these words may also be a homework assignment. *Suggestions:* eight basic color words, numbers from "zero" to "ten," words from the first book of the basal reading series, words from teacher-composed stories, and selected words found in word lists (see *Instant Words* on pages 137 through 140).

Easy-Read Books

Read books that have one patterned sentence per page with illustrations that help to determine the pattern for that page. Read the book over and over until the children can read it (memorized!) without assistance. Then cover the illustrations and practice reading without the help of the pictures. Next, write the sentences on sentence strips (no pictures!) using the color-coding technique. (See *Under the Sky* by Rozanne Lancsak Williams.). Practice reading these sentences.

Next, scramble the sentences and read them in various sequences. Finally, cut the words apart and give each child in the group one sentence to arrange in its correct order. For practice-work, the children may select one sentence to copy and illustrate. The papers may be assembled into a class book.

Under the sky, <u>there is</u> a tree.   **Color Key:**
Under the tree, <u>there is</u> a flower.   *Italics* = green
Under the flower, <u>there is</u> some grass.   <u>Underlined</u> = brown
Under the grass, <u>there is</u> a rock.   Matching nouns =
Under the rock, <u>there is</u> some soil.   (tree . . . tree) = any same color
Under the soil, <u>there is</u> a worm.
Hello, worm!

Reading Groups

If a basal reading series is used, begin the first reader when a majority from this readiness group seems ready to begin formal reading. At this point, it is best to keep this reading group small, preferably with no more than six students. If the group is larger, it may be advantageous to split it into two groups. Perhaps the school's reading teacher may work with one of the two groups; or an aide may work with half of the group while the teacher works with the other half. *Caution:* Aides and volunteer parents are very beneficial to the class, but the teacher is responsible for the teaching.

29

Vocabulary Flashcard Activities

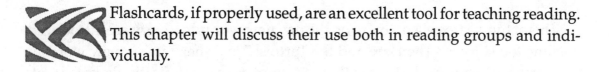Flashcards, if properly used, are an excellent tool for teaching reading. This chapter will discuss their use both in reading groups and individually.

Reading Groups

When working with flashcards in a reading group, all of the children should be involved as much as possible throughout the practice. The following flashcard activities can be very effective.

1. *I'm Thinking of a Word*

Place one-word flashcards (10-12) in a pocket chart. The teacher thinks of one of these words and says, "I'm thinking of a word." The children take turns guessing the word. If the guess is incorrect, the teacher points to the word and says, "not _____." The children need to listen to all of the guesses so that they can guess wisely when their turns come. When the correct word is chosen, the child gets to keep that flashcard until the end of the game. Some children will win more than once and others may not win at all. *Suggestion:* Those who did not win a flashcard may earn one by reading the final flashcard(s) in the pocket chart.

2. *Clapping Game*

First, practice clapping. The children's hands should not be too far apart, should not clap too hard, and should clap only once. The teacher holds the pile of flashcards and mentally selects one word that is not showing on top and tells the children what the word is. The teacher then tells the children to clap once when the selected word is showing on top. Slowly move the top flashcard to the back of the pile. This game requires the children to read each word silently in order to clap on the correct one. Keep selecting different words until the game is over. When this game is first taught, there are no winners. If someone claps at the wrong time, do not make an issue over the error. However, some children may decide to clap with every word. If so, institute a penalty for an error such as: "Fold your hands for one turn." To encourage quickness, the flashcard may be given to the child who claps correctly first. Don't forget to collect the flashcards when the game is over.

3. *Word Definitions*

This activity is excellent to use on the day new words to a story are introduced. Assume the story is "The Hare and the Tortoise" and there are six new words in the story. Put these six flashcards (hare, tortoise, race, start, finish, dawdled) into a pocket chart. The teacher gives a definition for one of the words, being careful not to use the actual word in the definition. Let the children take turns in choosing the correct word. If the correct word is chosen, the child keeps the flashcard until the end of the game. When only one word is left in the chart holder, the role reverses and the child needs to give a definition for that one remaining word. As the year progresses, the entire activity may be changed. One child gives a definition, and another child chooses the correct word. Definitions for the six new words might be:

    A.   This is another word for "turtle."   (tortoise)
    B.   This word means "to begin something."   (start)
    C.   This word means "wasted time."   (dawdled)
    D.   This is another word for "rabbit."   (hare)
    E.   This word is the opposite of "start."   (finish)
    F.   This word means "a contest."   (race)

4. You-Me Game

This game is a contest between "you" (the children in the reading group) and "me" (the teacher). The teacher nearly always loses, so the children love the game! On the chalkboard, the teacher writes the headings: "You" and "Me." Show the top flashcard to the first child. If the child knows the word, the teacher puts a tally mark under the heading "You." The next child reads the next flashcard. If the word is not known, a tally mark is placed under the heading "Me" and the same word is shown to the next child in order. Continue the game until all have had several turns. The score may look something like this:

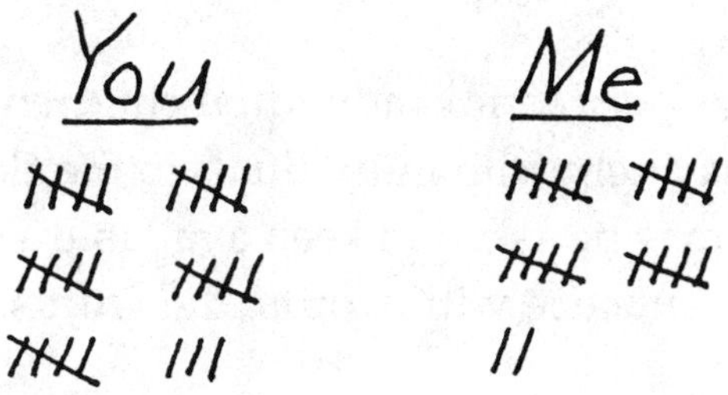

$$
\begin{array}{cc}
\underline{You} & \underline{Me} \\[4pt]
\cancel{||||} \ \cancel{||||} & \cancel{||||} \ \cancel{||||} \\
\cancel{||||} \ \cancel{||||} & \cancel{||||} \ \cancel{||||} \\
\cancel{||||} \ ||| & || \\
\end{array}
$$

Figure 29.1. You–Me

5. Hangman

This popular game works best if there are a lot of flashcards in the pile. It is a good game to play with the entire class. Do not show the flashcards. Select one of the new words, such as *tortoise*. Prepare the chalkboard (hanging stand and letter lines):

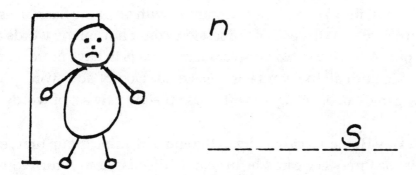

Figure 29.2. Hangman

NOTE: This is a sample "hanging." There is one line for each letter in the word.

Assume the first child guesses an incorrect letter ("**n**"). Write "**n**" at the top so others will not guess that same letter. Then draw a round head hanging from the stand. If the next child's guess is a correct letter ("**s**"), the letter "**s**" is placed on the second to last letter line. The game continues until the entire word is filled in or the man is "hung." Decide beforehand exactly what the finished man should look like. Make it a quick drawing with not too many details. *Suggestion:* Limit the drawing to about seven parts (no hair or fingers). The eyes, nose, and "sad" mouth are for the final wrong letter. Scoring may be similar to the tally marks in the "You-Me" game.

Individuals

Sometimes flashcards are needed for individual children to practice. Parents, aides, or cross-age tutors may help with individuals in the classroom and parents may help at home. Parents may be asked to keep available a supply of 3" × 5" file cards. If a child needs extra practice with words, the words are written on these cards.

1. Five-Star Words. Show the flashcard to the child. If the word is known immediately (no sounding out), a star (*) is drawn on the flashcard. If the word is not known immediately, the "helper" sounds out and says the word but does not draw a star. Continue until all of the words have been read one time around. Follow the same procedure at all sessions. At the end of the second session, some words may have two stars (**). When the words have five stars (*****), they have been mastered! Eliminate these five-star words and add new words as they are needed.

2. Say It Fast. Show the flashcard to the child. If the word is said "fast" (no sounding out), put that flashcard in the "say it fast" pile. If the word is not known immediately, the flashcard is put into a second pile. Continue with all of the flashcards, placing each in its correct pile. At the end of the session, count how many words are in the "say it fast" pile. At each successive session, the goal is to have more words in the "say it fast" pile until all the words are mastered. Do not add words during the game. A new game can begin again with a completely new set of words.

3. Earn Your Way Home. Occasionally, at the end of reading group time, each child may read two or three flashcards before being dismissed to return to his or her desk (home). Children who miss a word need to stay and try again at the end. The teacher may alternate words with the last two children so that there is no "last" child.

More Reading Strategies

The ultimate goal in reading is to be an independent reader who fully understands what is being read. Teachers need to help readers acquire the reading strategies needed to achieve this goal. These strategies should begin before the start of formal reading instruction, and if continuously reinforced, they will eventually become second-nature to the students.

As discussed in the introduction, the intent of this chapter is to incorporate the teaching strategies that did not seem to fit into any of the preceding chapters. The teacher should become familiar with the ideas presented in this chapter and plan to use them whenever appropriate.

Reading to Children

The teacher should establish good listening rules and see that they are followed. The environment needs to be conducive to listening. Listeners need to be positioned close to the reader. There should be no distractions.

Books that are read must be selected with care. Books should be selected from a broad spectrum that includes fiction and nonfiction. Some books are best read the first time for enjoyment and then reread for detailed comprehension.

A. Introducing Vocabulary

Understanding the meaning of words is essential for comprehension. The teacher should pre-read to determine which words will need to be defined. These words may be discussed prior to reading the book or when they are encountered during the first reading of the book. *Caution:* Too many interruptions during a reading can hinder the flow of understanding.

B. Developing Comprehension With Questions

When pre-reading a book, the teacher should also plan on the questions to ask. Vary the types of questions to incorporate different thinking skills. Allow "thinking time" after asking the question and before calling on someone to answer. Rather than having the children raise their hands if they know the answer, call on children at random and occasionally call on someone a second time. These techniques will encourage careful listening.

Questions may need to be tailored to fit the capabilities of certain students. Be sure that the children get equal chances to participate. Try to be positive when reacting to an answer, even if it is inaccurate. When reading a book, ask the children to predict what might happen next in the story. Good predicting denotes good listening and good comprehension.

There are three distinct types of questions that can best be explained by example. Several versions of the nursery rhyme *Over in the Meadow* have been compiled into books. The following is one adaptation of the first verse that might be found in such a book:

Over in the meadow on a rock in the sun
Lived an old mother snake and her little snake one.
"Hiss," said the mother. "I hiss," said the one.
So they hissed all day on a rock in the sun.

1. Pre-Reading Questions. Prior to reading any book, talk about the subject matter. For instance, prior to reading *Over in the Meadow*, develop an understanding of a meadow. Questions to ask might be: (a) What is a meadow? Contrast it to other types of land formations, such as a forest or a beach. (b) What animals might be in a meadow? (c) What might these animals be doing?

Next, prior to reading the first verse, discuss in detail the illustration that appears on the page. Questions for this particular page may be: (a) What animal is this? (b) How many animals are there? (c) Where are the animals? (d) What else do you see in the picture?

Read the verse. Then, ask similar questions about the illustrations of all succeeding verses before reading them.

2. Recall Questions. After reading the entire book, close it and ask specific questions that can be answered by remembering what was read. Such recall questions for the first verse may be: (a) Who is in the meadow? (b) Where are they? (c) What are the snakes doing?

3. "Higher Thinking" Questions. The goal of this type of questioning is to get the students to think about what was read and apply it to other related ideas. Often, there are no right or wrong answers to this type of questioning. "Higher thinking" questions for the first verse may be: (a) Where else could you find snakes in a meadow? (b) What time of the year is it? How do you know? (c) What else could the snakes be doing besides "hissing"? See if some children can answer this with one word, such as "slithering" or "sleeping." *Note:* Intersperse "higher thinking" questions with "recall" questions, rather than first asking the "recall" questions for the entire book and then going back for the "higher thinking" skills.

Students' Reading

When teaching students to read a story, the same techniques for developing vocabulary and comprehension should be followed as when a story is read to them. Prior to the reading, the teacher should discuss the meanings of any words that may be unfamiliar to the students. The same types of questions may be asked for comprehension: pre-reading, recall, and higher thinking.

A. *Deciphering Words*

Once children begin reading stories on their own, rather than having everything read to them, they need to know how to decipher unknown words. The teacher should teach strategies for figuring out any unknown words. These strategies may be taught whether working with a reading group or with individual children. When a child in a reading group does not know a word, only the teacher may help. After allowing about five seconds of "thinking time," the teacher prompts the reader with a series of four strategic questions. Progress through the questions until the child can decipher the word.

1. *Phonics:* What does the word look like? Can you sound it out?
2. *Reread:* Will it help to go back to the beginning of the sentence?
3. *Skip:* Can you skip the word and read to the end of the sentence?
4. *Guess:* What do you think the word is? Does that make sense?

If the child does not know the word after completing the four steps, say the word. The selection is undoubtedly above the child's reading level if this happens often.

The teacher needs to encourage and praise the children with specifics when one of the strategies has been successfully used. The words of encouragement also provide a restatement of the four strategies. Words of encouragement may be:

Phonics: "I like how you sounded out that word."
Reread: "I'm glad you remembered to go back to the beginning of the sentence and then figured out the word."
Skip: "I noticed that you skipped the word and then figured it out."
Guess: "That was a good guess."

As the children begin using the strategies on their own, ask them: "How did you figure out that word?" This questioning will continue to make the children aware of which strategies they are using. Eventually, these strategies will become so automatic that the children will use them without thinking about it.

Note: The four teaching strategies for deciphering unknown words should not be limited to beginning readers. As reading materials become more difficult, teachers must continue to see that each student is deciphering words independently and is understanding what is being read. Regular monitoring prevents reading problems that are "discovered" in later years.

B. Tracking

Beginning readers need to follow along visually while others are reading. Everyone needs to be reading. In a reading group, most students should move a pointer finger when following the text. This tracking discourages "wandering eyes." Some children may be able to read without tracking. If the teacher is positive that a student is following the text, then by all means allow that student to read without using a pointer finger. As the children become more proficient in their reading, they usually discontinue finger pointing naturally. Tracking may seem to be slowing down reading for a few; they may need to be encouraged to read with their eyes only. As the amount of print on a page increases, some students may need to use a book marker that reveals only one line at a time.

Note: Beginning readers should not be taught "speed-reading" techniques.

Guided Silent Reading

There are a variety of techniques for implementing silent reading. The teacher's manual of a basal reader will have suggestions for guiding the silent reading of a story. The following formats will work for guiding a reading group or individuals through the silent reading of any story. Format #1 is used with beginning-level readers. Because the stories are short, the teacher first reads the entire story to the group or individual.

Format #2 is used with more advanced readers. The stories are longer and the readers are more proficient, so the teacher does not read the story out loud. Most of the other suggestions covered in the first format may also be used in the second format. *Important:* Students should never be expected to read out loud during their first reading. They should have a chance to practice either by choral reading or silent reading.

Format #1. For a group that is reading short stories at the beginning level, the teacher begins by reading the entire story to the group, following the format discussed earlier in this chapter (see *Reading to Children* on pages 191-193).

The next day, the same story is read silently by the students. To prepare for this silent reading, the teacher plans specific questions. The questions should be arranged in sequential order from the beginning to the end of the story.

The procedure for this silent rereading of the story is as follows: New or unfamiliar words in the story are introduced (see *Step 3 (Sentence Strips)* and *Step 4 (Vocabulary)* on page 169). The books are opened to the first page. The teacher asks the first question, and the children begin reading silently until they come to the answer. They then look up at the teacher (no raising of hands) and quietly wait until everyone in the group has found the answer. When all of the children are looking up, the teacher selects one student to read the answer aloud. Continue with this procedure until all questions have been completed. After the last question, the teacher should tell the children to finish reading the story to themselves.

For a story of average length, five questions are sufficient. Sample questions for the story "Jack and the Beanstalk" might be:

1. Start from the beginning of the story and read to yourself until you find who gave Jack the beans.
2. Read on until you find what Mother did with the beans.
3. Read on until you find what Jack took from the giant first.
4. Read on until you find what Jack took next.
5. Read on until you find what Jack took last.

Format #2. This format is the same as Format #1 except that:

1. The teacher does not read the story to the children. They silently read the story themselves for the first reading.
2. The teacher guides the silent reading page by page, rather than question to question. When a book is open, the two open pages should be considered as "one page." The next page comes at the turning of the page.
3. Predicting is now possible during the silent reading because the children have not heard the story.

After the pre-reading discussion and the development of vocabulary, the teacher guides the students through a silent reading of a story, one page at a time. Discuss the picture, if any, on the first page. Either have the children predict what will happen on the page and then have them read the page to themselves to find out if they were accurate in their predictions; or, just as in Format #1, the teacher asks a specific question and they read to find the answer. For variety, use both of these techniques. Some pages lend themselves to predicting, but others may be better with questions from the teacher. After the first question is answered, other questions should also be asked. This further questioning helps ensure that the students read and comprehend the entire page, rather than stopping when they have found the answer. Continue this procedure for each page in the story. *Note:* If a child comes to a word that cannot be deciphered, even after trying the four strategies, that child points to the word and looks at the teacher. The teacher whispers the word to the child.

Silent Reading Without Guidance

More advanced readers may read an entire story without guidance from the teacher. The format for this type of silent reading is that the teacher meets with the reading group for the pre-reading discussion of the story and for vocabulary development. Then the students are given a definite reason for reading the entire story, such as: (a) The group will meet to discuss specific predictions, questions, or both. (b) The students will have to complete a paper related to the story. (c) The students will be assigned a project related to the story. (d) The students will need to be prepared to read the story out loud.

Once the silent reading assignment is given, everyone separates for the reading. They could sit on the floor in different parts of the room. The teacher should monitor the students. *Note:* Because everyone reads at a different rate of speed, it is not advisable to have a long story read silently at a reading table because those who finish first may disturb those still reading.

Sustained Silent Reading

"Sustained silent reading" (SSR) is a time when everyone (including the teacher) silently reads self-selected books. By the beginning of the second semester, first graders should be ready to have a scheduled sustained silent reading time. In all succeeding grades, SSR should be part of the daily schedule from the beginning of the school year.

There should be a large selection of varied reading material available for SSR, such as library books, class books, VIP stories, mascot stories, and collections of poems that have been studied. A child who had difficulty with a reading group story may be encouraged to reread that story.

A good time to schedule SSR is after lunch recess. Before sitting down at their desks, the children get any books that they will want to read. In order to give everyone an equal opportunity, there should be a plan for choosing popular books.

The following rules are suggested for SSR:

1. Children do not get up to get more reading material. Time must be spent reading, not looking for books!
2. Some beginning readers have a difficult time reading "silently," so remind them to "whisper" when they read.
3. No one may ask for reading help. This is a good time for independent practice using the four strategies for deciphering words.
4. As the children finish reading, they put their heads down.
5. The teacher signals that time is up when most of the children have their heads down.
6. The students are then dismissed by rows or tables to return books to their rightful places. Class books and reading group books should always be returned. Library books may be kept at their desks until finished (have bookmarks available).

Paired Reading

Occasionally, children should have the opportunity to read an entire story to another child. This activity should be the final reading of a story. There needs to be enough time to complete the readings. It is preferable to read to someone not in the same reading group, because then the story will be "fresh" for the listener. During the reading group time, the "readers" can select "listeners" from those working independently at their desks. Each pair needs to find an out-of-the-way place where they will not disturb or be disturbed. The teacher walks around and monitors the pairs.

Reading Friend

Find an adult volunteer to come into the classroom at least once a week to be a "reading friend." This volunteer does not help with other classroom activities. At the very beginning of first grade, the reading friend may read stories to each reading group during their practice-work time. When most of the students are beginning to read on their own, the "reading friend" becomes a listener yet continues to read to anyone still at the readiness stage. The reading friend can listen to a child read a wide variety of materials, such as basal reader stories, poems, chart papers, homework papers, class books, and library books. *Note:* If time is a factor, a child may read only a part of a story to the reading friend. The reading friend should have a form to keep track of who has read and for writing comments to the teacher.

Tape Recorders

Every primary classroom should have at least four tape recorders available for both listening and recording. It is best to have tape recorders with microphones that can be easily transported. These can be purchased at most toy stores.

Listening to Tapes. A listening center is very important! Two earphones can be plugged into an adapter so that two children may listen simultaneously to a story being read. There are numerous tape-recorded books that can be purchased. A good source for purchasing tapes is through the various book clubs that solicit business from schools. Bonus points may be used for getting free books with tapes.

Tapes prepared by the teacher are another source. Favorite books and stories may be recorded. When preparing the tapes, establish a signal for when the children need to turn the page. The signal may be the ringing of a bell or quietly saying, "Turn the page."

Reading Into a Tape Recorder. Reading into a tape recorder is a real treat for beginning readers. Students may read into a tape recorder as a free-time activity. These tape-recorded readings should be monitored by the teacher to discourage "playing around."

Reading into a tape recorder may also be an assignment. This can either be during practice-work time, as a "learning center" activity, or during the reading group time. With four recorders and no more than eight children in a reading group, two children may be assigned to read together. When reading together, they alternate reading the pages.

Another way to use a tape recorder with a reading group is to record the children as they take turns in reading a story. The teacher holds the microphone and moves it to the child who is reading. There needs to be time at the end for listening to the entire recorded story.

Using a Tape Recorder to Develop Fluency. Readers need to be taught to read with good expression (fluency). One way to work on fluency with individual children is for the teacher to read into a tape recorder a short story that is currently being read. The child will have the opportunity to listen to the teacher read the story, to read along with the teacher, to read and record the story individually, and finally to listen to his or her own reading. *Suggestion:* The tape and tape recorder may be sent home for a homework assignment. The following is a procedure for preparing this type of tape: Read the name of the story and tell the listeners that you will wait for them to turn to the correct page and look at the first picture. After waiting about 10 seconds, say "Get ready" and then read the page. At the end of each page, softly say, "Turn the page." With each new page, allow a little time for looking at pictures before saying, "Get ready." Upon finishing the reading of the story, the teacher concludes the tape recording by giving instructions, such as:

Rewind this tape back to the beginning of the story. Then push the "play" button and read the story *with* me. When we have finished reading the story together, you may read the story by yourself into the tape recorder. To do this, you first need to push the "stop" button and get out the microphone. Be sure that the microphone is turned on. When you are ready to read, push the "record" button. At the end, you may rewind the tape and listen to yourself read. You may begin now by rewinding this tape and reading the story with me.

Note: The verbal signal ("Get ready") is needed in order for the children to start reading with the tape recorder from the beginning of the page. The entire class should be taught beforehand the procedure for listening and then reading into a tape recorder. The verbal instructions on the tape serve as a reminder for what has already been taught.

Additional Pocket Chart Activities

A. Sequencing

Sequencing is an excellent technique for expanding comprehension skills. The teacher composes sentences that tell how to do something. In the beginning, compose only three sentences. For example, these three sentences tell how to drink milk:

Get a milk carton out of the refrigerator.
Pour the milk into a glass.
Drink the good, cold milk.

Place the sentences, out of order, into a pocket chart. Let the students work at getting them into the correct order.

Gradually increase the number of sentences. These eight sentences tell about making a snowman:

It snowed last night.
I put on my warm clothes.
I made a big snowball for the body.
Then I put a small snowball on top.
I finished decorating my snowman.
Everyone liked my snowman.
Then the sun came out.
My snowman is melting!

For practice-work, these sentences may be duplicated out of order. The children cut and paste them into the correct order. The story may then be illustrated.

B. Completing Sentences

The teacher writes enough sentence "beginnings" on sentence strips to fit each slot in a pocket chart. Write all of these "beginnings" (**bold**) in the same color, such as red. The teacher then writes "endings" (*italics*) for each sentence in a different color, such as green. Place the "endings" after the "beginnings" in the pocket chart, except not in the correct order. The children need to work at rearranging the sentences so that they all make sense. For practice-work, the children may copy and illustrate one sentence. The following sentences may be used at Christmas-time:

The stockings are	*hanging by the fireplace.*
The star is	*on top of the tree.*
Santa comes	*down the chimney.*
Reindeer can	*fly in the sky.*
The tree is	*tall and green.*

C. Patterns

Poems and songs that repeat words over and over are perfect to use in pocket charts. The traditional song "The Wheels on the Bus" has a pattern that is easy to change. Three sentence strips are enough to establish the pattern:

The _____ on the bus

Go _____

All through the town.

On sentence strips, cut to size, write the various choices, such as:

Line 1	Line 2
wheels	*round and round*
people	*up and down*
wipers	*swish, swish, swish*
horn	*toot, toot, toot*

The children take turns inserting the proper words.

D. Coloring Instructions

Duplicate copies of a picture out of a coloring book, enough for each child (see Form 30.1, *Large Scarecrow,* at end of chapter). Compose sentences giving the children directions as to how to color the picture. Write these sentences on sentence strips and place them into a pocket chart. The children must read and follow the coloring directions. *Suggestion:* Duplicate copies of the sentences for a homework assignment (see Form 30.2, *Scarecrow Sentences*, at end of chapter).

I am a scarecrow.
My hat is green.
My hair is yellow.
My shirt is red.
My bird is black.
My pitchfork is brown.
My pants are blue.
My gloves are orange.
My patches are purple.

Sign and return:

31

Reading at Home

Actually being able to read "real" books is the ultimate goal of all beginning readers. So far, the reading homework assignments have included flashcards, word lists, poems, songs, student-made materials, and teacher-composed stories. Once a student is able to read "real" books with a degree of independence, then the reading of these books should be included in the home-reading program.

Training Parents

Parents should be trained in ways to help with reading homework assignments. "Back-to-School Night" and parent-teacher conferences are good times for this training. A handout explaining the process should also be prepared (see Form 31.1, *Reading at Home, Letter to Parents,* at end of chapter). The handout can be explained at these meetings and can be given to parents who were not in attendance. Some parents will need to be reminded of the process during the school year.

Note: The *Letter to Parents* states that the rules for playing the "Say It Fast" and "Five-Star Words" games are attached (see page 212). Make a copy of the rules for these games (see page 190) and attach them to the letters.

Establishing the Homework Habit

There needs to be an understanding of the reasons for assigning reading homework. The three major reasons are: (a) It takes practice to become a proficient reader. The more you read, the better reader you will be. (b) By working with their child, the parents become aware of their child's strengths and weaknesses. Such an awareness can help prevent severe reading problems later on. (c) In order to ensure success in doing homework in the upper grades, the habit of doing homework in the primary grades needs to be established. It should be constructive homework, not just "busywork." If a child does not have homework on a given night at any grade level, the parent should give the child a reading assignment.

How much time to spend on homework is another issue. It is very important that children like to read. "Liking to read" cannot be forced on anyone. Setting the stage for success in reading should be a goal for all teachers and parents. Parents should start reading to their children at an early age. Students should not be pushed into reading before they are ready, and the reading material should not exceed their capabilities. Success must be attainable! The parents should know their child's interest level and attention span and fit the timing to suit their child. If the child resists reading, then it may be wise for the parent to read to the child the entire "homework time."

A guideline for minimum time spent on homework could be:

First grade—10 minutes
Second grade—20 minutes
Third grade—30 minutes
Fourth grade—40 minutes
Fifth grade—50 minutes

By the time students reach the sixth grade, they should be ready for 60 minutes of homework.

Should there be homework every night? Most jobs have a five-day week. Going to school is the student's job, so five nights of homework should be expected.

Suggestions: Students are required to do homework Monday through Thursday. They may choose their own fifth day (Friday, Saturday, or Sunday). Consider giving a grade for returning homework assignments. If there is not a spot for it on the report card, write it in somewhere.

"Read" and "Unread" Books

A homework book has either been read and studied at school ("read" book) or the child reads it for the first time at home ("unread" book). The children should be ready to read "read" books as a homework assignment with very little or no help. To ensure that the book is actually being "read" and not just memorized, they should be able to read with all pictures covered and find specific words out of order. *Note:* If the child is having difficulty, the parent should help the child as if it is an "unread" book.

"Unread" books may need to be worked with in a different manner. Proficient readers will require very little help with words. If books are selected at the appropriate reading level, these readers should be able to read the books aloud to their parents with little or no assistance. The parent should ask specific questions to make certain that the child is comprehending what is being read.

At the beginning level, most books can be read and returned the next day. However, when a child is not yet a proficient reader, the same book may need to be a three-day homework assignment. The following steps may be used for those children needing more help:

Day 1. The parent tracks and reads the entire selection to the child. The child follows the words as they are being read. When appropriate, the child may predict what will happen before the page is turned. The parent asks specific questions for comprehension. *Note:* The parent should talk about any pictures on a page before reading that page; otherwise, the child is liable to look at the picture rather than the words.

Day 2. The parent and child choral read the selection.

Day 3. The child reads the selection alone. If a word is not known, the parent allows for "thinking" time before saying the word. (Do not "sound out" words during a reading!) After the reading, the parent writes unknown words on flashcards

(3″ × 5″ file cards). The parent and child discuss ways to remember these words. This would be the time to "sound out" words. Play a game with all of the flashcards (see *Five-Star Words* and *Say It Fast* on page 190).

Determining Reading Level

Home-reading books that the child reads for the first time at home should not be too difficult. When parents work with their own children, it is better to have reading books below, rather than above, the child's reading level. The teacher needs to be sure that the child is ready to begin reading the first books (Level 1) of the home-reading collection. The teacher, or an aide, should listen to the child read in order to establish the correct reading level.

The "five-fingers rule" is an easy way to determine reading level. This is not an exact rule, but it does serve as an informal evaluation for determining anyone's reading level. The "five-fingers rule" is as follows: When the reader definitely does not know a word, the listener puts down one finger. (Misreading words does not apply, if the reader can go back and read the word correctly.) Five fingers down because of five unknown words means the reading level is too difficult for independent reading. This principle applies to an entire short, easy reader. For longer books with few pictures, the principle applies to a page without pictures. The "five-finger rule" should especially be followed for children with a low frustration level. Children eager to be challenged may have more leeway.

Collecting Home-Reading Books

Getting a home-reading book collection started is not an easy task. It can be expensive but is certainly worth it. Garage sales can be a good source. A letter may be sent home with students from the upper grades, requesting books that are no longer being read. It helps to collect home-reading books that belong to a series. There are many different series of books being published. A few suggestions are:

1. *A First Start Easy Reader* (Troll Associates)
2. *An Early I Can Read Book* (Harper Trophy)
3. *Bank Street-Ready to Read* (Bantam Books)
4. *Follett Just Beginning to Read Books* (Modern Curriculum Press)
5. *Get Ready . . . Get Set . . . Read!* (Barron's)
6. *I Can Read It All by Myself-Beginner Books* (Random House)

7. *Learn to Read . . . Read to Learn* (Creative Teaching Press)
8. *Let Me Read . . . Good Year Books* (HarperCollins)
9. *Phonics Practice Readers* (Modern Curriculum Press)
10. *Primary Phonics Series* (Modern Curriculum Press)
11. *Rigby Books* (Rigby Education)
12. *A Rookie Reader* (Childrens Press)
13. *Start to Read Book* (A School Zone)
14. *Step Into Reading* (Random House)
15. *Tiger Cub Books* (Peguis Publishers)
16. *Wright Group Books* (The Wright Group)

Managing the Home-Reading Library

Keeping track of books that the children take home can be cumbersome. I have tried many different methods, and the following seemed to be the quickest and most efficient for checking out books to individual students from the Home-Reading Library.

Numbering the Books. The books are categorized and labeled into 10 levels (see *X. Home-Reading Books* on page 22). Numbers, such as 3.16 (16th book in Level 3), are written with permanent ink on a small plain sticker that is placed on the outside top right-hand corner of each book. The books are arranged on a shelf from easiest to hardest. Duplicate the two "Home-Reading Book Record" pages (see Forms 31.2 and 31.3 at end of chapter) on lightweight tagboard with Levels 1-5 on the front and Levels 6-10 on the back. These forms provide for 30 books in each of the ten levels. If more than 30 books exist in any of the levels, then a supplement would be duplicated on another piece of tagboard with additional numbers. If there are multiple copies of a book, each copy will have the same number.

Sending the Homework Home. Place the tagboard(s) and the home-reading book into a large envelope, one per student (see *G. Homework Letter and Envelope* on page 18). Circle the book's number on the tagboard. When it is returned, the number is crossed out. Because the next book in order may not be available for everyone at the same time, it is often necessary to skip around within a level. It only takes a glance to see which books have and have not been sent home. *Note:* If a child is able to skip a level, cross out the entire level.

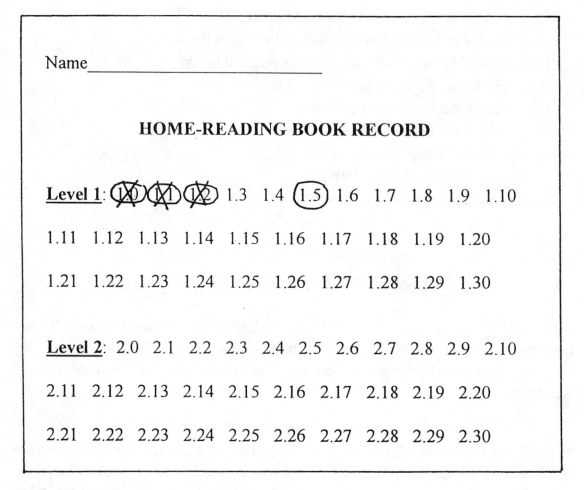

Figure 31.1. Home-Reading Book Record

Caution: The children must be told not to write on the tagboard and always to leave it in the envelope. Stress the importance of not losing the books, the envelope, or the tagboard inserts.

Signature Form. A signature form should be sent home with each book that is a homework assignment (see Form 31.4 at end of chapter). The form is signed by the parent. Comments are optional. The teacher may write a short comment in order to encourage the writing of a response.

Dear Parents,

The following information is to guide you in helping your child achieve success in learning to read. It takes practice to become a proficient reader. The more your child reads, the better reader your child will be. If we work together, we will set the stage for your child's reading success.

Reading homework will be assigned throughout this school year. Students who get into the habit of doing homework in the primary grades are likely to continue the habit in the upper grades. If your child does not have homework on a given night at any grade level, you should give your child a reading assignment.

How long should your child work on homework? This depends a lot on your child's capabilities, interest level, and attention span. A guideline for minimum time spent on homework could be: first grade—10 minutes; second grade—20 minutes; third grade—30 minutes; fourth grade—40 minutes; fifth grade—50 minutes; and sixth grade—60 minutes.

It is important that your child likes to read. If there are problems in achieving this goal, do not hesitate to contact me, and we will work out a special plan for your child.

Your child will receive a grade on the report card for returning homework. If for some reason it is impossible to complete an assignment on any given day, let me know. Reasonable excuses are accepted.

Homework guidelines and suggestions:

A. Establish a good time to do homework.

B. Determine the most suitable place to read—least noise, interruptions, and visual distractions.

C. Homework will come home in a large envelope. Establish a safe place to keep this envelope, so that it can be readily found when needed.

D. There will be a variety in types of homework. Whenever necessary, instructions will be included.   Contact me if you ever have questions. Generally, the types of reading homework and the techniques to use are:

1. Your child reads to you a poem, song, or story that is on a single sheet of paper. You child   should "track" (move a pointer finger under each word) to minimize memorization and ensure actual reading. At the end of the reading, ask your child to point to about five different words, in five different places. Knowing specific words is important.

2. Your child reads to you a list of words on a single sheet of paper. Instructions are to read them several times in different directions. Your child should come close to

mastering these words. If needed, help to "sound out" a word and discuss ways to remember it.

3. Your child "tracks" and reads a book that has been read and studied in class. Your child should be ready to read the book with little or no help. If you suspect that the words have been memorized and your child is not "reading," cover the pictures before beginning each page. Also, ask your child to point out specific words out of order.

4. Your child "tracks" and reads a book that he or she has never read. Talk about the pictures before reading each page. Ask questions to be sure that your child understands what is being read. If your child has difficulty in reading these books, be sure to let me know. The book can be a 3-day assignment with specific instructions to be followed for each of the 3 days.

5. When your child is reading and does not know a word, do not have your child "sound out" the word. "Sounding out" during a reading can take away from the enjoyment of reading and can make it difficult to understand what is being read. Instead, wait just a moment to be sure that he or she cannot figure it out, then say the word and remember it for working on after reading the book.

6. Have available a supply of 3" × 5" file cards. When your child does not know a word (see 5 above), write the word on a file card. Now is the time to work on "sounding out" the word and talking about ways to remember the word. Save all file card "flashcards" until the words are mastered. Suggestion: Play either the "Say It Fast" or "Five-Star Words" games when working with these flashcards. Instructions for these two games are attached.

E. When the reading of "real" books begins for your child, a sheet of tagboard paper will be inserted into the homework envelope. There will be numbers on this paper for recording which books are being sent home. All recording is done at school. You do not have to do anything. Please see that no one writes on the paper and that it always remains in the envelope.

F. When your child brings a book home to read, there will be a form for you to fill out and sign, verifying the reading of the book. You will need to check whether you feel that your child needs to read the book again or whether you feel that he or she is ready for another book. Return the book either way. It will be sent again if you request it.

Once again, please call me before or after school (333-3333) if you have any questions or concerns about your child's reading. We can discuss it by phone or schedule an appointment. By working together, we can help your child achieve success in reading.

(Teacher's Name)

Form 31.2. Home-Reading Book Record (Level 1 through 5)

Name _____

HOME-READING BOOK RECORD

Level 1: 1.1   1.2   1.3   1.4   1.5   1.6   1.7   1.8   1.9   1.10

1.11   1.12   1.13   1.14   1.15   1.16   1.17   1.18   1.19   1.20

1.21   1.22   1.23   1.24   1.25   1.26   1.27   1.28   1.29   1.30

Level 2: 2.1   2.2   2.3   2.4   2.5   2.6   2.7   2.8   2.9   2.10

2.11   2.12   2.13   2.14   2.15   2.16   2.17   2.18   2.19   2.20

2.21   2.22   2.23   2.24   2.25   2.26   2.27   2.28   2.29   2.30

Level 3: 3.1   3.2   3.3   3.4   3.5   3.6   3.7   3.8   3.9   3.10

3.11   3.12   3.13   3.14   3.15   3.16   3.17   3.18   3.19   3.20

3.21   3.22   3.23   3.24   3.25   3.26   3.27   3.28   3.29   3.30

Level 4: 4.1   4.2   4.3   4.4   4.5   4.6   4.7   4.8   4.9   4.10

4.11   4.12   4.13   4.14   4.15   4.16   4.17   4.18   4.19   4.20

4.21   4.22   4.23   4.24   4.25   4.26   4.27   4.28   4.29   4.30

Level 5: 5.1   5.2   5.3   5.4   5.5   5.6   5.7   5.8   5.9   5.10

5.11   5.12   5.13   5.14   5.15   5.16   5.17   5.18   5.19   5.20

5.21   5.22   5.23   5.24   5.25   5.26   5.27   5.28   5.29   5.30

Form 31.3. Home-Reading Book Record (Level 6 through 10)

Name _____

HOME-READING BOOK RECORD

Level 6:	6.1	6.2	6.3	6.4	6.5	6.6	6.7	6.8	6.9	6.10
	6.11	6.12	6.13	6.14	6.15	6.16	6.17	6.18	6.19	6.20
	6.21	6.22	6.23	6.24	6.25	6.26	6.27	6.28	6.29	6.30

Level 7:	7.1	7.2	7.3	7.4	7.5	7.6	7.7	7.8	7.9	7.10
	7.11	7.12	7.13	7.14	7.15	7.16	7.17	7.18	7.19	7.20
	7.21	7.22	7.23	7.24	7.25	7.26	7.27	7.28	7.29	7.30

Level 8:	8.1	8.2	8.3	8.4	8.5	8.6	8.7	8.8	8.9	8.10
	8.11	8.12	8.13	8.14	8.15	8.16	8.17	8.18	8.19	8.20
	8.21	8.22	8.23	8.24	8.25	8.26	8.27	8.28	8.29	8.30

Level 9:	9.1	9.2	9.3	9.4	9.5	9.6	9.7	9.8	9.9	9.10
	9.11	9.12	9.13	9.14	9.15	9.16	9.17	9.18	9.19	9.20
	9.21	9.22	9.23	9.24	9.25	9.26	9.27	9.28	9.29	9.30

Level 10:	10.1	10.2	10.3	10.4	10.5	10.6	10.7	10.8	10.9	10.10
	10.11	10.12	10.13	10.14	10.15	10.16	10.17	10.18	10.19	10.20
	10.21	10.22	10.23	10.24	10.25	10.26	10.27	10.28	10.29	10.30

Form 31.4. Signature Form

DATE:_____

STUDENT'S NAME:

_____

BOOK TITLE:

_____

I have listened to the reading of this book.

Check one: _____ Send home same book for more practice.

_____ Send home another book.

SIGNED: _____

COMMENTS (optional):

- -

DATE:_____

STUDENT'S NAME: _____

BOOK TITLE: _____

I have listened to the reading of this book.

Check one: _____ Send home same book for more practice.

_____ Send home another book.

SIGNED: _____

COMMENTS (optional):

32

Creative Writing

"Creative" writing comes from originality of thought. Ideas presented in this chapter are the beginning steps that lead to creativity. There needs to be a progression of instruction that precedes actual creative writing. Certain skills are needed before children can be expected to write on their own. Nevertheless, children should be encouraged by the teacher whenever they want to write.

Pre-Creative Writing

Creative writing instruction may begin with children "creating" sentences that have been planned by the teacher. The following four writing lessons fit this category.

A. *Magnetic Sentences*

Teacher Preparation. Purchase cookie sheets that can attract magnets. It is best to have one sheet for each student in a reading group. Use 4" × 6" file cards (cut to size) to write phrases that can be arranged into sentences. Each phrase card will need a small piece of magnetic tape placed on the back. Prepare enough sets for each student in a reading group.

Keep each set in a clear, resealable storage bag. If this is a practice-work activity, the materials may be shared, because each reading group is at practice-work at different times. When beginning to work with magnetic sentences, start with a few phrases. Delete and add to the collection when change is needed. Use three different colors of permanent-ink pens in writing the phrases. The beginning phrase needs an upper-case letter. The ending needs a period or exclamation point. The following examples may be used at Halloween:

Red	*Black*	*Green*
A <u>scary</u> pumpkin	**is**	*at the haunted house.*
One <u>black</u> cat	**sat**	*on the step.*
The <u>old</u> witch	**ran**	*on the broom.*
The <u>spooky</u> ghost	**flew**	*by the fence.*
		past me!

The adjectives are underlined so that the more advanced students may create and change them when writing their own sentences. The adjectives should not be underlined when students are writing on their own.

For teaching purposes, prepare the same phrases on sentence strips (cut to size). These phrases may then be put into three columns in a pocket chart . . . red column, black column, green column. The phrases in each column should be scrambled. Leave the bottom pocket empty for the activity that follows.

Student Participation. In the reading group, the children must first be able to read the words. Then they can create sentences by choosing a phrase from each column of the pocket chart and placing them into the empty pocket such as, "A scary pumpkin ran past me!" After the reading group instruction, a practice-work assignment may be as follows:

1. From the resealable storage bag, the student selects one beginning phrase, one verb, and one ending phrase. The phrases are placed in order on a cookie sheet to form a sentence that makes sense.
2. The student copies the sentence onto a one- or two-lined writing paper (see *Additional Resources*, pages 246, 247).
3. The student illustrates the sentence.
4. Repeat the process with different beginnings, verbs, and endings. *Suggestion:* Papers around a theme, such as "Halloween," may be assembled into class books, reading group books, or individual books.

B. Scrambled Sentences

Teacher Preparation. The teacher needs to think of a short sentence that can be readily illustrated, such as: "Columbus sailed on a big ship." The words of the sentence need to be scrambled (e.g., sailed / ship / a / big / Columbus / on). The scrambled sentence is duplicated (see Form 32.1, *Columbus Scrambled Sentence*, at end of chapter).

Suggested sentences to scramble are:

1. A black cat is on a fence.
2. An orange pumpkin is in the window.
3. The turkey has colorful feathers.
4. Santa is up on the rooftop.
5. Rudolph has a red nose.
6. The snowman is in the yard.
7. The kite is flying high.
8. Colorful flowers are in the garden.

Student Participation. The students practice reading the scrambled words. Guide the children to find the word that is capitalized and the word with the period or exclamation point. Now they should be able to figure out the order of the entire sentence. During practice-work time, use the Columbus paper as follows:

1. The student cuts apart the scrambled words.
2. The student glues the words in order in the long rectangle.
3. The sentence is written on the writing lines.
4. The sentence is illustrated at the bottom of the page.

Suggestion: Stickers or rubber stamps are great to use in illustrations. For instance, a jack-o-lantern sticker may be put into the window in Sentence 2. A rubber-stamp-pad picture of Santa may be stamped on the roof in Sentence 4.

C. Patterned Sentences

Teacher Preparation. The teacher needs to write a sentence pattern on the chalkboard, such as: Apples are _____.

Student Participation. Together, brainstorm for words that describe apples. List these words in a row beneath the pattern. Some ideas might be: *red, green, yellow,* *hard, crunchy, sweet, delicious, snacks, fruit,* and *good to eat.* During practice-work time, the children write as many patterned sentences as time allows. The final sentence may be an "opposite" sentence (e.g., Apples are not _____.). Do not brainstorm for an "opposite" idea. Instead, encourage creativity. One child's completed paper might read:

> Apples are red.
> Apples are green.
> Apples are crunchy.
> Apples are delicious.
> Apples are good to eat.
> Apples are not good for little babies.

Suggestion: The very first time the class writes patterned sentences, the teacher should guide the students throughout the entire lesson. The teacher writes on a transparency using an overhead projector. The children copy on their own writing papers.

Other ideas for patterned sentences with a final "opposite" sentence are:

1. I can _____.   I cannot _____.
2. A sign of winter is _____. A sign of winter is not _____.
3. The scarecrow has _____.   The scarecrow does not have _____.
4. Lincoln was _____.   Lincoln was not _____.
5. Some dinosaurs were _____. Dinosaurs were not _____.

Caution: Do not overuse this type of writing. Patterned sentences are mainly for beginning writers. Children need to learn to write in their own language.

D. "One Sentence per Page" Books

Teacher Preparation. The teacher needs to choose a theme such as:

1. September
2. October
3. Columbus
4. Halloween
5. Pilgrims
6. Workers in Our School
7. Community Workers
8. Wild Animals
9. Spring
10. Frogs

Student Participation. Together, brainstorm for sentences to fit the theme. Elicit complete sentences. Write the complete sentences on large chart paper. Other sentences may later be added to the list. During practice-work time, children select one of the sentences to copy and illustrate. They should write on one- or two-lined paper. Continue this writing activity every day until there are enough pages to put into individual books. Create covers for the books.

Suggestion: Select a "best" paper of each of the ideas (no more than one per student) and assemble these pages into a class book. The selected students will need to make an extra copy of the page that was chosen in order to have it for their own books. Before adding this book to the class library, have each student read his or her page to the class.

Beginning Creative Writing

Throughout most of first grade, students may need assistance with creative writing activities. Writing in small groups with the help of an adult is ideal. The students should be encouraged to compose the rough draft with as little help as possible. Then, the adult may help with proofreading: sentence structure (oral language), punctuation, and spelling. Usually, the errors are erased and corrected. Less capable students may need to dictate their sentences to the adult and then recopy them onto the writing paper. Time should be provided for the students to read their stories to others.

Spelling Dictionaries

When first graders are ready to begin creative writing, they may be given their own spelling dictionaries. All of the children are not ready to use a dictionary at the same time; nevertheless, give all of them their own dictionary so that no one feels left out. Getting a dictionary is exciting and is useful in varying degrees for all children. It is possible to purchase individual spelling dictionaries. The format that works best for beginning writers has at least one page for each letter with words that children use frequently when writing. There are additional lines for writing other words that a child may need.

Individual spelling dictionaries may be made out of bound composition books. There will be no words printed beforehand. Instead, all the words will be written as the individual child needs them. At first, to ensure proper spelling and legibility, the words should be written by an adult. As students become proficient, they can write their own words. *Caution:* Students must not become dependent on using their dictionaries for every word. They should be encouraged to sound out words whenever possible. Because the English language has so many different spellings for the same sound, the dictionary is a valuable tool. First grade is not too soon to develop good habits using a simple dictionary.

Story Writing

Next are two plans for teaching story writing. If properly instructed, the students should feel adequately prepared to write both types of stories.

A. *Sequencing Stories*

Teacher Preparation. Have pictures available that may be sequenced to create a story. Most teacher supply outlets have reproducible books on the subject of sequencing. If these sequencing books already have sentences provided, eradicate the sentences before reproducing the pages. Three excellent sources for sequencing at the primary level are: *Fairy Tale Sequencing* by Joy Evans and JoEllen Moore, *Picture Sequencing* by Helen Chirinian, and *Sequencing* by Phyllis Bass.

Select writing paper that is suited for sequencing pictures, two pictures on the left-hand side of each page (see Form 32.2 at end of chapter). In case more writing lines are needed, lines without pictures may be printed on the back. If your school's lined writing paper is used, the pictures can be glued, one under the other, on the left-hand side of the page.

Student Participation. The pictures need to be arranged in the correct sequential order and then glued onto a writing paper. The children brainstorm for key words that may be needed to tell about the pictures. These words are listed on the chalkboard. *Suggestion:* Assign a number to each picture and list the words under the appropriate numbers. The children refer to these key words when writing one or two sentences about each picture. The final result is a complete story.

The following is a sequencing story, "Goldilocks and the Three Bears," that was written by a first grader (Peter Cleek). His final page is included to show his handwriting and to reveal erasing instead of recopying. Notice that at this level, run-on sentences are not corrected.

Figure 32.1. *Goldilocks and the Three Bears*
NOTE: Permission to reprint *Goldilocks and the Three Bears*, by Peter Cleek, granted by Laura Cleek and N. Eugene Cleek (parents).

B. Mapping a Story

Teacher Preparation. Select a story from either a basal reader or a library book. Duplicate the story-mapping papers for illustrating the four components of a story: setting, characters, plot, and climax.

Setting	Characters
Plot	Climax

Figure 32.2. The Four Components of a Story

Student Participation

Level 1. As a reading group, brainstorm and decide upon the four components of the story. Let each child illustrate these four components in the proper squares on their duplicated story-mapping paper. Repeat this level of activity with other stories until the majority of the group displays competence. Then move on to Level 2.

Level 2. Without brainstorming, let each child decide on the four components of a story. They illustrate their own story-mapping papers. At this level, each child will need to explain orally his or her four illustrations to an adult. When competency is displayed by a majority of the group at this level, move on to Level 3.

Level 3. Again, brainstorm as a group and decide upon the four components of the story. This time the students orally dictate one sentence for each component and the teacher writes them on the chalkboard. Setting, characters, and plot may be written in any order, but the climax is written last. The students now have a completed four-sentence story. The children copy the sentences and illustrate only the climax. When a majority of the group display competency at this level, move on to the final level.

Level 4. The children write their own four sentences. Only the climax is illustrated. An adult should be available for assistance when needed. *Caution:* Do not hurry from level to level. The top reading group will reach Level 4 long before the low group. More advanced students should be encouraged to elaborate and write more than four sentences.

Motivating Techniques

In addition to the preceding suggestions, here are some final techniques to motivate young authors.

A. *Painting Stories*

Each child paints a picture around a theme, such as "bears." Then the child dictates one or two sentences about the painting to an adult. The dictation is written with a marking pen directly on the painting. As the year progresses, many children will be ready to dictate more than a two-sentence story. These longer stories are too much to write on a painting, so the format may change for everyone. Each child will still paint a picture around a theme; however, the dictated story will no longer be written on the painting. Instead, the adult will write the story on five-lined paper (see *Additional Resources*, p. 250). After everyone has had their dictated story written, the individual stories are returned to each child. During practice-work time, the children illustrate their stories in the space at the top of the paper. The illustration should be similar to the picture painted prior to dictating the story. Now all of the illustrated stories may be bound into a class book. The children may read their own stories before the book is added to the class library. *Note:* Student dictation of sentences offers a great opportunity to work on oral language (i.e., speaking in complete sentences, using proper grammar and syntax, and displaying a logical sequencing of ideas). *Suggestion:* Easel painting may be one of the "learning centers." A flat counter is an excellent location for this center. There is less dripping of paint on a flat surface. A painting sample may be placed up on the wall over the counter for the children to follow. They may add other details to their own paintings.

B. *Sticker and Rubber-Stamp Stories*

Stickers and rubber-stamp pictures are excellent for motivating children to write sentences and stories. The children should write their stories on a lined paper that has room for an illustration at the top. Select stickers and rubber-stamp pictures that generate a variety of interesting stories. Suggestions are:

Rubber Stamps	*Stickers*
1. Smokey the Bear	1. Scarecrows
2. Max (*Where the Wild Things Are*)	2. Jack-o-lanterns
3. Santa and his reindeer	3. Farm animals
4. Easter Bunny	4. Wild animals
5. Leprechaun	5. Toys
6. Clifford, the Big Red Dog	6. Whales
7. Mayflower (ship)	7. Circus

Again, it is desirable to write these stories in small groups with an adult available for assistance. The children may work on illustrations while waiting for their turn to receive help with the proofreading.

C. Pop-Up Books

Pop-ups are books the children can make that have one or two pictures that "pop-out" inside a folded piece of construction paper. Making a pop-up book is relatively easy. Most first graders can be taught to make their own. The following diagrams show how to construct one out of an $8\frac{1}{2}" \times 11"$ piece of construction paper:

Figure 32.3. Pop-Up Books

Instructions for making a pop-up book are as follows:

1. Fold the paper and cut on the two lines.
2. Push the cut tab through to the inside and make the folds indicated.
3. Position the tab so as to be able to glue the pop-up picture on the "X."
4. Glue the pop-up picture after the background picture is completed and the writing paper is attached.

Special writing paper should be designed to fit into the book (see Form 32.3, *Writing Paper for Pop-Up Book* at end of chapter). The writing paper may be placed at both the top and the bottom with only the picture or pictures being the "pop-up(s)"; or the writing paper can be only at the bottom with a background illustration added to the top behind the "pop-up." Pop-up books are well suited for patterned sentences, poems, short stories, and riddles. Examples of two riddles are:

I grow tall.	I am an animal.
Children like to climb me.	I hibernate all winter.
Birds live in me.	I come out on February 2nd.
I give shade.	My shadow scares me.
What am I?	Who am I?

Examples of patterned sentences in a pop-up book are:

(top)	Scary witch, scary witch What do you see? (pop-up picture of cat)	Turtles hatch from eggs. Turtles have shells. (pop-up picture of turtle)
(bottom)	I see a black cat Looking at me.	Turtles eat insects. Turtles are reptiles.

Note: Several "pop-up" pages may be glued back-to-back to make one book.

D. *Topic Sentences*

A topic sentence is written on five-lined writing paper and a copy given to each child. The children then complete the story.

Suggestions for topic sentences are:

1. Curious George came to our classroom.
2. This school bus is magic.
3. Santa has a problem.
4. We made a snowman.
5. I found a pot of gold!
6. A baby dinosaur lives at my house.

Topic sentences may be introduced in three different stages:

Stage 1. The duplicated papers with the topic sentence are given to the children. The teacher has an identical transparency to use on the overhead projector. The children brainstorm and compose a story together. The teacher writes the story on the transparency, and the children copy and then illustrate the story.

Stage 2. The topic sentence is given to the children in a reading group. The children in the group brainstorm and compose the rest of the story together. The teacher does not write the story but dictates the composed sentences, one word at a time. Again, the story needs to be illustrated. *Suggestion:* Read one example of each reading group's story to the entire class. Usually the stories are all quite different, even with the same beginning topic sentence.

Stage 3. The topic sentence is given to the children. After a brief introduction and discussion, the children create and write their own endings to the story. The stories from this stage may be illustrated and then bound into a class book. Let the children read their own stories to the entire class.

E. Rewriting Patterns

Pattern books, poems, and songs are often conducive to rewriting. Pattern books have the same words, or patterns, written through much of the book. When rewriting, the pattern stays the same, but key words are changed. The song "Ten Little Indians" lends itself to many different rewrites. A few suggestions are:

One little, two little,	One little, two little,
Three little snowmen . . .	Three little bunnies . . .
Ten little snowmen in the yard.	Ten little bunnies hopping around.

A House Is a House for Me by Mary Ann Hoberman is a pattern book suitable for rewriting. In this book there are many "houses," so it may be difficult to think of ones not already mentioned. Families may be involved by helping their children brainstorm for unusual "houses." Each child may be responsible for one rewrite (e.g., "A frame is a house for a picture.") The rewritings are written on two-lined paper and illustrated. Each page may be bound into a class book. The final page needs to read: "But a house is a house for me."

Rosie's Walk by Pat Hutchins is a final suggestion of a book that can be rewritten. Instead of Rosie the Hen, the "walker" may be:

Wanda the Witch
Tommy the Turkey
Rudolph the Red-Nosed Reindeer
Shaun the Leprechaun
Thumper the Easter Bunny

One class rewrote this pattern to go with their own community. Instead of illustrations, actual photos were taken around town. The "walker" was Frosty the Snowman. A rubber-stamp picture of Frosty was used in each illustration. The rewritten class book read:

Frosty the Snowman went for a walk
across the railroad tracks
around Lely Park
over Stony Creek Bridge
past Mill Street School
through the fairgrounds
under the arch
and got back to Pizza Palace in time for dinner.

This class book was added to the school library.

F. Journals

Writing journals is an excellent way to get children to express themselves. The question is: "When should journal writing begin?" First graders need to have enough writing skills to begin writing journals successfully. There are many writing activities that have been detailed so far that prepare students to become capable writers, so do not rush to begin journal writing. Most children are ready to begin about mid-year, when they have progressed far enough to be able to spell entire words (not just isolated sounds) and to write understandable sentences.

Creative writing should be planned for every day of the week; however, journal writing may be assigned only one day per week. Monday is a good day to write journals because the weekend usually provides a variety of happenings to generate writing ideas.

Journal writing is an "independent" writing activity. Independent writing means that there is no adult to help in spelling or proofreading. For this reason, inventive spelling must be accepted. The only other time that inventive spelling should be accepted is whenever children write during "free time" (not an assignment). The primary goal of writing journals and writing during free time is to get the children to write, write, write! They need not worry about the spelling. With a majority of the children, skills learned in the other spelling and writing lessons will carry over into these writings.

If children are making common errors in their independent writings, plan class writing and spelling dictation lessons to rectify these errors. Commonly misspelled words may be written by everyone in the individual dictionaries; however, an adult will need to check to see that they were all spelled correctly. *Note:* Some students may need individual help with patterns of errors that need to be corrected.

Suggestion: When reading the journals, the teacher can write comments on Post-it Notes and attach them wherever applicable. Frequently misspelled words may be written on Post-its. The children may be told to write these words in their own individual dictionaries. If they write words themselves, they are more liable to remember that the word is in their dictionary. *Note:* If there are a lot of misspelled words, select no more than five in any given week. More than that would be an overload and discouraging to the child. *Caution:* At the primary level, art and creative writing often go hand in hand. Nevertheless, writing should always be the main objective. Evaluate the time spent on the "art" part of the lesson. This time should be included in the total minutes allocated for "art" each week.

G. *Writing Letters*

Near the end of the school year, plan some lessons for teaching the children how to write letters. They need to be taught the format for letter writing. A letter must have at least one topic of interest.

Merely writing "How are you? I miss you." is not interesting! On the last day of school, all children may be given a letter from the teacher, such as:

June 8, _____

Dear _____,

   I enjoyed having you in my class this year.
I will miss you!
   Please write me a letter this summer. I
would like to know what you are doing.
   Try to write your letter so that it looks like
a letter and not a story. Make your letter interesting.
If you write an interesting letter, I will answer you.

   Your teacher,

_____

The children may be given some extra writing paper and a stamped envelope addressed to the teacher (address labels make this task easy!). Children who write interesting letters to the teacher (see Figure 32.4) will get a picture postcard sent back to them. Postcards are quicker to write and are cherished by the children.

Dear Mrs Talbot,

I am having a great summer. I went fishing. Stephie and I caught the same fish, it had both of our hooks in its mouth. We went to the ocean and went horseback riding on the beach. I have been

swimming a lot. I even went swimming in my dress, when I fell in. You are a good teacher! I hope to see you again!

        Your student,

        Shawn Cooper

Figure 32.4. Shawn's Letter
NOTE: Permission to reprint "Shawn's Letter," by Shawn Cooper, granted by Scott Cooper and Sherrie S. Cooper (parents).

sailed	ship.	a	big	Columbus	on

sailed ship a big Columbus on

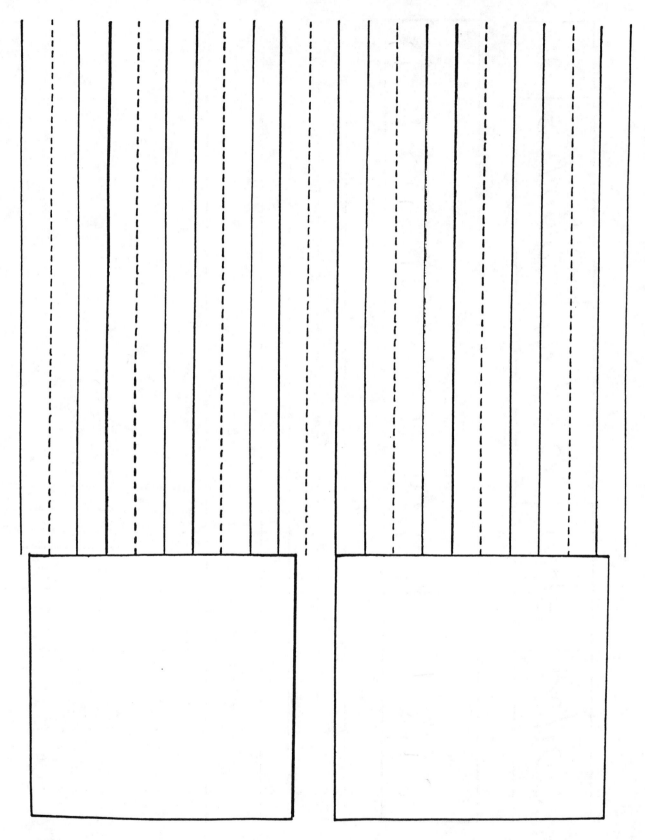

Form 32.2

↑ Cut ↑

(Writing paper for pop-up book. One duplicated paper will be suitable for one book with writing above and below the pop-up tab.)

↓ Cut ↓

Additional Resources

Dear Parents,

Today is the first day of school and the first day of homework. Getting into a homework habit is part of what is needed in order to be a successful and responsible student. At this level, the homework should take only a few minutes each day.

When your child comes home from school, there should be one special place to put all homework and school papers. The place should be conveniently located, yet out of the reach of smaller children and pets.

Today's homework is the flashcard "red." Your child should read the word to you. The word should not be "sounded out." This is a sight word, which means that the word is known on sight.

Keep the flashcard in the envelope at home. Tomorrow's homework will be another color word. For homework, your child will now have to read both color words. The next day, another color word will be sent home. Now there will be three words to practice. This homework pattern will continue until all eight color words (the colors in a crayon box) are complete. Save these flashcards in the envelope and have your child practice them until they are mastered.

After the color words, the homework will continue to be flashcards. The flashcards will then be number words (two per day) to learn as sight words.

Homework time should be a "fun" time. Contact me if there are problems. There are simple flashcard games you could play with your child. These games are difficult to explain in writing but easy to explain in person.

I look forward to working with you.

(Teacher's Name)

Resource 2. Homework Letter 2

Dear Parents,

Your child is now ready to begin reading sentences, stories, and books for homework. The reading homework will come home in this special envelope. There will always be something for you to sign, to acknowledge the fact that your child read the assigned homework.

If the assignment is to read a book, you will need to fill out a simple form: Date, Student's Name, and Book Title. You will also need to check whether you think your child needs to read the same book again or have another book to read. This will be your decision. It is optional whether you write any comments; however, hearing from you occasionally would let me know how you think your child is doing in reading at home.

School books for homework need to be returned. Something that is your child's creation stays at home, but the signature form is returned in the envelope. Sometimes the reading selection will be on a single piece of paper. There will be a place for your signature.

Some children are ready to read with little or no help. Other children may need more assistance. For those needing help, here is a suggested format:

1. Read the selection to your child, pointing to the words as you read.

2. Read the selection again, still pointing to the words. This time your child reads with you.

3. Now let your child read alone. Your child needs to point to the words as they are read. This is called "tracking." "Tracking" is important for beginning readers because it focuses on reading the words rather than saying what has been memorized.

4. If your child does not know a word, wait a little while before saying it. (Beginning readers need "thinking time.")

Teaching Reading, Writing, and Spelling. Copyright © 1997 Corwin Press, Inc.

Do not have your child "sound out" a word in the middle of reading. It is better for you to say the word. At the end of reading, look at the word again and discuss how it could be remembered. Make flashcards on 3" × 5" file cards of unknown words and have your child practice them.

5. Say a few words out of order from the reading selection. Have your child find these words.

Reading with your child should be pleasurable. Don't expect perfection. Learning to read takes time and a lot of practice. If reading becomes unpleasant, stop at that point and contact me at school (333-3333). We'll work together to solve the problem.

Good luck!

(Teacher's Name)

Dear Parents,

Today the class learned how to write the upper-case (capital) letter _____. Since this is the first letter of your child's last name, your child now needs to learn to write his/her last name. This paper is an additional homework assignment; thus, it does not have to be completed in one day. Do try to have it completed and returned to school within a week.

There are two sides to this paper. On the front side, your child first practices tracing and then writing the _____ to the end of the first writing line. Next, the last name needs to be traced and written on the remaining lines. See that all of the letters within the name are close together . . . close, but not touching.

On the back side, your child first traces the first and last name. Then the two names are written in "best" handwriting on each writing line. The letters need to be close together within both names, and there needs to be a space between the names. The space needs to be about the size of a nickel.

Thanks for your help!

Sincerely,

(Teacher's Name)

Teaching Reading, Writing, and Spelling. Copyright © 1997 Corwin Press, Inc.

Dear Parents,

Using parents as aides is an important part of our educational program. I hope that some of you will be able to work one day a week, starting around the 20th day of school.

You will need to be in the classroom for most of the morning. This will be during reading time (9:00-11:30). Your responsibilities will be varied. You will be kept busy!

If for some reason you are not able to work one day per week, perhaps you know someone who can (grandmother? aunt? neighbor?). Maybe mom and dad can take turns, coming every other week. Or perhaps you can take turns with a parent of another child.

We need to have at least five aides, one day per week. Detach, fill out, and return the following form as soon as possible. Do not hesitate to contact me if you have any questions. If you do volunteer to be an aide, I'll get in touch with you well in advance of your first day's work.

Thank you!

(Teacher's Name)

_____

_____ I cannot work. _____ I can work one day per week.

Check any days you can work. Circle the day you prefer:

____Monday ____Tuesday ____Wednesday ____Thursday ____Friday

Child's Name: _____

Signature: _____

Resource 5. VIP Letter

_____ is the VIP (*Very Important Person*) in our class next week (_____-_____, 19_____). We would like to get to know our VIP better! Please bring lots of pictures and special things to share. Ideas are: pictures of your family, pets, home, special events, and special trips. Other items to bring may include collections, favorite toys, souvenirs from trips, a collage of favorite foods, things made in preschool, and so on. Be creative! These things may be brought all week.

Clifford, our class mascot, wants to get better acquainted with our VIP. He is coming to visit in your home. Take good care of Clifford and be sure he comes back to school next Thursday. Someone else will be eager to take him home on Friday.

A writing journal is also coming home in the special Clifford bag. Please write one page, telling what happened with Clifford during the week. (An extra paper is being sent, in case there is a mistake.) Did Clifford go anywhere special? Did anything exciting happen to him? Where did he sleep? Whom did he meet?

Mom or Dad may need to do the *printing* in the journal for our VIP. Maybe later in the year, the VIP can do the printing. If so, then Mom or Dad can help plan what is to be written and help in spelling the words. Thanks, Mom and Dad!

Congratulations VIP! You are special!

(Teacher's Name)

green	red
blue	yellow
purple	orange
brown	black

zero	six
one	seven
two	eight
three	nine
four	ten
five	

Teaching Reading, Writing, and Spelling. Copyright © 1997 Corwin Press, Inc.

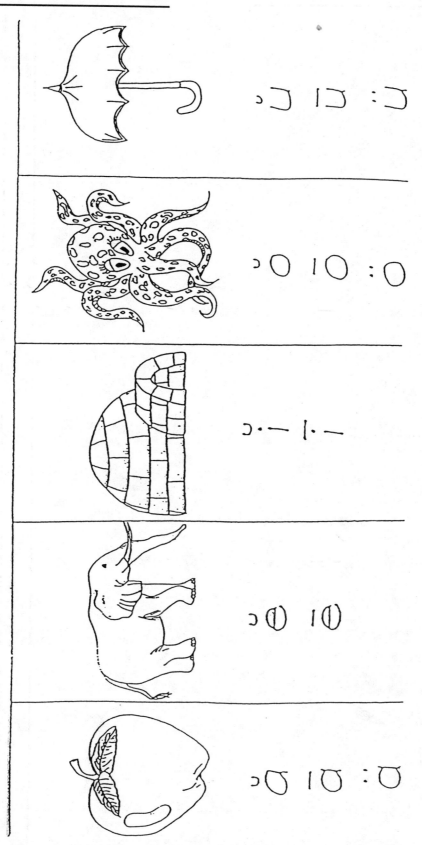

Resource 9. One-Lined Writing Paper

Resource 10. Two-Lined Writing Paper

Resource 11. Three-Lined Writing Paper

Teaching Reading, Writing, and Spelling. Copyright © 1997 Corwin Press, Inc.

Resource 12. Four-Lined Writing Paper

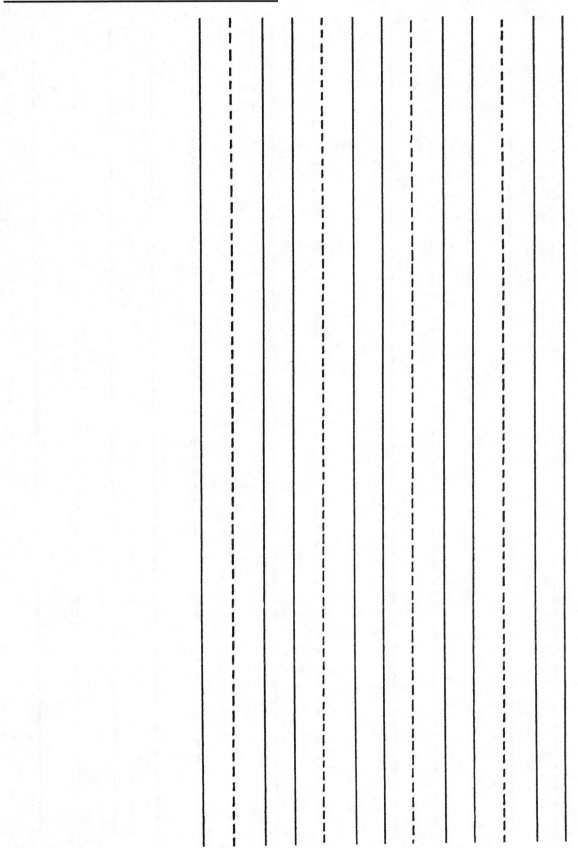

Resource 13. Five-Lined Writing Paper

Teaching Reading, Writing, and Spelling. Copyright © 1997 Corwin Press, Inc.

2

2

Teaching Reading, Writing, and Spelling. Copyright © 1997 Corwin Press, Inc.

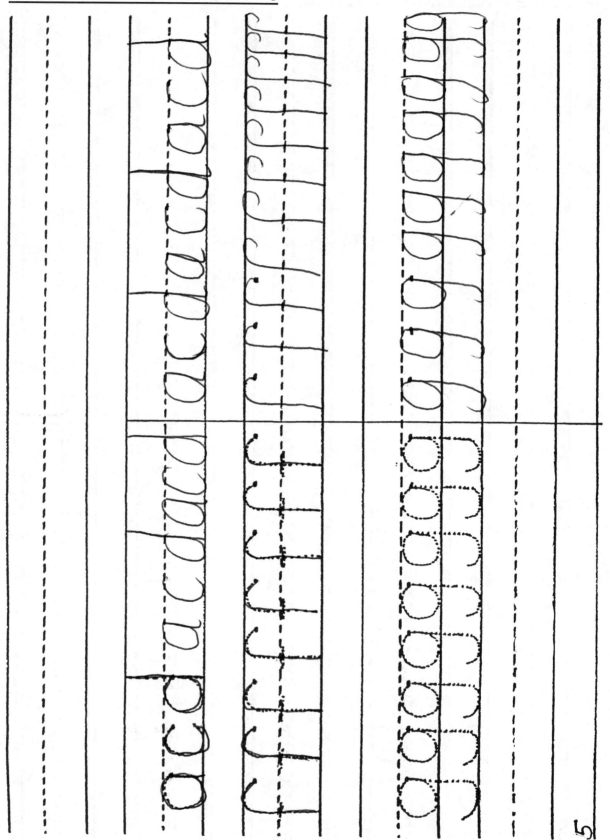

Teaching Reading, Writing, and Spelling. Copyright © 1997 Corwin Press, Inc.

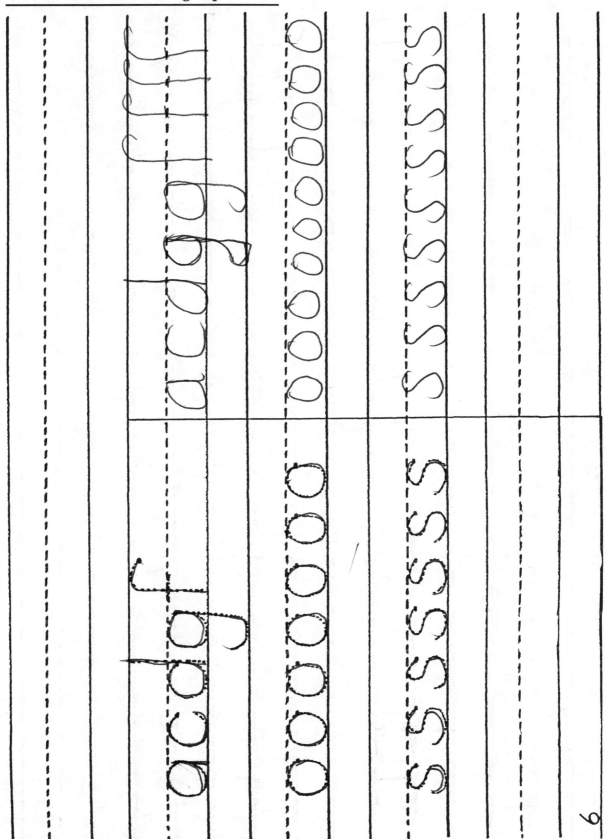

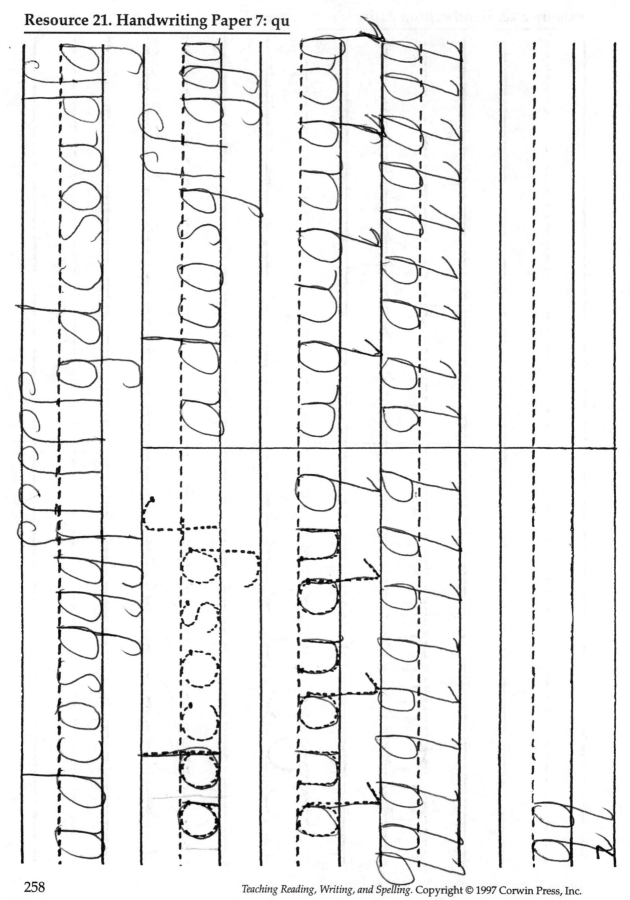

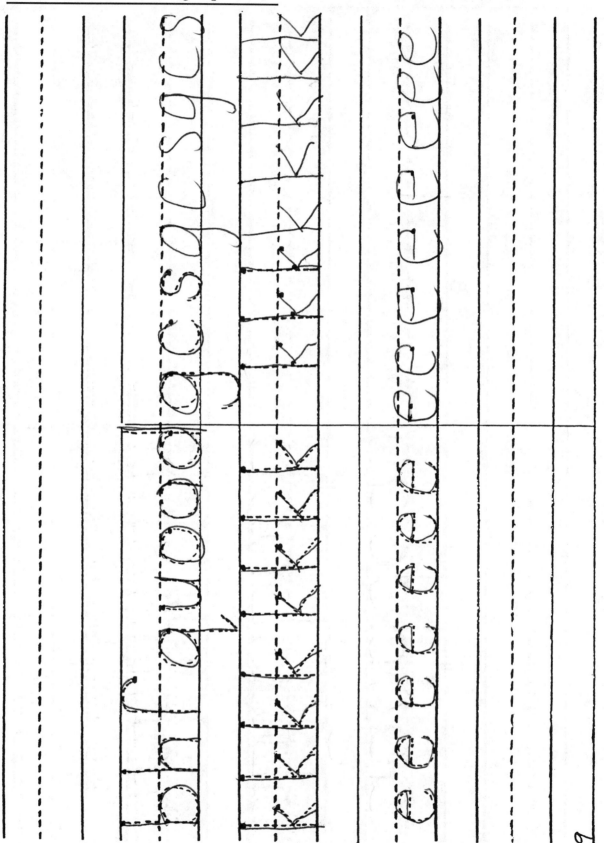

Teaching Reading, Writing, and Spelling. Copyright © 1997 Corwin Press, Inc.

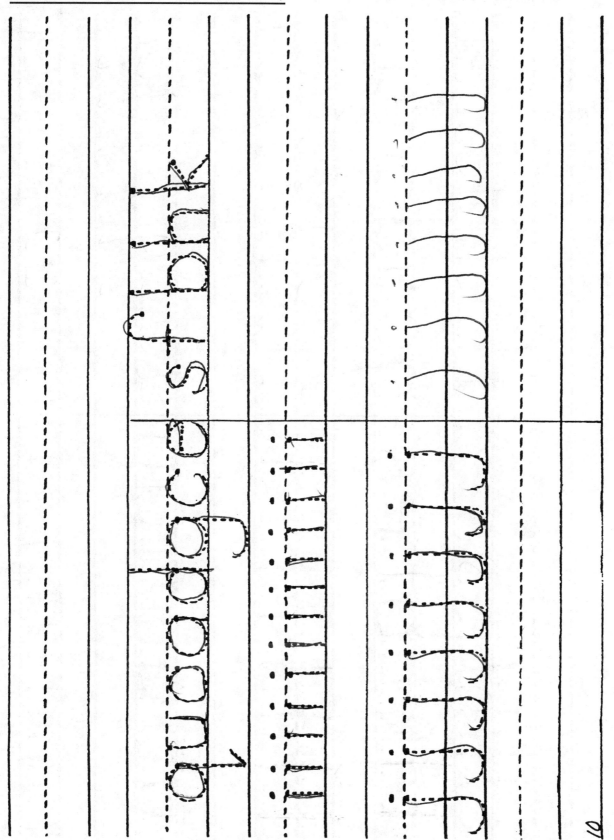

Teaching Reading, Writing, and Spelling. Copyright © 1997 Corwin Press, Inc.

Resource 26. Handwriting Paper 12: n, m

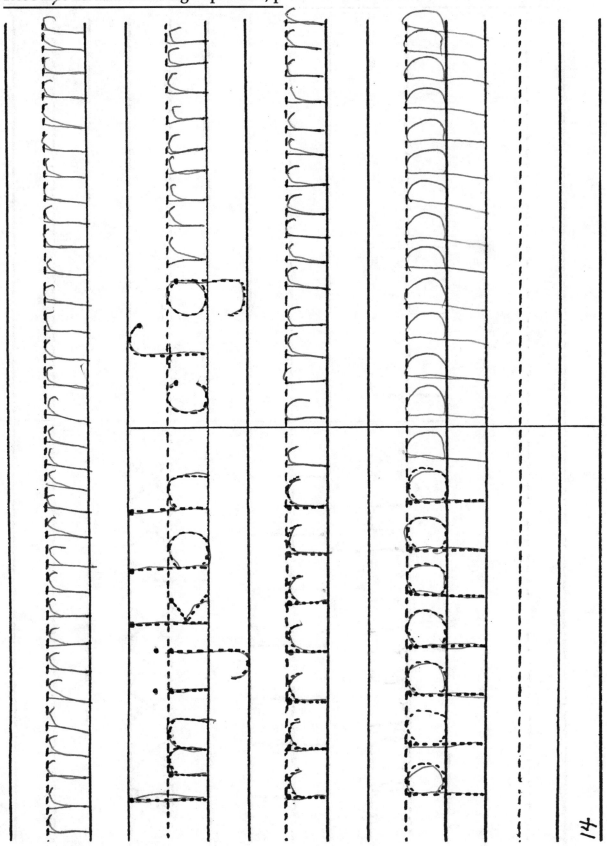

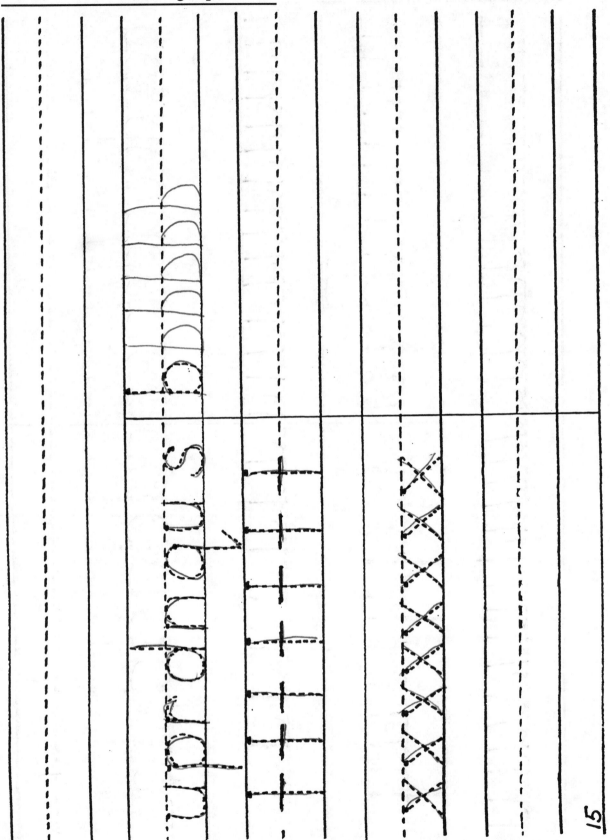

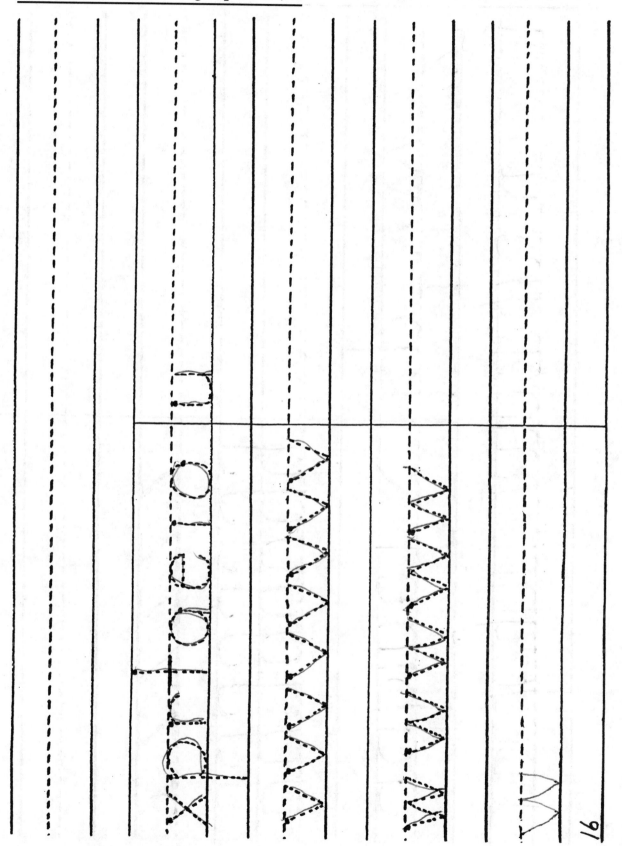

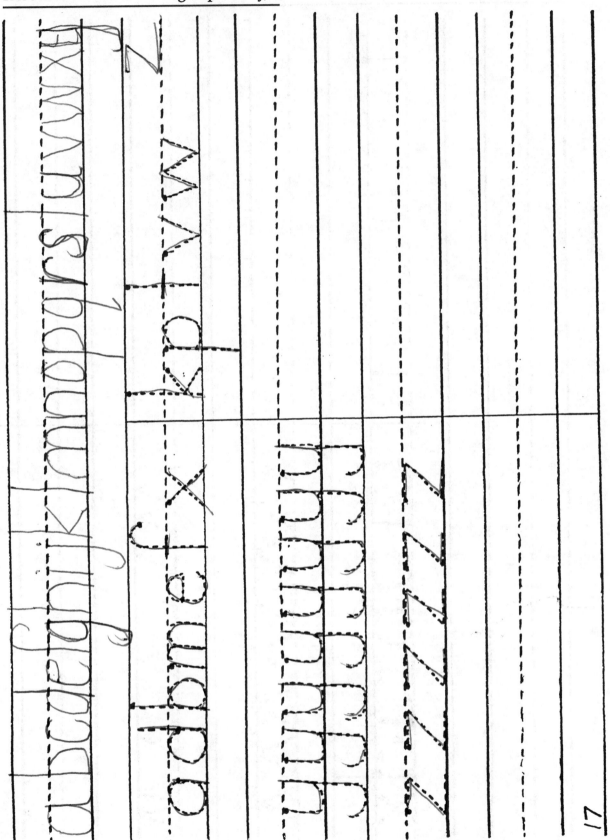

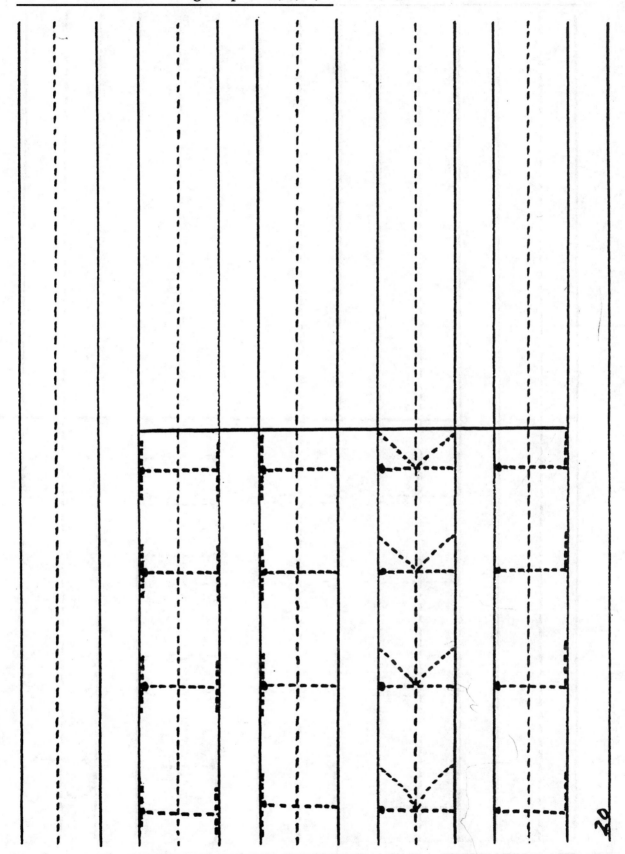

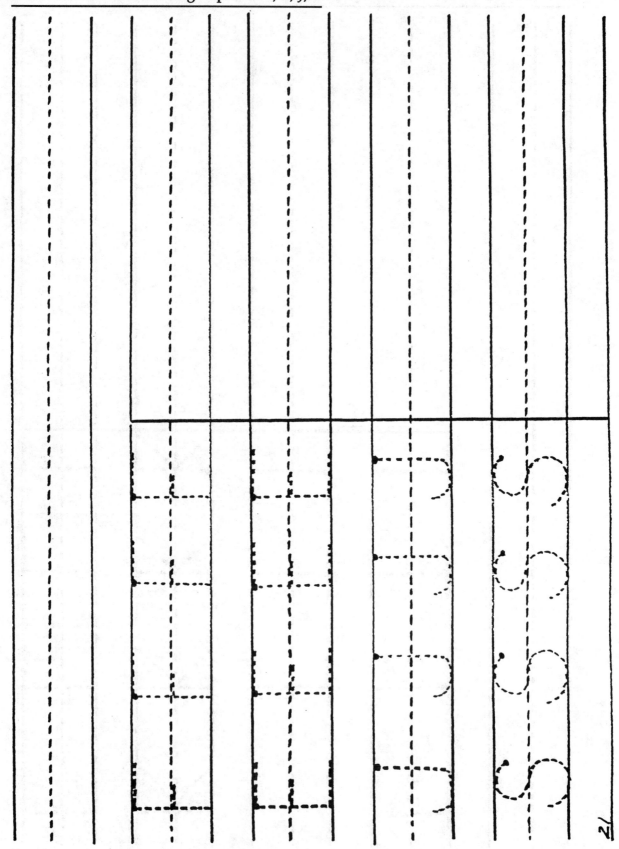

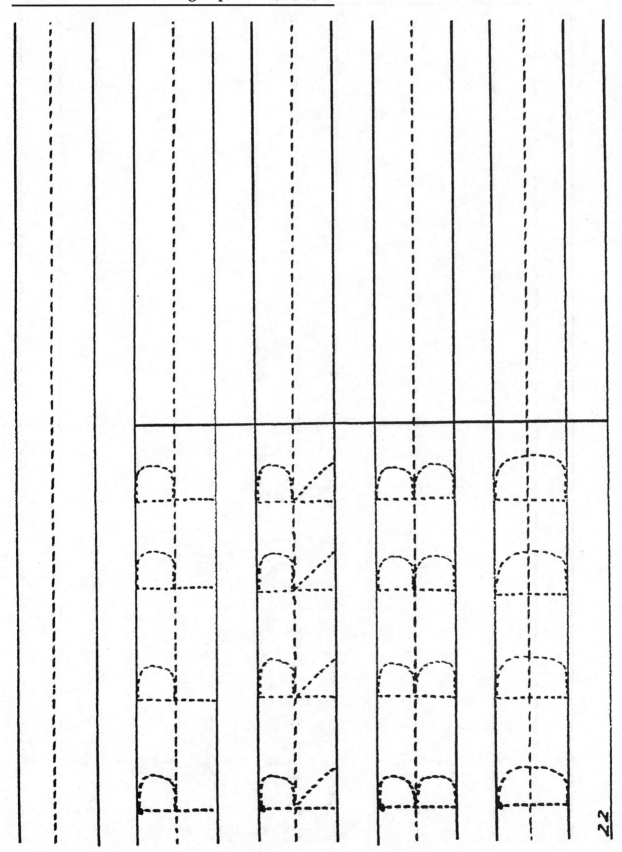

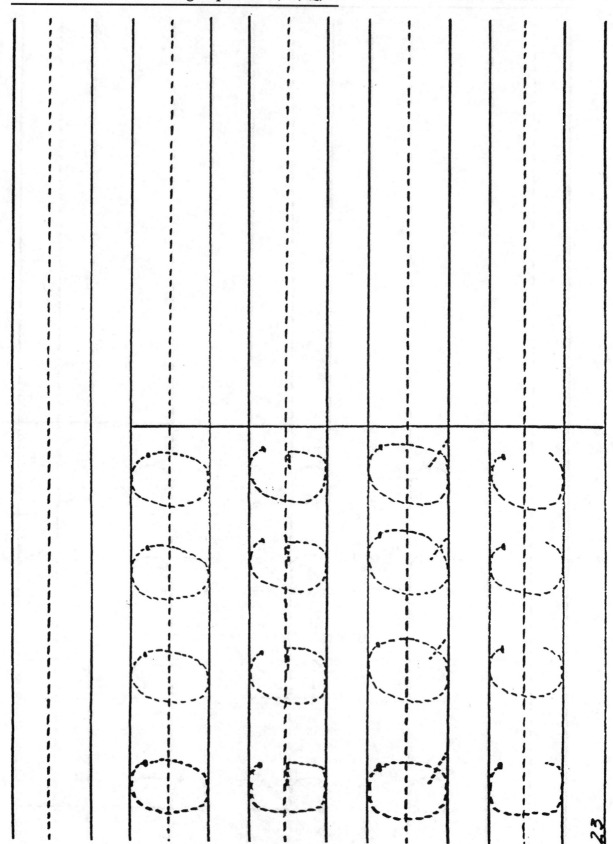

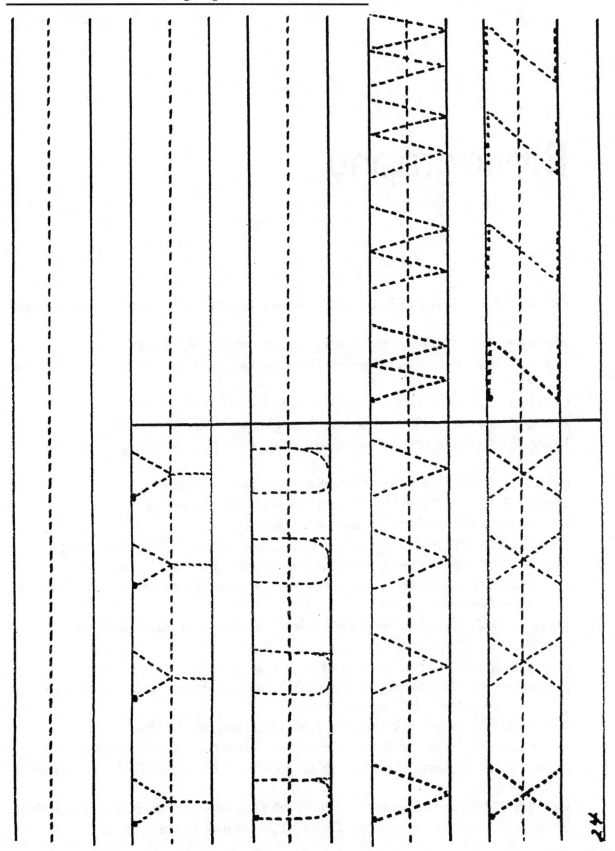

Bibliography

Adams, P. J., & Kronowitz, E. L. (1994). *Pathways to poetry.* Carthage, IL: Fearon Teacher Aids.

Alexander, R. (1990). *Poetry place anthology.* Jefferson City, MO: Scholastic Inc.

Chirinian, H. (1988). *Picture sequencing.* Palos Verdes Estates, CA: Frank Schaffer Publication.

Cunningham, P. M. (1995). *Phonics we use.* New York: HarperCollins College.

Evans, J., & Moore, J. (1988). *Sequencing.* Monterey, CA: Evan-Moor Corp.

Evans, J., & Moore, J. (1991). *How to make books with children.* Monterey, CA: Evan-Moor Corp.

Galdone, P. (1986). *Over in the meadow.* New York: Simon & Schuster.

Hoberman, M. A. (1978). *A house is a house for me.* New York: Viking.

Hutchins, P. (1968). *Rosie's walk.* New York: Macmillan.

Johnston, M. M. (1995). *Primary teaching manual.* Los Angeles, CA: Total Reading.

Kovalski, M. (1990). *The wheels on the bus.* Boston: Little, Brown.

Lillegard, D. (1986). *September to September: Poems for all year round.* Chicago: Childrens Press/Regensteiner.

Lobel, A. (1986). *Random House book of Mother Goose.* New York: Random House.

Lottridge, C. B. (1996). *Mother Goose: A sampler.* Toronto, Ontario: Groundwood Books.

Martin, B., Jr. (1992). *Brown bear, brown bear, what do you see?* New York: Henry Holt.

McCracken, R., & McCracken, M. (1986). *Stories, songs, & poetry to teach reading & writing.* Winnipeg, Manitoba: Peguis Publishers.

Peek, M. (1988). *Mary wore her red dress.* New York: Houghton Mifflin.

Rader, L. (1996). *The best smelling Mother Goose book ever.* New York: Simon & Schuster.

Rosen, M. (1993). *Poems for the very young.* New York: Kingfisher Books/Grisewood & Dempsey.

Ryono, S. (1989). *Fairy tale sequencing.* Palos Verdes Estates, CA: Frank Schaffer Publication.

Williams, R. L. (1994). *Under the sky.* Cypress, CA: Creative Teaching Press.

Index